# Essays and Studies 2007

Series Editor: Peter J. Kitson

# The English Association

The objects of the English Association are to promote the knowledge and appreciation of the English language and its literature, and to foster good practice in its teaching and learning at all levels.

The Association pursues these aims by creating opportunities of co-operation among all those interested in English; by furthering the recognition of English as essential in education; by discussing methods of English teaching; by holding lectures, conferences, and other meetings; by publishing journals, books, and leaflets; and by forming local branches.

## Publications

*The Year's Work in English Studies*. An annual bibliography. Published by Blackwell.
*The Year's Work in Critical and Cultural Theory*. An annual bibliography. Published by Blackwell.

*Essays and Studies*. An annual volume of essays by various scholars assembled by the collector covering usually a wide range of subjects and authors from the medieval to the modern. Published by D.S. Brewer.

*English*. A journal of the Association, *English* is published three times a year by the Association.

*The Use of English*. A journal of the Association, *The Use of English* is published three times a year by the Association.

*Newsletter*. A *Newsletter* is published three times a year giving information about forthcoming publications, conferences, and other matters of interest.

## Benefits of Membership

*Institutional Membership*

Full members receive copies of *The Year's Work in English Studies*, *Essays and Studies*, *English* (3 issues) and three *Newsletters*.

Ordinary Membership covers *English* (3 issues) and three *Newsletters*.

Schools Membership includes copies of each issue of *English* and *The Use of English*, one copy of *Essays and Studies*, three *Newsletters*, and preferential booking and rates for various conferences held by the Association.

*Individual Membership*

Individuals take out Basic Membership, which entitles them to buy all regular publications of the English Association at a discounted price, and attend Association gatherings.

*For further details* write to The Secretary, The English Association, The University of Leicester, University Road, Leicester, LE1 7RH.

# Essays and Studies 2007

# Slavery and the Cultures of Abolition

## Essays marking the Bicentennial of the British Abolition Act of 1807

Edited by
Brycchan Carey and Peter J. Kitson

for the English Association

D. S. BREWER

ESSAYS AND STUDIES 2007
IS VOLUME SIXTY IN THE NEW SERIES
OF ESSAYS AND STUDIES COLLECTED ON BEHALF OF
THE ENGLISH ASSOCIATION
ISSN 0071–1357

First published 2007
D. S. Brewer, Cambridge


D. S. Brewer is an imprint of Boydell & Brewer Ltd
PO Box 9, Woodbridge, Suffolk IP12 3DF, UK
and of Boydell & Brewer Inc.
668 Mt Hope Avenue, Rochester, NY 14620, USA
website: www.boydellandbrewer.com


ISBN 978–1–84384–120–3


A CIP catalogue record for this title is available
from the British Library

The Library of Congress has cataloged this serial publication:
Catalog card number 36–8431


This publication is printed on acid-free paper

Typeset by
Frances Hackeson Freelance Publishing Services, Brinscall, Lancs
Printed in Great Britain by
Antony Rowe Ltd, Chippenham, Wiltshire

# Contents

# Notes on Contributors

**George E. Boulukos** is an Assistant Professor at Southern Illinois University Carbondale. His book, *The Grateful Slave: The Emergence of Race in Eighteenth-Century British and American Culture* is forthcoming from Cambridge University Press. The book argues for the impact of eighteenth-century fictions of slavery on modern conceptions of racial difference. He is also beginning a new project, tentatively entitled Eighteenth-Century Incoherence, on the interpretive problems of applying nineteenth- and twentieth-century analytical categories to eighteenth-century culture.

**Brycchan Carey** is Reader in English at Kingston University, London. He is the author of *British Abolitionism and the Rhetoric of Sensibility: Writing, Sentiment, and Slavery, 1760–1807* (Palgrave, 2005) and the editor (with Markman Ellis and Sara Salih) of *Discourses of Slavery and Abolition: Britain and its Colonies, 1760–1838* (Palgrave, 2004). He has also authored a number of articles on slavery and abolition for scholarly journals and books. He is currently completing a book on the origins and development of Quaker antislavery rhetoric in the seventeenth and eighteenth centuries.

**Deirdre Coleman**, Robert Wallace Chair of English at the University of Melbourne, researches eighteenth-century literature and cultural history, with a particular concentration on racial ideology, colonialism, natural history, and the anti-slavery movement. She is the author of *Romantic Colonization and British Anti-Slavery* (Cambridge University Press, 2005) and *Maiden Voyages and Infant Colonies: Two Women's Travel Narratives of the 1790s* (London: Leicester UP, 1999). Her work has appeared in *Eighteenth-Century Life* and *Eighteenth-Century Studies*, and she has recently edited the Australia volume of *Women Writing Home, 1700–1920: Female Correspondence across the British Empire*, 6 vols (Pickering and Chatto, 2006). She is currently writing a biography of the flycatcher Henry Smeathman (1742–86).

**Maroula Joannou** is Reader in Late Victorian and Early Twentieth-Century Women's Writing at Anglia Ruskin University in Cambridge. She is the author of *'Ladies, Please Don't Smash These Windows': Women's Writing, Feminism and Social Change 1918–1938* (1995) and *Contempo-*

*rary Women's Writing: From The Golden Notebook to The Color Purple* (2000). She has edited *Women Writers of the 1930s: Gender, Politics and History*, co-edited a volume of essays on the women's suffrage movement with June Purvis and a *festschrift* to Margot Heinemann with David Margolies. Most recently she has published a critical edition of Ellen Wilkinson's novel, *Clash*, with Ian Haywood.

**Peter J. Kitson** is Professor of English at the University of Dundee. Recently he is the author of *Romance Literature, Race and Colonial Encounter, 1780–1830* (Palgrave 2007) and the editor (with Debbie Lee) of the eight-volume edition of *Slavery, Abolition and Emancipation: Writings from the British Romantic Period* (London: Pickering and Chatto, 1999).

**Gerald MacLean** is Professor of English at the University of Exeter. Recent books include *The Rise of Oriental Travel: English Travellers to the Ottoman Empire, 1580–1720* (2004: Turkish translated 2006); (ed.) *Re-Orienting the Renaissance: Cultural Exchanges with the East* (2005); (ed.) *Writing Turkey: Explorations in Turkish History, Politics and Cultural Identity* (2006); *Looking East: English History and the Ottoman Empire before 1800* (2007).

**Felicity Nussbaum** is Professor of English at the University of California, Los Angeles. She is the author most recently of *The Limits of the Human: Fictions of Anomaly, Race and Gender in the Long Eighteenth Century* (Cambridge UP, 2003) and editor of *The Global Eighteenth Century* (Johns Hopkins UP, 2003). Her current projects include a book on women in the eighteenth-century British theatre and a collection of essays on *The Arabian Nights* in historical context. She is President of the American Society for Eighteenth-Century Studies (2006–2007).

**Diana Paton** is a Senior Lecturer in History at Newcastle University. She is author of *No Bond but the Law: Punishment, Race, and Gender in Jamaican State Formation, 1780–1870* (2004), co-editor of *Gender and Slave Emancipation in the Atlantic World* (2005) and editor of *A Narrative of Events, since the first of August, 1834, by James Williams an Apprenticed Labourer in Jamaica* (2001).

**Sara Salih** is Associate Professor of English at the University of Toronto. She is currently working on a book about representations of 'brown' women in Jamaica and England from the Abolition era to the present day (Routledge, forthcoming 2008). She is the author of *Judith Butler* (Routledge, 2002), and the editor of the *Judith Butler Reader* (Blackwell, 2004), *The History of Mary Prince, a West Indian Slave* (Penguin, 2000), and *Wonderful Adventures of Mrs Seacole in Many Lands* (Penguin, 2005).

**Lincoln Shlensky**   is an Assistant Professor of English at the University of Victoria, in British Columbia, where he teaches postcolonial literature and Jewish Studies. He is currently preparing a manuscript entitled *Islands of Memory: Postcolonialism, the Holocaust, and Literary Politics*, which examines modernist literary influence and the politics of traumatic remembrance in Hebrew and Caribbean literatures.

**Marcus Wood**   is a painter and performance artist; he is also Professor of English and American Studies at the University of Sussex. He is the author of *Radical Satire and Print Culture 1790–1822* (Cambridge University Press, 1994), *Blind Memory: Visual Representations of Slavery in England and America 1780–1865* (Manchester University Press, 2000) and *Slavery, Empathy and Pornography* (Oxford University Press, 2002). The book of his exhibition, 'High Tar Babies' was published by Clinamen as *High Tar Babies: Race, Hatred, Slavery and Love* in 2001. He is also the editor of *The Poetry of Slavery: An Anglo-American Anthology 1764–1865* (Oxford University Press, 2003).

# Introduction

## BRYCCHAN CAREY AND PETER J. KITSON

Twelve negresses from Nubia brought a price
   Which the West Indian market scarce would bring,
Though Wilberforce at last has made it twice
   What 'twas ere abolition.
               (Byron, *Don Juan* (1821), Canto IV, st. 115)

BYRON'S MORDANT COMMENTARY on the economic effects of the British Abolition Act upon the market for human beings in both the Caribbean and the Levant (West and East) sets an appropriate tone and context for this volume of essays which *mark*, but do not celebrate, this historical moment, much fetishized in nineteenth- and twentieth-century British historiography. In 1807 Christian evangelicals of the stamp of Hannah More and William Wilberforce might proclaim the marvellous gift of the British abolition of the trade to the peoples of Africa, but the actual benefits of this, like those of the later Emancipation Act of 1833, are rather more complex and conflicted. On 25 March 1807, the Bill for the Abolition of the Slave Trade within the British colonies received the Royal Assent and passed by an overwhelming majority in the House of Commons, became law from 1 May 1807. Introducing the Bill into the House of Lords, Lord Grenville proclaimed that its enactment would be 'one of the most glorious acts that had ever been undertaken by any assembly of any nation in the world'. That same year the African Institution was formed to seek the enforcement of the Abolition Act and to further the market for trade with Africa in commodities other than those of human beings. Henceforth the British Royal Navy took up station outside the post of Freetown in Sierra Leone pursuing and capturing slave traders and liberating their 'live cargoes'. In the same year, President Thomas Jefferson signed into law a bill prohibiting American citizens from participating in the African Slave Trade.

Yet the trade was continued clandestinely by the Americans under other national flags. Rio de Janeiro recorded its largest annual import of African slaves (18,677) in 1810 and total slave imports to the Americas rose again in the 1820s. Despite the Emancipation Act of 1833, British abolitionists were sorely discomfited to learn that, by 1840, there were more slaves in British India than had ever been emancipated in the British colonies of the Caribbean. For many, the Abolition Act was not regarded as the prelude to the end of slavery, but the curtailing of a cruel and unnecessary activity. If plantation owners took better care of their slaves, it was argued, then their slaves would procreate and obviate the need for the maintenance of a Transatlantic trade with which only the most callous or disinterested were entirely comfortable. Attacking the institution of slavery was conceived as an attack upon the rights of property and a much more serious issue than the trade itself. Of course, many abolitionists, such as Thomas Clarkson and Granville Sharp, fully understood the strategic importance of attacking colonial slavery through the abolition of the trade – as did the West Indian planters themselves who realized that, so pitiless were the conditions of the field labourers combined with a punishing tropical environment, that the achievement of a self-sustaining workforce was never very likely, although it would prove possible in the less severe conditions of the United States.

The British Abolition Act (like the later Emancipation Act) has been subject to intense scrutiny from revisionist historians who have debated its importance and significance. The most influential, and one of the most contested, revisionist accounts of British abolition and emancipation was provided by Eric Williams, the postcolonial Prime Minister of Trinidad and Tobago. Williams attacked the consensus view that the abolition of the Transatlantic slave trade was accomplished by a group of high-minded evangelicals and Quakers. His seminal work, *Capitalism and Slavery* (1944), argued that the profits derived from colonial slave labour were important in financing the Industrial Revolution in Britain and Williams also claimed that both abolition and emancipation, rather than being the results of altruism for and empathy with African slaves, were the inevitable consequences of a decline in the profitability of the West Indian colonies and of an overproduction of sugar in 1806–7 and again in 1833. Plantation slavery, famously criticised as an unproductive mode of labour by Adam Smith in *The Wealth of Nations* (1776), thus belonged to the old world of protectionist, mercantilist empires at odds with the rise of a new economic system of wage labour, laissez-faire economics and colonial exploitation. Williams's beguiling linkage of the rise of capitalism and the growth of antislavery feeling, however, was subsequently criticised by historians of the trade (Anstey 1975; Drescher 1977; Bender 1992; Thomas 1997) who point to the economic success of the West Indian plantations in the decade from 1790 onwards as well as to the general profitability of the trade. David Brion Davis who believes that 'the emergence of an international antislavery opinion represented a momentous turning point in the evolution of man's moral perception, and thus in man's image of himself' (Davis 1975, 42) argued for a more sophisticated discussion of the interrelation between ideas and economics in the period, attempting to show the process by which the anti-slavery idea was translated into a social fact and became a means to enable collective action. Davis claimed that the new awareness of the unacceptability of colonial enslavement might very well serve the hegemonic function of legitimizing free labour, but he also argued that those putting forward antislavery ideas remained unaware of the hegemonic function served by their ideology.

The Slave Trade, however, was only abolished when, rightly or wrongly, it came to be perceived as against the economic and national interests of the British. What in the mid–1790s was seen by many as, at best, a sentimental and quixotic endeavour and, at worst, a politically radical and seditious business in sympathy with the most dangerous tendencies of the French Revolution, came to be viewed in an entirely different light in the years of amelioration prior to abolition. With the rise of Napoleon's military despotism and his restoration of slavery to the French colonies in 1802, abolitionism lost its radical colour and became something akin to patriotism in spirit. Of even greater significance was the French Emperor's failure to subdue the new free former slave republic of Haiti (1804) which effectively removed French competition in Caribbean sugar production. As Britain assimilated one French West Indian colony after another, she also acquired a surplus of tropical produce at a time when Napoleon's 'continental system' was hampering her access to European markets. With the Act of Union in 1801, new Irish members, traditionally sympathetic to the abolitionist cause, arrived at Westminster. Opposition to the trade was also significantly strengthened by the emergence of a cohort of younger and energetic abolitionists: most notably James Stephen, Zachary Macaulay (now returned from Sierra Leone), and the ambitious Utilitarian reformer Henry Brougham, politicians of a different calibre from the patrician Wilberforce.

The situation had been further complicated by the question of whether or not such British West-Indian conquests (and virgin territory) should be supplied with slaves. It was argued that they should not because, first, to bring new lands into sugar production would damage the established sugar colonies and, second, if the captured lands were ever to be returned to the French it would be foolish to return them enriched with British capital. These arguments were ably put forward in James Stephen's strategically ingenious *The Crisis of the Sugar Colonies* (1802). Abolition of the foreign trade in slaves thus now could be seen as working for the national interest rather than acting against it. It was also widely assumed that the United States would end the slave trade by 1808. The unexpected death of Wilberforce's friend the Tory Prime Minister William Pitt in 1806 was a boon to the abolitionists, leading to the formation of a ministry dominated by politicians strenuously opposed to the trade: the so-called 'Ministry of All the Talents' led by Lord Grenville as Prime Minister with Charles James Fox as Foreign Secretary. Both men were looking for an appropriately reforming measure to unite their coalition. The abolition of the transatlantic trade in slaves was that measure. The Foreign Slave Trade Bill of May 1806 prohibited the British trade in slaves to foreigners and to newly-conquered territories, bringing to an end the majority of the trade itself. In June 1806 a general motion for abolition was introduced into the Commons which, despite Fox's sudden death and an ensuing election, became law on 25 March 1807. From 1 May 1807 the British trade in slaves was formally, legally abolished.

Slavery and the traffic in human beings, of course, was never simply a British phenomenon. True, the British, though late-comers to the trade, established themselves as the most important dealers in human misery in the eighteenth century; yet slavery was, and, sadly still remains, a global blight and one that is not time bound by the important but regionalised history of the Transatlantic. As the essays in this volume make clear, slavery was practised by Christian and Muslims, in the colonies of the West Indies, in the Americas, in the Levant, along the 'Barbary Coast' of North Africa, and throughout sub-Saharan Africa. It was practised in the British, French, Ottoman and Qing empires (chattel slavery was not formerly abolished in China until the final decade of Manchu rule, though legal forms of servitude still remained until the 1950s). In the Romanov Empire serfdom rather than slavery was the norm for agricultural labourers throughout the nineteenth century. Though by the end of World War I chattel slavery and the slave trade had been largely eradicated and existed legally in only a few places, or as an illegal trade, other forms or practices which restricted human freedom, such as serfdom, forms of indentured labour, child labour, and forms of forced labour came to be defined as kinds of slavery. The struggle against such practices still, of course continues. (Drescher and Engerman 1998, 163–8).

Marking 1807 as point of transformation is an Anglo- or Eurocentric act. Other dates are equally as significant. In March 1792 the Danish government abolished the importing of slaves from Africa into their possessions. In 1791 the struggle for the independence of the slaves of Saint Domingue began. The French civil commissioner to the island, Léger-Felicité Sonthonax, issued a general emancipation decree in 1793. In Guadeloupe, a revolutionary army of freed slaves led by the Jacobin Victor Hughes defeated the royalist planters and their British allies and abolished slavery on the island. On 4 February 1794 the French National Convention outlawed slavery in all the French colonies, extending the rights of citizenship to all. Had not Napoleon restored slavery to the French colonies in 1802 it may well be that we would associate the acts of abolition with radical, free-thinking French revolutionaries such as Robespierre, Hughes and Sonthonax, rather than with the conservative Christian British evangelicals, Wilberforce and More. In any case, as Marcus Wood points out in his essay in this volume, freedom from slavery was first properly achieved by the slaves themselves with the establishment of the republic of Haiti, the New World's second independent nation, in 1804. Even earlier Black loyalist slaves secured their freedom by serving in the British army against the American revolutionaries. Their story has recently been retold by Simon Schama, who argues that the American Revolution, at least in the South was 'a revolution, first and foremost, mobilized to protect slavery.' Thousands had rallied to Earl Dunmore's declaration of 7 November 1775 promising freedom for all 'indentured servants, Negroes or others' willing to bear arms for the British. Dunmore's promise was kept by the unlikely figure of Sir Guy Carleton in the negotiations with General Washington, determined to reclaim his nation's (and his own) property, at the conclusion of the War (Schama 2005, 73, 80, 146). While Wilberforce piously, and by and large ineffectively, opined against the trade in the Commons, Black activists like Olaudah Equiano and later Robert Wedderburn agitated extensively in meetings up and down the land.

The essays in this volume emerge for the most part from recent debates about the culture, language and literature of slavery and abolition that have taken place within the field of English literary studies. While historical study of the British abolition movement has generated an extensive historiography, commencing with Thomas Clarkson's seminal *History of the Rise, Progress and Accomplishment of the Abolition of the African Slave Trade* (1808), literary and cultural scholars have become interested in British colonial slavery and its abolition only rather more recently. Writing separately in 1942, the American scholars Eva Beatrice Dykes and Wylie Sypher were the first critics to pay sustained attention to the representation of Africa and Africans in British literature of the Romantic era. Their findings, although now well known to scholars, failed at the time to inspire much interest in the literature of abolitionism. A quarter of a century later, in the late 1960s, a new generation of scholars led by Phillip Curtin and Paul Edwards began to raise questions about the published accounts of African visitors to eighteenth-century Britain, and Edwards made available facsimile editions of the works of Olaudah Equiano and Ignatius Sancho. Still, however, most academic inquiry into slavery and abolition was being conducted by historians, very few of whom were interested in looking either at slave culture or the culture of abolitionism.

In the 1980s, and more particularly in the 1990s, the study of the literary and cultural forms of slavery and abolition emerged as a distinct area of specialism within literary studies. In the 80s, David Dabydeen and Keith Sandiford's examinations of the representation of Africans, and of African self-representation in eighteenth-century English literature, offered important new readings of the 'black presence' in canonical literature, as well as demonstrating the rhetorical sophistication of African self-representations of the period. By the end of the 1990s, a growing number of critics, several of whom are represented in this volume, had approached the topic from a range of angles: Vincent Carretta, Angelo Costanzo, Helena Woodard and Helen Thomas had transformed our understanding of the slave narrative; Deirdre Coleman, Moira Ferguson and Felicity Nussbaum had demonstrated the relationship between abolitionism and British women's writing; Markman Ellis had shown that antislavery and sentimentalism were closely aligned, while Joan Baum, Deirdre Coleman, Tim Fulford, Peter Kitson, and Helen Thomas had explored the multiform ways in which the concerns of the emerging Romantic movement interacted with the ideals of the abolition, and later, the emancipation campaigns. Literary and cultural critics struck out beyond the written text: David Dabydeen and Marcus Wood explored representations of slaves and slavery in art, while the sociologist Paul Gilroy introduced the now widely recognized category of the 'Black Atlantic'. The texts of the abolition movement, long confined to remote library archives, were made available to a wider readership as well. By 2000, a dozen anthologies of eighteenth and nineteenth-century literature both by and about slaves in the British colonies had appeared; several editions of important African self-representations, such as those by Olaudah Equiano and Ignatius Sancho, had been issued, and a generous selection of original texts in facsimile had been edited by Peter Kitson and Debbie Lee.

These writers and editors, among others, laid the groundwork for what, in the first decade of the twenty-first century, has become an important sub-field in the areas of eighteenth-century literature and the literatures of the Romantic era. It is no longer possible in 2007, as it was even a mere decade ago, to teach or to research eighteenth and early nineteenth-century literature without paying attention to issues of race and empire, and without recognizing that Britain's participation in what Wordsworth called 'this most rotten branch of human shame' was both a violation of all the 'polite' and 'rational' principles of the Enlightenment tradition-ally seen as the hallmarks of the period, and a human tragedy on an unimaginably vast scale (Wordsworth 1926, X, 226). Having become established as an important sub-field of literary studies in the 1990s, the study of the literature of slavery and abolition is now seen as occupying an important position at the heart of all our attempts to understand the culture and thought – as well as the politics and economies – of those many societies tangled up in the complex web of slave trading and slave holding.

The essays in this collection cover a wide range of texts associated with slavery, the slave trade or abolitionism, from the sentimental writings of eighteenth-century abolitionists and ameliorationists to Black writers such as Olaudah Equiano and the contemporary novelist Caryl Phillips. They range from the literary, legal and historical to the visual, addressing the cultures of slavery and abolition in the widest sense. In the volume's first essay Marcus Wood addresses the articulation of abolition and emancipation as a gift of the European in a variety of visual works from contemporary paintings and statuary to Pontecorvo's powerful film *Burn* (aka *Queimada*). Taking his critical bearings from Frantz Fanon (among others) Wood shows how the 'white art of emancipation' is deeply imbricated in a Hegelian model of slavery which denies the enslaved the agency of recapturing a freedom which was never their enslavers' right to restore, any more than to take from them in the first place. The issue of slave revolt also features in the next two essays in the volume. In an authoritative scholarly discussion of the various representations of the renegade slave, Jack Mansong or 'Three Fingered Jack', Diana Paton shows how metropolitan readers and audiences interpreted this troublesome figure. Drawing on the noble Negro tradition of writing, Jack alternately represents an heroic avenger of British and plantocratic duplicity or a dangerous and unstable criminal; his image adapted to the changing contexts of British responses to slavery in the early nineteenth century. Sara Salih extends Paton's concerns to cover a wide range of literary and historical texts deriving from the abolitionist and ameliorationist phase of writing about slavery. She focuses, in particular, on the representation of the suppression of slave insurrection arguing that 'the repeated, almost obsessive, representation of insurrection and the punished black body constitutes a double "putting down," i.e. textual depiction as a form of textual quelling whereby the unruly black body is disciplined and delimited'. Salih arraigns writing about the tortures and punishments inflicted on slaves as involved in a contradictory aesthetic of sentimental sympathy which is, at best, quietist and, at worst, demonstrates a covert sadistic pleasure in the suppression of unruly subjects whose status as human beings was never clearly accepted. Salih also addresses the troubling issue, recently raised by Marcus Wood's *Slavery, Empathy and Pornography* (2002), of the ethics of white representations of slave sufferings and their complicity in a politics of subjugation and oppression.

George Boulukos focuses on a key text published in 1804 at the height of the debates about slave revolt and the violent but successful Saint Domingue slave revolution. Locating Charlotte Smith's *The Story of Henrietta* in the context of the contemporary debates about amelioration, rather than emancipation, Boulukos argues that the text presents a pessimistic view of the possibilities of improvement combined with a 'pronounced belief in racial difference'. Arguing that Smith's despair results from a belief in the racial depravity of the slaves combined with despair at the reactionary intransigence of the planters, Boulukos shows how Smith's ideas anticipate the racist master/slave dialectic of Hegel (also discussed by Wood). Lincoln Shlensky returns the focus of the collection to one of the subjects of the slave trade: the Black writer, Olaudah Equiano. Shlensky deftly surveys the recent debates about the authenticity of Equiano's narrative occasioned by the historical findings of Vincent Carretta. Situating these debates in the contexts of memory he asks the question as to what our concern with 'the focus on textual authenticity' in Equiano's *Narrative* may foreclose, or overshadow, in terms of a critical methodology? Focusing on the conversion episode as an allegory of his life story, Shlensky argues that Equiano offers not an authentic autobiography but a 'symbolically distilled and emblematic account of the barriers to, and possibility of, creating a truly representative collective identity in the West'. Uncovering some of the assumptions underlying representations of the slave trade is also the subject of Deirdre Coleman's commentary and transcription, for the first time, of the fascinating and important essay by the naturalist and 'flycatcher', Henry Smeathman,

'Oeconomy of a Slave Ship' written some time after 1775. Coleman shows how Smeathman's description of the slaver he sailed on is underpinned by Hobbesian conceptions of the polity of nature and Linnaean ideas about the centrality of insects to the grand vision of nature.

The next two essays move the focus of the volume eastwards to look at the issue of eighteenth-century Islamic slavery and its representation in two texts, one fictional and the other autobiographical. Felicity Nussbaum addresses the issue of Islamic forms of slavery in the collection and translation of tales we know as the *Arabian Nights*. Taking the case of one of the most influential, and least authentic, tales in the collection *Aladdin*, Nussbaum argues that its Africans and slaves do not fit easily into the concerns of abolitionist discourse. The *Nights* operates outside of Paul Gilroy's influential formulation of the Black Atlantic, yet, never-theless, offers traces of the origins of a modern black Diasporic subject related to, yet distinct from Islam. Gerald MacLean, in a challenging and polemical essay, also discusses the issue of Islamic slavery, this time that of Christian Europeans by the Muslim rulers of North Africa, recently popularised in contemporary accounts by Linda Colley, Robert C. Davis and Giles Milton. MacLean presents a close analysis of a little-known captivity narrative of the mid-eighteenth-century: Elizabeth Marsh's *The Female Captive: A Narrative of Facts Which happened in Barbary, in the Year 1756*. He argues that Marsh's narrative presents a romance depicting the anguished sufferings of its heroine within an exotic and oriental setting which is worryingly suitable for historical recovery at a time when a re-current strand of Western Islamophobia is present. MacLean critiques a recent study of European slavery in the Mediterranean and Barbary Coast and its reception. The volume concludes by returning to Transatlantic slavery and other forms of Black experience in Maroula Joannou's discus-sion of Caryl Phillips's novel *Crossing the River* (1993). Joannou argues that Phillips is the most significant contemporary Black British novelist to re-vision the history of slavery and the continuing impact on the re-lationships between white and black people in the modern world. Joannou discusses, among other issues, the problematics of Phillips's appropriation of John Newton's *Journal* for the section of his novel deal-ing with the Middle Passage and the ethics of how we discuss, talk about, memorialize or otherwise represent the trauma of slavery and the trade in human beings, which we never ourselves could experience in 2007, some two hundred years after one particular bill was enacted as a piece of legislation.

## Works Cited

Anstey, Roger, 1975. *The Atlantic Slave Trade and British Abolition*. New Jersey: Humanities Press.

Bender, Todd, ed., 1992. *The Antislavery Debate: Capitalism as a Problem in Historical Interpretation*. Berkeley: University of California Press.

Clarkson, Thomas, 1808. *History of the Rise, Progress and Accomplishment of the Abolition of the African Slave Trade*.

Davis, David Brion, 1975. *The Problem of Slavery in the Age of Revolution*. Cornell: Cornell University Press.

Drescher, Seymour, 1977. *Econocide: British Slavery in the Era of Abolition*. Philadelphia: Pittsburgh University Press.

Drescher, Seymour, and Stanley L. Engerman, eds., 1998. *A Historical Guide to World Slavery*. Oxford: Oxford University Press.

Schama, Simon, 2006. *Rough Crossings: Britain, the Slaves and the American Revolution*. London: BBC Books.

Smith, Adam, 1776. *The Wealth of Nations*.

Stephen, James, 1802. *The Crisis of the Sugar Colonies*.

Thomas, Hugh, 1997. *The Slave Trade: The History of the Atlantic Slave Trade, 1440–1870*. London: Picador.

Williams, Eric, 1944. *Capitalism and Slavery*. Chapel Hill NC: University of North Carolina Press.

Wood, Marcus, 2002. *Slavery, Empathy and Pornography*.

Wordsworth, William, 1926. *The Prelude* (1805 Text) ed. Ernest de Selincourt (Oxford: Oxford University Press) Book X, lines 203–228.

# Emancipation Art, Fanon and 'the butchery of Freedom'

## MARCUS WOOD

> Willy nilly the black has to wear the livery that the white man has sewed for him.
>
> (Fanon [1967] 1991, 3)

| | |
|---|---|
| Soldier: | But then after a while maybe they will free you. |
| José Dolores: | It does not work like that friend. If a man gives you freedom it is not freedom. Freedom is something you alone must take. Do you understand? |
| Soldier: | No. |
| José Dolores: | But one day you will because you have already begun to think about it. |

> (Pontecorvo 1968)

MEDITATING UPON the sheer power which the myth of the emancipation moment[1] exerts over the black, and white, imagination, Frantz Fanon wrote the following bizarre words:

> Some thirty years ago a coal black Nigger in a Paris bed with a 'maddening' blond, shouted at the moment of orgasm 'Hurrah for Schoelcher!' ... it was Victor Schoelcher who persuaded the Third Republic to adopt the decree abolishing slavery ... (Fanon [1967] 1991, 63)

For Fanon that black man's orgasmic roar, 'Hurrah for Schoelcher' exists against the backdrop of several statues showing black youth, clothed to various degrees, standing next to the over-coated figures of Victor Schoelcher. They are late nineteenth- and early twentieth-century developments of a body of imagery perfected by the British and celebrating white philanthropists, at the moment of black release from bondage, as

---

[1]   As far as I know David Brion Davis coined the term 'emancipation moment', see, 'The Emancipation Moment', 22nd Annual Robert Fortenbaugh Memorial Lecture. The text was published as Davis 1983. This remains the most succinct and enlightening discussion of the rhetorical limits and methods of Abolition narratives of emancipation.

*Fig. 1.* Richard Westmacott, *Memorial to Charles James Fox*, marble, 1815.
Photographed by the author.

'the friend of the slave'. I want to open inductively with Fanon because
of the insights he has into the constrictions and erasures which are operated by the visual art generated by emancipation.

   In Britain Charles James Fox, William Wilberforce, Granville Sharp
and Thomas Clarkson all appeared in text and image as 'the friend of the
slave'. Fox's monument in Westminster Abbey might serve as an introductory example for the manner in which European memorial and emancipation sculpture encoded the Black body. **(fig. 1)** Fox had certainly
been a consistent 'champion of freedom' whether it was for the rights of
American and then French revolutionaries, English radical labourers,
Catholics or slaves. He died days before the Slave Trade Abolition Bill
went through parliament, and made a suitably grand death bed statement about how this measure was the one thing that allowed him to:
'consider my life well spent'. The monument which Richard Westmacott
made for Westminster Abbey nearly a decade later showed Fox in classical toga, as a latter day Roman Senator, gazing heavenwards at the moment
of death. He is embraced by a beautiful female figure of Liberty, while a
tragically smitten female figure of Peace has collapsed over his feet and

*Fig. 2.* Society for Effecting the Abolition of the Slave Trade, *Abolition seal,* jasperware, 1789. Private collection.

ankles. On the ground near the foot of the great statesman's couch, and physically separated from him and the females, is the kneeling figure of a liberated black male slave. This slave is a precise three dimensional adaptation of the enslaved black shown on the Seal of the Society for the Abolition of the Slave Trade, who in 1789 was famously allowed to ask: 'Am I not a man and a brother?' **(fig. 2)** The only major alterations are that the chains and shackles around the wrists of the original figure have gone, and that the black physiognomy is now sculpted according to European norms of facial beauty, rather than according to the distorted race stereotypes of the original seal. I shall be returning to the long term, indeed immovable, grip which the Abolition Seal exerted on subsequent emancipation art across Europe and the Americas. What I want to emphasise here, in the context of Fanon, is that even though this black has been given his freedom, and has had his chains physically removed, he is still imprisoned within the posture and gestures which the Abolitionists invented and which white society considered the most acceptable official icon of the Atlantic slave. The black slave has been given a strange form of freedom, and is now frozen forever within a gratitude which imprisons him.

*Abolition's Catch 22: 'the gift of freedom'*

Victor Schoelcher, the veteran abolitionist and confirmed scientific racist referred to by Fanon, died aged eighty-nine. Soon afterwards the colonies in which he had worked set up memorials. **(fig. 3)** In Louis Ernest
Barriat's 1896 statue there is a definite homo-erotic charge. The lithe
black youth in his loin-cloth, is beautiful, with his slender legs, his almost
female belly, reminiscent of a Cranach Venus, and his hands covering his
heart, but caressing his nipple. The old patriarch wears an overcoat and
his arm is raised. He seems to be telling the young black to grow into his
freedom, to go off and enjoy himself. Yet as we shall see, Fanon's savage
satire is all about refusing the freedom which Schoelcher, like so many
other sculpted white emancipators, lays on youthful black masculinity
with, seemingly, such an easy innocence.[2]

Fanon hated these statues of colonial heroes which littered the capital
of Martinique, he saw in them the stultifying symbols of 'a motionless,
Manichaeistic world, a world of statues ... a world which is sure of itself,
which crushes with its stones the blacks flayed by whips'. (Fanon [1961]
1967, 40) What Fanon is saying is that under the terms of this contract of
liberation the black man's expression of freedom will always be intimately
bound to this original moment of controlled white donation. For Fanon
each of these statues, and each image which shows a black with a white
man on his shoulder telling him to walk out into the life a free man, is a
semiotic trick.

Within such images is an encoded expression of the continuation of
slavery. The black man is theoretically free, he can even enjoy carnal
relations with white women, but whatever he does, and wherever he does
it, he can never get Schoelcher out of his mind. That statue, Schoelcher
exhibiting on the one side a light, superior and un-intimate embrace, on
the other a mighty raised arm embodying the 'gift of freedom', is a haunting image. Like a nightmare it pervades, it saturates, liberated black existence, it floods black consciousness with its knowing superfluity. Even
at the most intimate moment of adult life, the moment when life is created and human physicality and spirituality glimpse the possibility of a
complete liberation through union with another, old Victor Shoelcher is
still there with his hand on the shoulder of the beautiful black youth.
Under what might be termed a white sentence of freedom the black eter-
nally performs for the amusement of the white Patriarchal voyeur: 'Hurrah for Schoelcher!' indeed. The following analysis of the representation

---

[2]   For Schoelcher, the colonies and race theory see Cohen 1980, 198–270.

*Fig. 3.*    Louis Ernest Barriat, *Schoelcher memorial*, plaster, Musée Saint Nazaire, 1896. Musée Saint-Lazaire, Bourbon Nancy.

of black freedom by white cultures is an attempt to do justice to Fanon's tremendous insight. I shall be taking a series of images which grew out of the 1807 Abolition Bill, in order to illustrate the controlling semiotic apparatus Fanon has isolated. As a first step, however, it is necessary to explain how Fanon's strangely neglected theory works.

### Fanon seeing through Hegel and seeing Hegel for what he is

At one of the most charged points in *Black Skins, White Masks* Fanon uncovers the metaphorics of slave liberation as they work through the officially sanctioned arts of emancipation. He shows us how, again and again, but in an instant, white metropolitan government commanded the slave power to cast an official, formalised, in some ways abstracted, cultural construction of freedom upon the slave population. Fanon searches deeply into the appalling moral *aporia* lying within the myth that freedom can ever be 'given' by any master to any slave. Fanon's insights enable us to see the tumultuous artistic production erected around the myths of white freedom within the slave Diaspora as a deeply damaging control fantasy.

Fanon produces a transformative engagement with the power dynamics disguised and encoded within the archive generated by the emancipation moment. His thesis is carefully worked out of a quite new construction of Hegel's master slave dialectic. Fanon transforms the terms of the discussion by approaching the implications of the Hegelian theory from the perspective of emancipation. Fanon's analysis deserves a core position within the ever-growing body of work dedicated to thinking about how Hegel's meditation on the limits of power and enslavement might be related to the Atlantic Diaspora.[3] In the second section of the seventh chapter of *Black Skins, White Masks* entitled 'The Negro and Hegel' Fanon confronts the celebrated formulation of the master slave dialectic. He initially summarises the conflictual dynamic set out by Hegel in order to explain how a consciousness develops its humanity, its sense of self. Fanon summarises that it is only through struggle, a struggle even to the point of death, with the consciousness of another (the master) that the consciousness of the slave can attain a sense of its own being, a sense of being in reality free. In Hegel's world of macho spirituality an independent consciousness can only be forged through what is basically a duel. Hegel provides what might be described as a 'no pain, no gain' theory of spiritual birth: 'The individual who has not staked his life may, no doubt, be recognised as a *person*, but he has not attained the truth of this recognition as an independent person.' (Hegel 1949, 233) Fanon's crucial insight is to take Hegel's abstract model into the specific racialised power dynamics of the Diaspora.[4] For Hegel's crucial struggle into a heightened

---

[3]    Hegel casts his spell upon a variety of major intellectuals working on Atlantic slavery from different disciplines and with different political agendas. The two most forceful applications of Hegel within Diaspora studies are David Brion Davis in his 'Epilogue' (Davis [1975] 1999), 557–564; and Gilroy 1992, where he applies the master slave dialectic to Frederick Douglass's account of his battle with the slave master Covey in the *Narrative of the Life of Frederick Douglass*.

[4]    It is relevant that Hegel had very specific ideas about black Africans, and that his thought in this area is primitive and clearly circumscribed by contemporary dogma on race. As far as Hegel was concerned Africa and Africans were shut out of the terms of the master slave dialectic, and indeed the concerns of Hegelian philosophy generally. For Hegel, Africans constituted a lower form of life. Their

state of free consciousness recognition of 'the one' by 'the other' is essential. In order for the struggle between master and slave to occur the mutual recognition of difference must occur. But what, Fanon asks, if you exist in a crazy world, where the Master, with no warning, decides to pull the rug out from under the feet of the master–slave dialectic by saying: 'I abolish slavery'? Suddenly the master gives you your freedom for nothing, whether you want it or not, and there is nothing to be done about this filthy gift. Fanon sums it up humorously, indeed with a very strange 'black' humour:

> Historically the Negro, steeped in the inessentiality of servitude was set free by his master. He did not fight for his freedom.
> Out of slavery the Negro burst into the lists where his master stood. Like those servants who are allowed once every year to dance in the drawing room, the Negro is looking for a prop. The Negro has not become a master. When there are no longer slaves, there are no longer masters. (Fanon [1967] 1991, 219)

Fanon reveals the cunning robbery at the heart of the decree of emancipation. At a stroke slavery is abolished, and so slave and master suddenly cease to exist. In Hegelian terms this means that there is suddenly no 'other' whose destruction will enable the spiritual birth of the slave, and this means that the slave is forever locked out of the possibility of fighting

---

consciousness is explicitly described as comparable to that of the dog, and consequently they are creatures not capable of the basic spiritual self-consciousness required in order to embark on the Hegelian quest towards enlightenment. The position is set out with a brutal clarity in the fascinating 'Appendix C on Africa' included in Hegel's *Lectures on the Philosophy of World History* (Hegel 1975). This appendix has proved a rather unpleasant choke-pear for elevated Hegelian philosophical scholarship. It must however be frankly admitted that Hegel emerges as a clumsy cultural analyst, who exhibits a crude but wholly conventional set of assumptions about Africans. The perusal of a handful of popular history and travel books on sub-Saharan Africa provided Hegel with the materials for an extended and generalising account of the African continent. In the pages of his 'Appendix C' he recycles with an ignorant enthusiasm the full range of stereotypes generated by contemporary European racist fantasies of the 'Dark Continent'. It is *not* surprising that philosophical scholarship has sidestepped this material, or insisted that it can only be comprehended within the larger mysteries of the Hegelian schema. It *is* surprising that post-colonial and Diaspora theory has not considered the implications of this extended race diatribe (a crazily, indeed comically, exaggerated catalogue of atavistic blood lust and Dahomanian cannibalistic excess) in terms of where it places the African in relation to the master slave dialectic.

for his or her freedom. The black slave can only celebrate under licence, and in that image of the servant dancing in the drawing room Fanon gestures towards the multitude of emancipation art which shows the liberated black capering while white Benevolence gazes on with a controlling amusement.

White imposition of the abolition of slavery suddenly shuts down the iconic possibility of slave revolution, slave rebellion, the slave as freedom fighter. And in a final piece of white devilry the master has been magically transformed, with a sudden bang, into a refulgent benefactor, bestowing that very thing which according to the logic of the Hegelian dialectic could never be given, freedom. It is of course a sleight of hand, moral smoke and mirrors, an abolition dodge, which suddenly generates myriad cultural fictions. There they are in the massed crowds, in the statuary and friezes erected in city squares and town halls, in every commemorative newspaper showing the slave kissing this or that white hand. All this art of emancipation plays out endless variations in which the jubilantly submissive slave jumps for joy, while the shackles fall, and in which the kneeling slave expresses unending gratitude. Suddenly slavery has gone, and the memory of slavery, has been replaced in a flash by a space of celebration and thanks, which insists on the fiction of an enforced equality of black and white.

Fanon has deep insights into how this violently imposed fiction of freedom really works:

> One day a good white Master who had influence said to his friends, "Lets be nice to the niggers ..."
> The other masters argued, for after all it was not an easy thing, but then they decided to promote the machine-animal-men to the supreme rank of *men*.
> *Slavery shall no longer exist on French soil.*
> The upheaval reached the Negroes from without. The black man was acted upon. Values that had not been created by his actions, values that had not been born of the systolic tide of blood, danced in a hued whirl around him. (Fanon [1967] 1991, 220)

Fanon describes a perpetual process of daylight robbery, freedom has been stolen from the blacks in the original act of enslavement. Then, in the very act of giving freedom back, it is stolen away for a second time, for there can now never be any process of cleansing revolutionary violence. Fanon sees in this process of deception a tragic legacy, the removal of the possibility of revolutionary black consciousness and its replacement with a black frustration and confusion so intense as to be pathological:

> The liberation of the black slaves produced psychoses and sudden deaths.
>
> It is not an announcement that one hears twice in a lifetime. The black man contented himself with thanking the white man and the most forceful proof of the fact is the impressive number of statues erected all over France and the colonies to show white France stroking the kinky hair of this nice Negro, whose chains had just been broken.
>
> 'Say thank you to the nice man' the mother tells her little boy … but we know that the little boy is often dying to scream some other expression … (Fanon [1967] 1991, 220)

Fanon, with the prescience of a true artist, creates an articulate space here, poised between silence and furious utterance. What is the little boy dying to scream in the place of silence? Maybe he doesn't even know, because all he has is a sense that he has been robbed blind. This is not a fantasy, but a commentary on a whole genre of art works produced in the form of prints, paintings and statues. Fanon refuses to see this inheritance from the perspective of the white paternalistic forces which generated it, but forces his reader to come at it with a new set of eyes, the eyes of the ex-slave tortured by the gift of liberty.

The great emancipation swindle is set up in order to refuse the ex-slave's consciousness both the historical memory of the trauma of slavery, and the enabling presence of an antagonistic white patriarchy: 'When it does happen that the Negro looks fiercely at the white man, the white man tells him: "Brother there is no difference between us." And yet the Negro knows that there is a difference. He *wants* it. He wants the white man to turn on him and shout "Damn Nigger!"' (Fanon [1967] 1991, 221) Fanon sees in the mythology of emancipation the foundations of today's benign liberal racisms. Such racisms have found in the easy fictions of equality, parity, sameness, a way of avoiding any real engagement with the difficult aspects of the inheritance of Atlantic slavery. In this sleek but savage equation the 'gift of liberty' is also the gift of invisibility. We are in the territory so majestically mapped in Ellison's *Invisible Man*, and yet that territory was first discovered, maybe even first invented, in the successive waves of emancipation propaganda which flooded Europe and the Americas from 1807 to 1888. Fanon argues that the slave power, even at the moment of its dissolution, set a terrible mechanism in place that forever compromised and destabilised black access to a pure rebellious hatred. In this sense the amassed cultural archive of the emancipation moment is a dark and destructive phenomenon. In the piles of broken chains, in the endlessly repeated smiles of dancing blacks, and in the refulgent masses of myriad female allegorical embodiments of Liberty, Justice, Britannia, Columbia or Brasilia we do not have something merely misleading. What Fanon demands that we see in the organisation of this colossal fantasy, so consistent across the Black Atlantic, is nothing less than a brilliantly constructed aesthetic system for the control of white guilt and black suffering, and for the disguise of white culpability and black outrage.

Fanon ends with an incensed lament on cultural belatedness: 'The former slave needs a challenge to his humanity, he wants a conflict, he wants a riot. But it is too late.' (Fanon [1967] 221) And yet, like Aimé Césaire before him, Fanon although he has seen through this white fiction of black belatedness, will simply not let it go at that. In the final page of the analysis of Hegel and the inheritance of abolition Fanon enters both pro-phetic and parodic mode and creates a tragico-satiric interpretation of emancipation art. It is a triumphantly bitter finale in which Fanon firstly enacts the ecstatic outbreak of cleansing revolutionary blood lust which emancipation had robbed the blacks of. He then, however, shifts from this vision straight into an ironic assault upon those very forms of white state art built to shut out the possibility of remembering a slave revolution:

> "The twelve million black voices" howled against the curtain of the sky. Torn from end to end, marked with the gashes of teeth biting into the belly of interdiction, the curtain fell like a burst balloon.
>
> On the field of battle, its four corners marked by the scores of Ne-groes hanged by their testicles, a monument is slowly being built that promises to be majestic.
>
> And at the top of the monument, I can already see a white man and a black man *hand in hand*. (Fanon [1967] 1991, 222)

Just when we feel certain that the monument to this fantastic spectacle of failed black rebellion will be a barbaric exhibition of sexually tortured black bodies Fanon has the last laugh. Fanon steps in as hands on satirist and erects a fantastic monument both to black suffering and to white complacency. The official vision of a false and effortless black and white equality, was enacted in thousands of emancipation monuments, statu-ettes, dinner services and engravings. In this sense Fanon both sets up, and simultaneously sends up, a body of work that has remained remark-ably consistent in its symbolic essentials across the entire slave Diaspora from 1807 onwards. Fanon instructs us to see, rising above the real bodies of black men strung up by the balls, something far more vicious – the benign lie of the emancipation moment. What Fanon exposes is the inability of white European and American cultures to understand that freedom, in a terribly real sense, was never something they had the power to give the slave populations they had created.

*Semiotic ghosts and the 'gift of freedom': the long shadow of the Abolition Seal*

From time to time I receive correspondence from the Wilberforce House museum. The envelopes are always embellished with one or more white stickers showing a crude photographic reproduction of the figure of a kneeling black male, shackled at the wrists, hands extended out before him as if in prayer, wearing a white loin cloth.(**fig. 4**) He kneels under the caption 'Wilberforce House Hull Est. 1906 Britain's First Slavery Museum'. The figure is an adapted version of the image we have already briefly considered in the context of the black figure on Fox's monument. (**fig. 1**) What does it mean that this figure is still considered the appropriate factotum of a slavery museum dedicated to a white abolition leader? What does it mean that this figure is still endlessly cut up, reproduced, or morphed into a variety of other figures in illustrations, graphic satires and advertisements?

Fanon explained that at the rhetorical heart of white emancipation propaganda was its assumption that freedom remain the gift of the white.

*Fig. 4.*  Wilberforce House, *Sticker adapted from the Abolition Seal*, printed paper, 1998. Collection of the author.

This was his great insight, because once you understand this, then it doesn't really matter whether the colonial imagination that talks of black freedom claims to be pro-slavery or abolitionist. The controlling mechanisms were put in place from the outset of Abolition as a Euro-American phenomenon, and have remained monolithic. I am going to use the Abolition Seal, and the history of its adaptations through time and place, as a proof of this assertion. The famous Seal combined image and word with ruthless economy to create a most Fanonian impasse for the emergence of a free black subject.

It is no exaggeration to say that this little icon provided a distillation of the rationale for the entire body of visual art which was to be generated under the pressures of a series of emancipation moments within the  Atlantic slave diaspora. The Abolition Seal is a semiotic nexus, a net for containing the black male and female. In England, France, North America and Brazil, from 1807–1888 successive emancipation moments generated successive waves of emancipation statues, paintings, envelopes, mezzotints, stipple engravings, woodcuts, samplers, cups, saucers and plates. These objects, with their often elaborate allegories of freedom, have one constant ingredient. They invariably carry images of slave men, women and children, who, although emancipated and no longer enchained, still replicate with ominous precision, the precise posture of the supplicant black who asked in 1789 'Am I not a man and a brother?', and a little later in the version produced showing a female slave 'Am I not a woman and a sister?'[5]

The image places the viewer in a one on one relation with the slave body, the caption gives the power of instant manumission to the viewer. David Brion Davis has posited that 'the idea of emancipation was profoundly influenced by the model of manumitting individual slaves'. (Davis 1983, 17) He further argues that manumission constituted a rite of passage in the same way that a birth, death, marriage or baptism did. If one applies this brilliant insight to the Abolition Seal and its motto, then the crucial element must be that it is the viewer who is given absolute power over this intimate rite of passage. What the Abolition Seal bestowed on the white viewer was the power to manumit.

In many ways the Abolition Seal was the first great piece of liberation propaganda to generate an international, indeed intercontinental, impact

---

[5]  For reasons of economy I concentrate fairly exclusively upon adaptation of the male version of the Seal in this article. The adaptive history of the female version in the nineteenth century within the North American context is conveniently plotted by Yellin 1989, 3–29.

# Library Services

No. 084 117

# Library Services

No. ....................

Self Collection of holds

(Last 6 digits of barcode no.

located on the bottom of

your University card)

Please issue the item at

the self service machine be-

fore you leave this area.

mu.ac.uk    LIBRARY SERVICES

upon the slave diaspora. Its instant, ubiquitous, and, judging from the stationery of Wilberforce House, continuing success, may be explained by the manner in which it encoded an entire anti-liberation philosophy. Within the racial dynamic of this print the white power to say yes (which of course implicitly tenders an antithesis, the right to say no) is the necessary pre-condition by which the possibility of black freedom is allowed to be introduced. This image with its accompanying aphorism laid down the ground rules for how white abolitionists liked to envision their power over prospective emancipated blacks. Kneeling, supplicant and still enchained, the slave must ask for the right to possess a gender and a human status.

## The conflicted evolution of the Abolition Seal

When it came to developing a white controlled semiotics for the configuration of the emancipated slave the inheritance was a tricky one. Emancipation as a large-scale phenomenon in the Atlantic diaspora did not first arrive in 1807, or 1833, or any of the later watershed dates across Europe and the Americas. It first came in two contexts, both of which had the effect of generating a deeply confused set of symbols and art narratives: the first context was the American War of Independence, the second was the Haitian War of Independence. As early as 1775 the British began to implement a policy of liberating any black slave who would fight with them, or work with them, against the rebel colonies. The first three hundred slaves who joined up with the British army became the Royal Ethiopian Regiment. The first widely used abolition motto was not 'Am I not a man and a brother', but the rather more forthright words 'Liberty to Slaves' which the British had embroidered on the uniforms of this first black regiment of free slaves some fifteen years before the creation of the Abolition Seal.[6] As the war progressed British hypocrisy, uneasiness and confusion over their policy of liberating slaves through enlistment became increasingly manifest. At the end of the war the cessation of hostilities between white English and white American was not carried over to blacks, no matter what national identity they embraced. The slave population was treated with casual duplicity by the defeated British. Their ex-slave army was broken up amidst confused negotiations with the victorious colonists, who wanted their property returned. Some

---

[6]   Quarles 1961 remains the standard account of the treatment of slaves in the revolutionary war.

black soldiers ended up back in enslavement. A group of about three thousand were evacuated *en masse* to found a new colony of freed blacks in Nova Scotia. Given the moral miasma surrounding this monumental failure of British nerve and American moral vision it is not surprising that neither the victorious colonists with their pro-slavery agenda, nor the British, still a mighty slave power in the Caribbean, felt obliged to generate propaganda celebrating this first 'emancipation moment' within the slave Diaspora.[7]

It should be clear even from the necessarily scanty overview set out above that the War of Independence, and the celebration of the gift of liberty within the graphic culture of North America, were set up to gen-erate some bizarre semiotic cross currents. The black slave body was fig-ured in circuitous and obfuscatory ways. Of course the first extended graphic works to deal with the process of bestowing freedom on Ameri-cans forced to endure the yoke of colonialism depicted not blacks but whites and 'indians'. As early as 1766 North America had developed an elaborate iconography relating to the 'gift of Freedom' from Britain. The crucial point is that this tradition shut out the black slave body. The first recorded political engraving to come out of the colonies is an elaborate representation in four panels of the obelisk which was erected on Boston common to celebrate the repeal of the British Stamp Act. The 1766 print *A View of the Obelisk erected under Liberty-Tree in Boston* sets out the four narrative allegories which adorned each facet of a giant ithyphallic and illuminated monument.[8] Presiding over each of the narrative panels are quadruple portraits of British aristocrats, royals and politicians deemed to be the dispensers of Liberty to the colonies. Throughout the panels the colonies are represented symbolically as a native American, with a skirt of foliage and a bow and arrow. In the second of the panels this figure kneels in supplication before British figures who stood out against the stamp tax and implores protection from the enemies of Liberty. The gesture of suppli-cation anticipates that of the slave in the Abolition Seal, yet the African-American slave body is conspicuous throughout this design by its absence.

The final panel in the print shows the symbolic native American now standing upright, with bow still in hand greeted by the figures of Liberty and Britannia. In other words the emblematic figures who were to populate the abolition prints produced in their thousands in England to mark the 1807 Slave Trade Bill (prints which then provided the basis for endless adaptations in subsequent emancipation propaganda) had already been

---

[7]   Hochschild 2005, 98–105.
[8]   For the discussion and reproduction of this print see Reilly 1991, 1766 – 1, p. 1.

developed in the context of the War of Independence. Few prints seem to have survived representing American liberation, but those which have maintain the essential symbolic elements of this early design. So for example prints evolved out of the elaborate allegoric representation of the War of Independence by British artist Robert Edge Pine continue to show the liberated America as a supplicant native American female. **(fig. 5)** In the 1781 engraving *America to Those who wish to Sheathe the Desolating Sword of War* she kneels, barefoot, wrapped in furs, with her left breast exposed, hands clasped in supplication. The allegorical figures of Liberty, Concord and Plenty approach her, while refulgent, and breaking through the clouds of war the figure of Peace descends from the sky with an olive branch. Again this figure of America closely anticipates the posture and attitude which were to be projected onto both male and female slave bodies initially in the designs of the Abolition Seals.[9]

*Fig. 5.* Robert Edge Pine, pinxit [1778], Joseph Strutt sculp., *America to Those who wish to Sheathe the Desolating Sword of War*, stipple engraving on copper, 1781. Ashforth Collection.

[9] The most detailed historical commentary on the prints generated by the War of Independence in America is *American Political Prints 1766–1876. A Catalogue of the Collections in the Library of Congress* ed. Bernard F. Reilly, Jr. (G. K. Hall,

It is a sad fact that when it came to celebrations of the 1807 Slave Trade Abolition Bill in American visual art black freedom was in fact savagely ridiculed within print satire. Blacks do not seem present in North American political graphics on the subject until 1808, and fascinatingly then they appear in crude racist satires from the North ridiculing the Black commemoration of American Abolition of the Slave Trade. This was traditionally celebrated by free Black communities in the Northern states on the 14 July, although the date of Abolition of the Trade was actually Jan. 1 1808. Black abolitionists immediately became the butt of white ridicule, which manifested itself in a tradition of racist satires known to historians of the American prints as the 'Bobalition' series. 'Bobalition' (a supposed black dialect corruption of abolition) prints endlessly reworked the notion that any black attempt to talk about, or formally celebrate emancipation would be ridiculous. **(fig. 6)** In this example *Grand Bobalition, or 'GREAT ANNIBERSARY FUSSIBLE'* the blacks are shown

*Fig. 6.    Grand Bobalition, or 'GREAT ANNIBERSARY FUSSIBLE'*, wood-engraving, c. 1808. Ashforth Collection.

Boston, 1991) see prints for 1766–96; see also Gwyn Williams, *A Cartoon History of the American Revolution* (London, London Editions, 1977); and Peter D. G. Thomas, *The English Satiric Print 1600–1632* (Cambridge, Chadwyck Healey, 1986).

as a ludicrous militia, marching to celebrate the anniversary of the abolition of the slave trade. The text is an elaborate parody of the toasts, songs
and speeches made to mark this important commemoration all framed
within a parodic letter of instruction from one 'Cesar Crappo'. There is a
dark irony in the fact that these 'Bobalition' prints dominate early white
representations of black freedom in political satire. To summarise: if one
looks at the overall patterns of the representation of emancipation in
early American graphic art it seems the slaves were kept out of prints
celebrating the end of the War of Independence. Then when blacks attempted to mark the American passage of the Slave Trade Abolition Bill
they were mercilessly mocked. This tradition of mockery runs consistently through from 1808 to reach a new intensity in 1832–3, maybe to
coincide with American free black responses to British Abolition.[10]

The fluctuating responses of the French nation to its involvement
in slave trading and the existence of its San Domingo plantations was
to generate a fascinating body of visual material in Paris from 1789 up
until English abolition of the Trade in 1807. The French context for
the figure of the kneeling slave in emancipation prints is complicated.
The French revolutionary intelligentsia were exposed to the first great
wave of English abolition propaganda from its originatory point in 1789,
when a young Thomas Clarkson visited the newly formed *Amis des Noirs*
in Paris. He was equipped with substantial packages of visual propaganda, including copies of the Plan of the Slave Ship *Brookes*, and versions of the Abolition Seal. His accounts, and those of people exposed
to the materials he brought, indicate the impact of this material.[11] The
*Amis des Noirs* were apparently behind an attempt to mass-produce copies of the Wedgwood medallion of the Abolition Seal for French distri-
bution. This immediately aroused the horror of French administrators
who pressured the Sèvres porcelain factory into abandoning the scheme
on the grounds that the medallions, now suitably inscribed *Ne suis-je
un homme? Un frère?* would, if sent to the French colonies, foment instant rebellion.[12]

Yet, it would be a mistake to assume that French designs using the
figure of the kneeling slave were solely developed out of the English design.

[10] See Reilly 1991, 1819–1, 1821–1, 1825–1, 1827–1, 1832–4 for other examples; collections of 'Bobalition' satire 1808–1835.
[11] For a detailed account of these interactions and particularly for the effect of
the propaganda on Mirabeau see Wood 2000, 26–9; also Oldfield, 1995.
[12] See letter 8 April 1789 from Compt d'Agiviller to the director of the Sèvres
factory, quoted in Honour 1989, 79.

*Fig. 7.* Chambon, Laurent sculp., *Le Commerce de l'Amérique par Marseille*, plate *Marché d'esclaves*, copper engraving, 1764. Collection of the author.

French travel literature of the mid-eighteenth-century contained images which seem to anticipate, with some precision, the emancipation prints which incorporated the image of the kneeling slave from the English Abolition Seal. Take for example the upper plate from Chambon's *Le Commerce de l'Amérique par Marseille*. **(fig. 7)** The image would appear to represent a benevolent eighteenth-century gentleman either commiserating with a slave, or embracing him, and telling him what freedom meant. In this sense it seems an early pre-cursor of that body of public sculpture which was to culminate in the Lincoln Emancipation Monument in Washington. In fact the image carried an entirely different set of meanings and occurred in an objective account of French colonial trade practises produced in 1764. At this date there was very little public sense, in France or in England, that there was anything morally suspect about the Guinea trade. What appears to be a tender embrace and a kiss is nothing of the sort. The explanatory text attached to the number 3 within the engraving reads: 'An Englishman licking a Negro's chin to ascertain his age, & to determine from the taste of his sweat if he is sick.' (Quoted in Honour 1989, 56) This is clearly at one level not anything to do with abolition philosophy. And yet it is surely troubling that, in the manner in which white domination is exhibited as enforced intimacy, the print does share a lot with the subsequent emancipation prints and statues showing

*Fig. 8.* Pierre Rouvier, in *La Cause des esclaves nègres*, plate *Soyez libre et citoyens*, copper engraving, 1789. Collection of the author.

white standing males embracing kneeling black males in order to thrust freedom upon them.

In fact the earliest graftings of the figure of the kneeling black into visual representations of black liberation tended to introduce a white female as the emancipator and not a male, and came not out of Britain but France and the newly self-liberated United States. So as early as 1789 the frontispiece to Frossard's *La Cause des esclaves nègres* (**fig. 8**) which argued in abstract political terms for the abolition of the slave trade, showed a crowned female personification of France bestowing liberty upon

a group of kneeling slaves all of whom seem still locked in the supplicatory position of the black in the Abolition Seal. The male figure in strict
profile in the fore-ground is quite precisely replicated from the Wedgwood
medallion, and although unchained his clasped hands are now locked in
place by the grasping white hand of the standing female liberator. One
year later Samuel Jennings began work on a large allegory for the Library
Company of Philadelphia *Liberty Displaying the Arts and Sciences*.[13] This
big oil painting exists in a tense relationship to libertarian rhetoric coming out of revolutionary France. Liberty has a pole topped with a cap of
liberty propped on her arm, and in the background there are a group of
blacks dancing around a tree of liberty. Yet this untrammelled black celebration of freedom is set off against the bottom right hand corner of the
painting, where a group of blacks kneel in submissive homage to liberty.
The kneeling black infant is, in this example, the figure who most precisely maintains the posture and gesture of clasped outstretched hands
from the Abolition Seal. Again the visible chains are gone, but the slave
body is still imprisoned.

Jennings's image was to provide a lasting formula when it came to the
prints produced to celebrate British abolition in 1807 and 1833. **(fig. 9)**
So for example this elaborate engraving entitled *Freedom* was mass-
produced in both finely coloured and black and white versions in 1833
and takes up the central elements developed by Jennings. Here Britannia
carries the spear with the liberty cap on top of it, she stands on a dis-
carded whip and shackles, and hands a sealed scroll inscribed with the
single word 'freedom' to a male slave, who perfectly replicates the figure
from the original Abolition Seal. As in Jennings's design this static re-
spectful figure exists as a counter balance to the groups of happy dancing
slaves, middle ground left and middle background right. When the slave
trade was abolished in Britain in 1807 a great majority of the commemorative prints played out variants on this symbolic tradition, choosing to
show the black still kneeling in the position of the Seal before abstract
personifications of Liberty, Justice and Britannia.

When the campaign to abolish slavery in the British colonies gath-
ered steam in the mid-1820s the British Abolitionists mass-produced stationery which made wide use of the figure from the Abolition Seal. So for
example this envelope uses the old symbolic structures to make a striking
claim for the different status of Liberty on the British mainland and in
the colonies. **(fig. 10)** In this engraving the left hand part of the

[13]    The picture is reproduced and discussed in Honour 1989, 4:1, p. 49.

*Fig. 9. (above)* Anon., *Freedom*, hand coloured copper engraving, 1833. Private collection (reproduced from slide, original unlocatable).

*Fig. 10. (below)* Anon., *Abolition Envelope*, copper engraving on coloured paper, c. 1825. Collection of the author.

composition shows Britannia with raised shield and spear protecting a supplicating black locked in the inevitable posture, although supposedly manifesting the fact that he is free because on British soil. The slogan "Am I not a Man and a Brother?" has been changed to the biblical quotation "God Hath Made of One Blood All Nations of Men". (Acts 17:26) In the background across the sea are miniature scenes showing planter atrocities against slaves. A British slave patrol ship, irradiated by lines of divine sanction, sails across the horizon line.

The image was so ubiquitous that it was circulating as printed ephemera in contexts where its relation to an original abolition context are difficult to determine. Take for example the following elaborate dinner invitation to the London Guildhall in 1824. **(fig. 11)** The dinner was given by the Lord Mayor of London and his Sherriffs and was attended by Britain's leading big businessmen. The invitation which they had been sent demonstrates how abolition of the slave trade had been enshrined at the heart of an economic mythology which showed Britannia as essentially compassionate, though unstoppable. Britannia rises triumphant above the whole scene extending shield and trident with her right hand and gesturing towards her heaped imperial wealth with her left. This wealth is represented by an enormous cornucopia which spills its produce out before a kneeling black and white infant. The white infant confidently turns his back on the National Matriarch, and clasps a large globe with his right hand; immediately above the white hand and globe stretch; the Thames, with St Paul's rising on its far bank. The black is seen in three quarter profile from the back, he gazes in supplication and awe at the figures of Britannia and Justice, who reclines on a mighty sword to Britannia's lower right. He adopts precisely the same posture as the slave in the Abolition Seal. With nearly one million slaves still labouring in the British sugar colonies the status of this black child is ambiguous. Is this little black boy a freed slave, triumphantly liberated by the Act of 1807, or a slave awaiting his freedom in the British Caribbean, or even an African child waiting and watching as Britannia expands relentlessly into Africa? He may be all of these things, but if we set him against the iconography which greeted the abolition of slavery in 1807 he seems firmly contained within the parameters of popular graphic imagination. He is exactly what the British business community hoped he would be, grateful, supplicatory, undemanding and passive.

The adaptations and variants of the black male and female from the Abolition Seal were to continue to proliferate within a great variety of abolition visual propaganda on both sides of the Atlantic up to and beyond

1865. Yet it is important to note that the image also generated another adaptive tributary in popular art dealing with the expression of freedom. In British graphic culture the earliest adaptation of the Abolition Seal within debates around emancipation involved what was to become a classic pro-slavery gesture of iconic substitution. In 1789, just at the moment when the Abolition Seal in the form of a Wedgwood medallion had gained wide popular currency, a primitive and anonymous satiric etching ap-

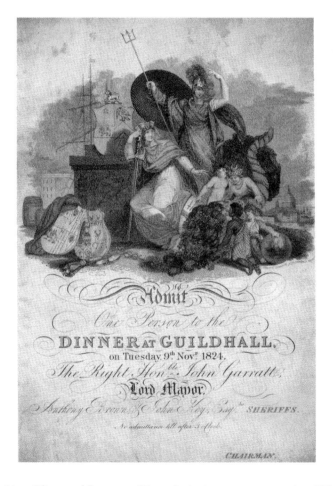

*Fig. 11.*    Oliver and Sampson, *Dinner Invitation*, copper engraving, 1824. John Lewis Collection, original lost, reproduced John Lewis, *Printed Ephemera*, Suffolk: W. S. Cowell, 1962, p. 157.

peared entitled *Abolition of the Slave Trade or The Man the Master*.[14] In this print a white man, kneeling in the posture of the black from the Abolition Seal, and naked apart from a bizarrely elaborate loin-cloth, screams in pain. A black in gentleman's attire grabs the white man's long unkempt hair with one hand and holds aloft in the other a large length of thick sugar cane. This print, and its fellows, were based on a sort of graphic scare-mongering which refused the reassuring visual rhetoric of British abolition. A whole string of subsequent prints would use the iconography of the seal to suggest that the suffering of the white labouring classes in Britain was being overlooked at the expense of sympathy for the colonial slave. **(fig. 12)** So for example Hone and Cruikshank's notorious parodic

*Fig. 12.* William Hone, George Cruikshank, *Peterloo Medal*, wood engraving, 1819. Collection of the author.

[14] The image is reproduced in Honour 1989, 4:1, p. 73.

medal brought out in response to the Peterloo Massacre in Manchester
in 1819 took up the inheritance of the Abolition Seal in complicated
ways. Although this powerful work undoubtedly brings into dramatic focus the plight of northern textile workers, it does so at the expense of the
absent black.[15]

It is ironic that it was, amongst British radicals, the wonderful proto-
feminist firebrand Elizabeth Heyrick who provided one of the only rein-
terpretations of the Abolition Seal to place an autonomous black slave
at the centre.[16] **(fig. 13)** Heyrick's pamphlet *Immediate Not Gradual Abolition* carried a frontispiece showing a confident, upstanding black man,
with arm outstretched in the gesture (as we have seen from the Schoelcher
statue) customarily reserved for the white emancipator. The slave stands
in a tropical landscape before a plantation with a long whip and shackles

*Fig. 13.*    Anon., *I Am a Man, Your Brother*, frontispiece to Elizabeth
Heyrick, *Immediate Not Gradual Abolition*, wood engraving, 1824.
Collection of the author.

[15]    Wood 1994, 210–13, for a detailed discussion of this image and its race implications within British radicalism.
[16]    For Heyrick and her ambivalent relationship with British Abolition, see
Ferguson 1992, 249–59.

on the ground at his feet. Above him is the tremendous sentence "I am a man, your brother" which in one daring move decimates the interrogative double negative of the original slogan, and by substituting 'your brother' for 'a brother' enforces intimacy between black and white. It is most significant that it was a radical female consciousness which finally swept away the sinister shroud of negativity in which the statement of black equality had been so comfortably shrouded for three decades. Yet despite Heyrick's valiant attempts to transform both the word and image of the Abolition Seal, the original remained the most long-lived and effective package allowing white audiences to imagine freed slaves.

In this context the words were as important as the image, and it is consequently worth dwelling on the precise terms of a formula which so perfectly encapsulated the conditions under which black freedom was allowed to ask for its right to be. In any context there is a vast amount at stake in the simple inversion of the two words 'I am' and 'Am I?' The former proclaims its vitality; the latter asks to be assured that it is alive. The slave is asking what is for the white audience a real question, and one which influential white intellectuals in Britain were still answering in the negative in the mid-nineteenth century. Take, for example, the brutally frank negrophobia of William Makepeace Thackeray, who, touring the United States as the Civil War was about to explode meditated upon the status of the black slave: 'They are not my men and brethren, these strange people with retreating foreheads, and with great obtruding lips and jaws ... Sambo is not my man and brother'. (Quoted in Sutherland 1970, 441) When it comes to thinking through the basics of his relation to black people Thackeray's racism instinctively takes cover in, and asserts its legitimacy by, going back to the terms of the renowned question on the Abolition Seal. For Thackeray this is not a rhetorical question, but a real question which can only be answered with an emphatic negative.

Throughout the middle decades of the nineteenth century there remained a graphic tradition which pictured the emancipated slave in terms of degraded victim-hood. This tradition generated some of the most extreme and negative variations upon the imagery of the Abolition Seal. Take for example the lithograph of the early 1830s *An Emancipated Negro*. (fig. 14) The figure is a compositional masterpiece. It is as if the slave in the Abolition Seal has been raised from his knees, and his body has been attenuated, and dried out. This moving black skeleton operates compositionally on a powerful diagonal running from the foot in the bottom left corner, to the desperate finger tips in the top right. The profile is a horrible example of the stylistic distortions of nineteenth-century racialism – vast

*Fig. 14.* J. Busle, *An Emancipated Negro*, coloured lithograph, 1833. Collection of the author.

fleshy lips, concave nose and colossal mandible. This black figure is a sneering development of the kneeling slave from the Abolition Seal. Armed, liberated from his chains, this figure no longer asks us to identify him as human, his language has been reduced to an atavistic level where thought and action are fused. As he shouts out 'Food', rather than 'Freedom', he simultaneously sees and pursues the concept which controls him. This emancipated slave has no interest in whether we see him as a man or a brother, his entire existence has been reduced to avoiding starvation. Of course the implicit message buried within that grotesque race stereotyping is precisely that enunciated so brutally by Thackeray. This specimen is not a man and a brother, and therefore his liberation was a game not worth the candle.

### Pontecorvo's Burn: *an art of emancipation beyond the 'gift of freedom'*

And so it seems the more one looks into the adaptive history of the Abolition Seal the more Fanon's analysis of the gift of freedom as a terrible semiotic con trick is revealed as true. But I want to end by suggesting that there may be other interpretative traditions and options which challenge the negative orthodoxies of white emancipation art. I opened this writing with a quotation from the dialogue between an anonymous soldier, and the leader of a nineteenth-century slave revolution in the fictional Caribbean island of Queimada. The words occur at the climax of *Burn*, Gillo Pontecorvo's unforgiving and beautiful film of the late 1960s which analyses slave insurrection and white mercantile hypocrisy in the Atlantic diaspora. (Pontecorvo 1968) The leader of the slave revolutionaries, José Dolores, speaks these lines when he is finally captured. Led in bonds he turns to one of his black guards, himself an ex-slave, and talks about his fate, and why he would rather die than be given liberty by his captors, who are terrified that Dolores's execution will make him into a martyr.[17] The last twenty minutes of the film focus on a single issue, the machinations of his captors, and Dolores's insistence upon dying to keep the theory of freedom alive. He dies, not as a Christian martyr, but as a slave revolutionary, because that is his only moral choice. He wants to die in order to defend the right to achieve an abstract freedom, rather than have the lie of white physical freedom foisted upon him.

The debate on freedom is primarily conducted through the inter-relationship and dialogue of Dolores and the political entrepreneur Sir William Walker. Sir William, played with great subtlety by Marlon Brando, is the man who first created Dolores as a slave revolutionary.[18] He then returns to Queimada in the second half of the film as an employee of the imperial powers in order to defeat and capture his revolutionary protégé when the politics of empire and the sugar markets have shifted.

---

[17]   The finest analysis of the film in the context of slavery and cinema is Davis 2000, 41–55.

[18]   Brando took on the part of Sir William for a minimal fee, and acted alongside a cast of minor and unknown actors. The blacks were played by people with no acting experience at all. Brando had titanic conflicts with Pontecorvo, and maintained to the end of his days that the film contained his most significant and finest performance. See Davis 2000, 47–8.

The final point that Pontecorvo makes in the film is not that Dolores possesses a beautiful and un-corruptible soul that enables him to die a truly heroic death in the cause of black liberty. The final point is that Sir William, for all his Machiavellian brilliance, and strategic intelligence, cannot understand why Dolores refuses to cut and run when given the chance. The colonisers attempt every ingenious ploy in order to get Dolores to agree to leave the Caribbean a free and rich man. He laughs at the offers. At the eleventh hour, as the gallows are being set up, Sir William sneaks into Dolores's quarters, cuts him free and tells him to run. There are, quite literally, no strings attached this time, and as the silent Dolores refuses to accept this proffered liberation Sir William must live out the vast bewilderment of the coloniser when finally faced with the rejection of his power to liberate. The dialogue runs as follows:

> Come on you are free. Jose you are free, free. Don't you understand? Why, what good does it do? What meaning does it have José? Is it a revenge of some sort? What sort of a revenge is it if you are dead? I don't know José, it just seems madness. Why? (Pontecorvo/Solinas 1968, 115–116 minutes)

So very many questions from a man, supposedly in a position of absolute authority, and intellectual superiority. Where does this obsessive insecurity originate? The Sir Williams of this world never have understood and never will, Dolores's actions. Sir William believes he is making an offer that cannot be refused. Of course Dolores says nothing, he doesn't need to. Sir William's tragedy, and that of any individual who believes they can simply hand out liberty to the oppressed, is that he cannot enter into a moral and political space which denies any validity, indeed any existence, to his proffered gift of freedom. Sir William, like the Anglo-American abolitionists, and the generations of historiographers who have culturally enshrined them, cannot see that there are certain things that it is beyond the power of any human, and most especially a politician, to endow another human with. The final thing about a gift is that it can always be rejected. Sir William tells Dolores that he is a man and a brother and sets him free, Dolores knows that what he is offered is not freedom but a lie. Pontecorvo uses film to shatter the white myth of the emancipation moment.

The terrific message of Fanon, refined and developed within the aesthetics of film by Pontecorvo, is one that if read properly, allows us to approach the hidden rhetorical codes of all emancipation propagandas with new eyes. As we think back on the 1807 Act and the visual propaganda it both fed off and generated it is vital that we look upon the tired moral chicanery of these images with new eyes. The final image of Dolores led to execution, laughing and staring in true freedom at Sir William, with the gallows in the background, shows a very different vision of black liberty from that offered in the Abolition Seal and the body of art it enabled. In an aesthetic context the choice of violent death, a real political martyrdom, at the hands of the coloniser proves the final semiotic antidote to the stultifying white gift of freedom. The potential of the slaves to die in the cause of their own liberty was something which both the masters and the abolitionists found too frightening to celebrate in art. In the end it was this fear of black moral and martyrological superiority, and terror of the fires of San Domingo, which generated the bizarre narrative falsehoods celebrated by the white art of emancipation.

## Works Cited

Anstey, Roger, 1981. *The Atlantic Slave Trade and British Abolition 1760–1810*. London: Macmillan.

Cohen, William B., 1980. *The French Encounter with Africans: White Response to Blacks 1530–1880*. Bloomington and London: Indiana University Press.

Davis, David Brion, (1975), 1999. *The Problem of Slavery in the Age of Revolution 1770–1823*. Oxford: Oxford University Press.

Davis, David Brion, 1983. *The Emancipation Moment*. Gettysburg: Gettysburg College Press.

Davis, Natalie Zemon, 2000. *Slaves on Screen: Film and Historical Vision*. New York: Vintage.

Fanon, Frantz, (1961), 1967. *The Wretched of the Earth*. Harmondsworth: Penguin.

Fanon, Frantz, (1967), 1991. *Black Skins White Masks*. London: Pluto Press.

Ferguson, Moira, 1992. *Subject to Others: British Writers and Colonial Slavery, 1670–1834*. New York: Routledge.

Gilroy, Paul. 1992. *The Black Atlantic: Modernity and Double Consciousness*. London: Verso.

Hegel, G. W. F., 1949. *The Phenomenology of Mind*. Translated by J. B. Baillie. London: Allen and Unwen.

Hegel, G. W. F., 1975. *Lectures on the Philosophy of World History*. Translated by H. B. Nisbet. Cambridge: Cambridge University Press.

Hochschild, Adam, 2005. *Bury the Chains: The British Struggle to Abolish Slavery*. London: Macmillan.

Honour, Hugh, 1989. *The Image of the Black in Western Art*. Vol. 4 *From the American Revolution to World War*. Part 1: Slaves and Liberators. Cambridge MA: Harvard University Press and Menil Foundation.

Oldfield, J. R., 1995. *Popular Politics and British Anti-Slavery: The Mobilisation of Public Opinion against the Slave Trade 1787–1807*. Manchester: Manchester

University Press.

Pontecorvo, Gillo (dir)/ Solinas Franco (screenplay), 1968. *Burn!* (aka *Queimada!*) France/Italy: Alberto Grimaldi.

Quarles, Benjamin, 1961. *The Negro in the American Revolution*. Chapel Hill: University of North Carolina Press.

Reilly, Bernard F., Jr, ed., 1991. *American Political Prints 1766–1876. A Catalogue of the Collections in the Library of Congress*. Boston: G. K. Hall.

Sutherland, John, 1970. 'Thackeray as Victorian Racialist', *Essays in Criticism* 20

Thomas, Peter D. G., 1986. *The English Satiric Print 1600–1632*. Cambridge: Chadwyck Healey.

Williams, Gwyn, 1977. *A Cartoon History of the American Revolution*. London: London Editions.

Wood, Marcus, 1994. *Radical Satire and Print Culture*. Oxford: Oxford University Press.

Wood, Marcus, 2000. *Blind Memory: Visual Representations of Slavery in England and America 1780–1865*. Manchester: Manchester University Press.

Yellin, Jean Fagan, 1989. *Women and Sisters. The Anti-Slavery Feminists in American Culture*. New Haven and London: Yale University Press.

# The Afterlives of Three-Fingered Jack

## DIANA PATON

### I

THE MUCH-RETOLD STORY of the man who came to be known as Three-Fingered Jack, along with other fictions of slavery, intertwined with genres such as history-writing and political polemic in the formation of an emergent British 'public opinion' as first the slave trade, then slavery itself came under attack. One of many enslaved men and women who managed to escape the plantation regime, Jack operated in Jamaica's Blue Mountain region in 1780 and 1781. He lived on the margins of slave society and led a group of around sixty maroons, reportedly gaining subsistence primarily through attacks on travellers. His group's actions posed sufficient threat to the stability of the slavery-based regime for the Jamaican Governor and House of Assembly to offer substantial rewards for his capture. About six months after the Jamaican press first reported his existence, Jack was killed and the rest of his group were dispersed. A group of maroons, led by one John Reeder, received the reward for Jack's death. The fictions and dramas that recounted Jack's life and death over the next decades were an important site for the formation of opinion about slavery for British readers and theatre-goers in the period of the debates about the abolition of the (British) Atlantic slave trade and of British colonial slavery.[1]

The shifting tellings of Jack's story intersect with developments in the controversies regarding the slave trade and slavery. In 1800, when interest in Three-Fingered Jack was at its height, the legislative goal of opponents of slavery was 'abolitionist' rather than 'emancipationist': focused on the campaign to abolish the Atlantic slave trade rather than slavery itself. The year 1800 marked the trough between the defeat of Wilberforce's 1792 bill to abolish the slave trade and the eventual success of the

---

[1]  For details of the performance histories of the pantomime and melodrama see Cox 2002; Hoskins and Southern 1996; Rzepka 2002a, 2002b; Warner *et al.* 2001, 7. Cundall 1930 and Eyre 1973 both list many of the pamphlet renditions. According to Errol Hill 1992, 101, *Obi* was performed only once in Jamaica, in 1862.

campaign in 1807 (Drescher 1977; Oldfield 1998). More pressing in 1800 was the ongoing revolution in Haiti, which raised the possibility of successful rebellion in the British colonies, and was closely watched for the answers it was supposed to provide to the question of how former slaves would behave as free people (Drescher 2002, 100–5). By 1830, the year of the first performance of the melodrama based on Jack's life, the terrain of debate had dramatically changed. The slave trade had been outlawed for more than twenty years without any sign of the shift to a free labour system for which anti-slave-trade campaigners had hoped. Antislavery activists had concluded that only a campaign for the immediate abolition of slavery would work (Midgley 1992, 107–16). The middle-ground argument for a reformed 'ameliorated' slavery was increasingly revealed as a cover for proslavery forces as the campaign shifted towards the passage of the Emancipation Act in 1833.

This essay examines the implications for the slavery debates of the various adaptations of Three-Fingered Jack that, as Michael Warner notes, 'promiscuously circulated' in the early nineteenth century (Warner *et al.* 2001, 8). It examines the source materials for the story and then focuses on two prose-fiction versions by William Earle and William Burdett respectively, on John Fawcett's 'serio-pantomime,' and on the melodrama adapted from Fawcett's play in the late 1820s. It argues that the potentially strong antislavery case to be made through the heroic outlaw figure of Jack was consistently undermined in the writing or staging of the story. This was particularly so for the pantomime and melodrama, which included extensive scenes in which happy slaves displayed their devotion to kind masters. It was also true, however, of the prose versions, despite their being more explicitly critical of slavery. Both Earle's and Burdett's novels personalize and individualize Jack's struggle and his hostility to slavery. Both root Jack's resistance in his need for revenge for personal betrayal, rather than presenting it as a consequence of slavery's inherent injustice.

Distinctively among contemporary fictions of slavery, the writings and stagings of Three-Fingered Jack's adventures were based on the life of a historically real person who was defeated in his anti-slavery activities.[2] Jack's story originates in the actual practice of enslaved insurgency against the colonial plantation regime, but this practice was only accessible to British writers and dramatists through the textual records of counter-

---

[2]   For some recent important discussions of fictions of slavery, see, for example Botkin 2004; Boulukos 1999, 76; Carey 2005; Ellis 1996; Richardson 1997.

insurgency (Guha 1983). This dynamic between insurgency and counter-insurgency produced a contradictory narrative in which admiration for Jack's heroism and, sometimes, explicit authorial antislavery sympathies, were nevertheless told through a plot culminating in the death of the rebel and the installation of a new hero: Jack's killer John Reeder (known in many versions as Quashee). Because of this plotting, the versions which present Jack least sympathetically are the most ideologically coherent. Versions of the story in which Jack is heroic, most notably William Earle's *Obi, or Three-Fingered Jack*, are much more contradictory.

The original textual references to Jack form a fragmented narrative gradually published in 1780 and 1781 through articles, advertisements and proclamations in the Jamaican newspaper *The Royal Gazette*, produced for the needs of the Jamaican state authorities and planter class.[3] The first of these articles, published in August 1780, refers to a 'gang of run-away Negroes' captained by 'BRISTOL alias *Three-finger'd Jack*' which has 'rendered travelling … very dangerous'.[4] Later articles report Jack's 'depredations', and the arrest of his 'wife'.[5] In December 1780 the *Gazette* published notices promising official rewards of three hundred pounds and juridical freedom for 'any slave that shall take or kill the said Three-fingered Jack'.[6] In early 1781 the *Gazette* reported the 'death of that daring freebooter Three Fingered Jack' at the hands of 'a Maroon Negro named John Reeder, and six others'.[7]

Some of these short pieces of writing were clearly known by later writers, but they did not constitute the major source for later versions of Jack's story. That was provided by a short account published in 1799 by Dr Benjamin Moseley, an English physician who practised in Kingston from 1768 to 1784, and was thus resident in Jamaica when Jack was active (Brunton 2004; Moseley 1799).[8] Moseley's account was followed the next year by a stage version and two prose fiction reworkings of Jack's story. The successful serio-pantomime *Obi; or Three-Finger'd Jack*, with words by the comic actor John Fawcett and music by Samuel Arnold,

---

[3]   These articles have recently been reproduced in Aravamudan 2005, 10–13.
[4]   *Supplement to the Royal Gazette*, 29 July 1780 – 5 August 1780, 458.
[5]   *Supplement to the Royal Gazette*, 25 November 1780 – 2 December 1780, 698; and 16 December 1780 – 23 December 1780, 747.
[6]   *Supplement to the Royal Gazette*, 30 December 1780 – 6 January 1781; and 13 January 1781.
[7]   *Supplement to the Royal Gazette*, 27 January 1781 – 3 February 1781, 79.
[8]   The relevant extract is reprinted in Cundall 1930, 9–10; Moseley 2005; and Arnold 1996, Appendix, 17–18.

opened at the Haymarket Theatre in July 1800.[9] The pantomime form meant that the story was told through written signs, action, gesture and song, but had no spoken dialogue. As Jane Moody (2000, 88) notes, pantomime's emphasis on physical theatre produced an exaggerated, 'diagrammatic' portrayal of political issues. Pantomime plots tended to emphasize the production and resolution of suspense. The pantomime *Obi* considerably altered and expanded on the bare outlines of the narrative given by Moseley in order to introduce new elements of tension. Most notably it introduced a pair of white lovers: Captain Orford, who is kidnapped by Jack, and Rosa, the planter's daughter, who braves Jack in order to rescue Orford. According to the *Royal Gazette* sources, the historical Jack had little contact with white people – the only whites involved are authorities offering rewards and passing resolutions, distantly removed from the action. By introducing Orford, Rosa, and Rosa's father Ormond, Fawcett made the fate of white people the play's emotional centre.

William Burdett's sixty-page novelette, *Life and Exploits of Mansong, commonly called Three-finger'd Jack, the Terror of Jamaica* (1800), seems to have been written as a 'novelisation' taking advantage of the success of Fawcett's pantomime. It has received no critical attention. Its preface explains that its 'Editor' published it in response to the public's 'general curiosity and ... wish to become farther acquainted with the Hero' of the 'popular pantomimical Drama of Obi; or Three-Finger'd Jack' (iii). It includes at the end a four-page 'Accurate Description' of the pantomime, and largely follows the pantomime's plot, although it also includes a long section that takes place prior to the action of the stage version. Like the pantomime, the emphasis in Burdett's novel is on action and adventure. Burdett's Jack is African, and is originally known as Mansong. Taking his cues and his information from Mungo Park's recently published and very successful *Travels in the Interior of Africa* (2000), Burdett carefully locates his story, telling us that Mansong was born in '*Simbing*, in the interior of *Africa*, adjoining the country of the *Moors*', and close to the 'large Moorish town' of Jarra (Burdett 1800, 5–6). Mansong is betrayed in a war between the Kingdoms of Kaarta and Bambarra (*sic*), in which Simbing, led by

---

[9]   The same theatre staged the first performance of the Caribbean and slavery-themed play *Inkle and Yarico* in 1787 (Felsenstein 1999, xii). The original pantomime script is the manuscript version submitted to the censor for licence (Fawcett 1800), reproduced in Arnold 1996. Further references are to the most accessible edition, Fawcett 2002, unless stated otherwise.

Mansong, allied with the former.[10] This treachery leads to Mansong's sale to an African slave merchant and his eventual sale 'on the banks of the Gambia ... to an English Captain' who brings him to Jamaica (Burdett 1800, 16). This extensive African section makes Burdett's narrative more sympathetic to Mansong/Jack than the pantomime. For the first third of Burdett's text, Mansong is clearly the hero, although he later shifts to a more villainous role. In contrast, the pantomime opens with Jack already a predatory outlaw in Jamaica. The audience is introduced to Jack through the plantation slaves' terrified reaction to his name (Fawcett 2002, I.i).

The third version of the story produced in 1800 was William Earle Junior's *Obi, or Three Fingered Jack* (Earle 1800).[11] Earle's version was considerably longer than Burdett's, was independent of the pantomime and may have preceded it in publication.[12] Like Burdett, Earle devotes about a third of his text to describing events in Africa that precede the action described by Moseley, although Earle's Jack is conceived in Africa but Jamaican-born. Earle's Africa contrasts with Burdett's. Where Burdett's Africa is urban, made up of towns and states that mobilize substantial armies against one another, Earle's is rural, cattle-raising and much less social. The only named African characters in Earle's novel are Amri, Makro, Feruarue, and Mahali, Jack's parents, maternal grandfather, and friend, who Amri describes as 'Feloops' from a country that 'borders on the Gambia' (74).[13] They interact with no other Africans, only with two Europeans, Captain Harrop and the adolescent William, who they rescue from the wreck of what can only be assumed to be a slaver. Despite the use of a number of unfamiliar words which purport to be from the Feloop language and the description of specific Feloop foodways, the effect is to produce a decultured and static Africa, without any sense of real location or continuing history (see Sypher 1942, 9; Carey 2005, 48).

[10]   Park's *Travels* includes an account of a war between Kaarta and Bambarra (2000, 135–9). The King of Bambarra, according to Park, was called Mansong, but Park's Mansong does not become enslaved (128).

[11]   This text has recently been edited by Srinivas Aravamudan (Earle 2005). Further citations are to Aravamudan's edition unless otherwise stated.

[12]   Rzepka (2002a, para. 1), claims that the pantomime drew on Earle as well as Moseley, but does not provide evidence for this.

[13]   According to Park (2000, 76), the 'Feloops' are one of four groups of 'natives of the countries bordering on the Gambia', the other three being 'the Jaloffs, the Foulahs, and the Mandingoes'. This and other contextual information suggests that the 'Feloops' were members of the Senegambian polity more widely known as 'Jola' (French 'Diola').

Like Burdett, Earle draws on Mungo Park's *Travels in the Interior of Africa* for his knowledge of Africa. Earle's characterization picks up on Park's description of the Feloops as people who 'never ... forgive an injury. They are even said to transmit their quarrels as deadly feuds to their posterity, insomuch that a son considers it as incumbent on him, from a just sense of filial obligation, to become the avenger of his deceased father's wrongs' (Park 2000, 76). Earle's Amri uses very similar language: 'Remember that the spirit of our nation is, Never to forget an injury, but to ripen in our breasts the seeds of hate for those who betray us. We are to transmit our quarrels to our posterity, and it is incumbent on a son, from a sense of filial obligation, to resent the injuries done to his parents' (74).

The emotional heart of the narrative is located in the relationship between Jack and his mother, Amri. Earle presents the story as an epistolary novel in fifteen letters from 'George Stanford' in Jamaica, who appears as an embattled voice of hostility to slavery in a planter-dominated society, to his friend 'Charles' in England. Incorporated into Stanford's letters are other narratives, including a long section in which Amri tells the young Jack the story of how she became a plantation slave in Jamaica, inculcating in him the desire for revenge as she does so (75–103).

Earle's digressive and epistolary structure and sentimental self-reflective narrator contrast with Burdett's episodic but straightforwardly told plot and unengaged omniscient narrator. They share, however, the practice of including extensive quotations from other sources within their texts or as footnotes. Both include a near-identical verbatim quote taken from Bryan Edwards's discussion of obeah in his *History, Civil and Commercial, of the British Colonies in the West Indies* (Edwards 1793, I, 88–99; Burdett 1800, 18–30; Earle 1800, 72–82).[14] Both insert it immediately after the introduction of the first obeah practitioners in their novels, Amalkir (Burdett 1800, 18) and Feruarue respectively (Earle 2005, 97), and use it to explain the meaning and history of obeah. In addition, both use quotations from Benjamin Moseley and insert the texts of the Jamaican Governor's and House of Assembly's proclamations and resolutions of December 1780. Burdett thus intertwines a proto-ethnographic style with the adventure story structure of the rest of his text. Earle's novel becomes almost a collage, presenting itself as an ethnographic source through which readers can learn about the unfamiliar ways of the Feloops

---

[14] This quotation from Edwards was itself a quotation from the responses of Edward Long and other leading Jamaican planters to the Lords of the Committee of the Privy Council in 1789.

and the Jamaicans as well as being entertained and emotionally moved by the suffering of Amri, Makro, and Jack.

These three refashionings – Fawcett's pantomime, Burdett's *Life of Mansong*, and Earle's *Obi* – became models for many further adaptations of Jack's story. The pantomime was performed at regional theatres across Britain and traveled to New York. Brief descriptions of the action including song lyrics, sheet-music versions of the score, and the music and/or lyrics of individual songs were published. Reprints and shorter chap-book editions of Earle's and Burdett's texts were produced. Perhaps because it followed the version with which theatrical audiences were familiar, Burdett's retelling proved the more popular.[15]

The final substantial early-nineteenth-century revision of the Jack story was a stage melodrama with spoken dialogue, based on the pantomime. William Murray produced it for the African-American Shakespearian actor Ira Aldridge, who first played the role of Jack at the Bristol Theatre Royal in 1830 (Cox 2002, n. 2; Rzepka, 2002a, para. 6).[16] The melodrama opens with Jack already a rebel in Jamaica, and does not include the detailed African scenes of the prose versions, although it does briefly refer to Jack's African past. It played for many years and was performed in regional theatres across Britain.[17]

The theme of obeah, or the use of African-derived spiritual power, was clearly an essential part of the story for British audiences. Three of these four main versions use the term 'Obi' in their titles, and the fourth, Burdett's *Life of Mansong*, also includes important scenes involving obeah. The connection of Jack's story to obeah did not appear in the *Royal Gazette* articles, although it is likely that the historical Jack's contemporaries believed that he used spiritual power as a weapon to protect himself against the plantocratic regime and its allies.[18]

For British readers, Benjamin Moseley introduced the emphasis on Jack's powers of obeah into the narrative. Indeed, for Moseley, the story

---

[15]  For reasons of space it is not possible to give details of the subsequent versions here. A full list is available online at http://www.brycchancarey.com/slavery/tfj/index.htm.

[16]  The most accessible text of the melodrama is the online edition (Murray 2002), which is based on an 1850 edition. This is the version cited here unless otherwise stated. It differs in some significant ways from *Obi or, Three Fingered Jack* (nd).

[17]  For instance at the Theatre Royal Durham in 1859 (Playbill in Durham University Palace Green Library, Special NSR Planfile C 18/17).

[18]  Oral tradition regarding Three-Finger Jack collected by Ken Bilby among contemporary Jamaican Maroons appears independent of the British writings and suggests this (Bilby 2005, 308–12).

of Jack's banditry and capture provides an entertaining digression from a wider explanation of the nature of obeah, which itself was a digression from a discussion of the symptoms and treatment of the chronic disease yaws (Aravamudan 2005; Lee 2002). Sufferers who were acutely afflicted by yaws, Moseley tells his readers, were banished to huts on the outskirts of plantations, where they learned 'the occult science of OBI' (Moseley 2005, 162). Moseley describes this 'very extensive' 'science' at some length before introducing Jack, who is relevant because of his association with obeah. Moseley suggests that Jack has access to obeah's power because of his possession of the physical object of an 'obian bag'. In the subsequent versions, Jack himself is not an obeah practitioner but gains protection through a charm obtained from an unnamed 'Obi Woman' (in the stage versions) or an obeah man (Amalkir in Burdett's *Life of Mansong*; Bashra in Earle's *Obi*). All of these characters are presented as grotesque. Drawing on English representations of the haggish witch, the Obi Woman was always played by men (Rzepka 2002, para. 4; Cundall 1930, 37). The pantomime stage directions describe her as 'an old decrepid Negress, dressed very grotesequely' (Fawcett 2002, I.iii) while in the cast-list to the melodrama she is called 'a Negro Hag' (*Obi or, Three Fingered Jack* nd, 1). Both Burdett's Amalkir and Earle's Bashra are clearly based on Moseley's version of the obeah-man as a repulsive yaws sufferer. Amalkir 'dwelt in a loathsome cave', was 'old and shrivelled', and suffered from a disorder that had 'contracted all his nerves' (Burdett 1800, 17). Earle's Bashra was 'wrinkled and deformed' (Earle 2005, 104) and was 'affected by a disorder prevalent in the West-Indies' (119). As noted above, both include extensive quotation from Bryan Edwards that would have guided the reader's response to obeah and the obeah practitioners.

Alone among the revisions, Earle presents a relatively complex view of obeah. While he subscribes to Moseley's hostility to obeah insofar as Bashra is physically repulsive, this repulsiveness is quickly passed over in favour of constructing Bashra as a paternal figure: he is 'astonished at the noble appearance of the hero-minded Jack, and embraced him with all the fervor of a father' (105). In addition, Earle's text includes another obeah practitioner, Feruarue, who as Amri's father receives the reader's sympathy. In a narrative nested inside Amri's 'African tale', Feruarue tells how he was, like his daughter and son-in-law, tricked into enslavement and once in Jamaica 'vowed revenge, and for that purpose, studied Obi' (99), a decision which in the circumstances seems entirely reasonable. Earle's presentation of obeah as in some ways a legitimate tool of enslaved resistance is rare in a period when obeah was represented either as exotic other or as hostile opponent of Christianity.

While the newspaper accounts and Moseley's version of Three-Fingered Jack were produced in Jamaica or by people who had spent extensive time there, the other four are in essence British elaborations of the story. Earle's and Burdett's fictions claim a direct Jamaican connection, the former asserting that it consists of letters 'from a resident in Jamaica to his friend in England' (Earle 2005, 67) and the latter describing its author as 'many years overseer of a plantation in Jamaica,' (Burdett 1800, title page) but both contain serious misrepresentations of Jamaican society and history that suggest that the authors were not directly familiar with the colony.[19] Rather, they drew on Jamaican accounts as source material for what were essentially British narratives that purported to be authentically Jamaican. The stage versions placed less emphasis on claims to authenticity, but equally drew on Jamaican accounts. Three-Fingered Jack as a cultural figure, then, can be seen as a Jamaican-British co-production, shifting in meaning as he moved from early tellings in Jamaican newspapers to much more elaborate fictional and dramatic reworkings.

## II

The original newspaper articles about Three-Fingered Jack provide little information to enable readers to locate him in a specific personal context. They do not reveal the plantation from which he had escaped, nor how long he had been operating as a maroon, nor do they attempt to explain how he acquired his nickname. It is also not clear if Jack was born in Jamaica or Africa, though one article referred to his group as 'chiefly Congos'.[20] Almost certainly, the lack of detail in the newspaper articles reflects their authors' lack of concrete knowledge. Like bandits everywhere, Three-Fingered Jack's indeterminacy made him an attractive figure, around whom a wide range of plots could be constructed (Hobsbawm 2001; Joseph 1990). The fictions and dramas of Jack's life fill in the elements missing from the original sources in different ways.

---

[19]  The 'Advertisement' to the fourth edition restates this claim to direct knowledge of Jamaica, but retains the misrepresentations (Burdett 1801, 3).
[20]  *Supplement to the Royal Gazette*, 29 July–5 August 1780, 458. Aravamudan (2005, 11) interprets this to mean that Jack's group were 'likely Koromantyns' (from one of the Akan peoples of today's Ghana). A more likely interpretation is that Jack was – or was in 1780 believed to be – from the West-Central region of Africa, today's Congo or Angola.

Despite their brevity and lack of detail, the newspaper sources clearly state that Jack's killer John Reeder was a maroon. Benjamin Moseley's account echoes this, reporting that Jack's killers were maroons from the settlement of Scots Hall.[21] According to Moseley, the maroons were originally named Quashee and Sam, but Quashee was christened in advance of the search for Jack, and changed his name to John Reeder. As maroons, Quashee and Sam were already free people, and therefore for them the Assembly's offer of the reward of freedom was irrelevant.

Later tellings of the story almost completely ignored this point, instead presenting Quashee as enslaved and balancing his desire for freedom against Jack's. Burdett tells us that Quashee and Sam are from 'Scots Hall, Maroon Town' but also indicates that they are enslaved (Burdett 1800, 46). In Earle's *Obi*, Quashee is 'a brave black of Scots-Hall, Maroons-town' who is motivated by 'the promise of that liberty which was dear to him' (Earle 2005, 123). Neither author seems to have understood that the residents of maroon settlements, including 'Scots Hall, Maroon Town' had previously secured free status through armed conflict and negotiation with the Jamaican colonial state.

The pantomime and melodrama versions pay even less attention to the historical Reeder's maroon status. In both, Quashee and Sam are firmly located as slaves. They are among the first characters the audience sees in the first scene, which takes place on 'an extensive plantation in Jamaica', and are the slaves of the 'benevolent master', Mr Ormond (Murray 2002, I.i). Neither performance refers in any way to maroon communities.

Discarding the maroon element of the story had multiple implications and purposes. For Burdett and Earle, it established an equivalence between Quashee and Jack. If Quashee and Sam are maroons, there is an unsatisfying lack of resolution to the state's offer to exchange freedom for Jack's death, and Quashee and Sam risk appearing as mere bounty-hunters. For the producers of the pantomime and melodrama, Quashee's enslaved status explicitly tied him into a vision of the integrated and harmonious plantation community, with an easy racial hierarchy and happy, grateful slaves. In the pantomime, Quashee and Sam decide to pursue Jack because he has captured Captain Orford, after the planter chides the 'Negroes' as a group for their cowardice in fearing Jack. In the melodrama, Quashee is explicitly motivated by loyalty to the master: he volunteers to

---

[21]  The contemporary Jamaican village is known as Scott's Hall. I retain 'Scots Hall' because it is used in the texts with which I am concerned, and is the spelling preferred by maroons today (Bilby 2005, 425–6 n. 5).

hunt Jack because 'you have been kind massa to me … I now show you
that black man's heart beat warm as white'.[22] Maroons, as autonomous
black characters, even if tied to the plantocratic state through treaties,
would have disrupted such a vision. The adaptors of the Jack story may
also simply have lacked the knowledge to make sense of the information
that Quashee and Sam were 'blacks of Maroon Town'. The British understanding of the place of black people in the Caribbean located them firmly
as slaves.

Forgetting the maroon status of Jack's killers also made sense because
the tension it raises was less relevant to British audiences than to Jamaican. In a Jamaican context, there was ongoing tension between maroons
and enslaved people on plantations because the maroons had made treaties with the colonial state that gave them security while obliging them
to act at times as allies of the colonists (Craton 1982, 89–92). The Jamaican maroons were mobilized to suppress slave rebellion on several occasions between the making of the treaties in 1739 and the abolition of
slavery (Craton 1982, 130, 311). As Ken Bilby (2005, 23) notes, these
and other actions which can seem 'distasteful … to those with the privilege of hindsight … were calculated, under extreme circumstances, to
ensure the survival of those they had come to identify as their own'. For
Jamaicans, the relationship between Jack and Quashee might have provided an opportunity for reflection on the wider issues raised by the division between those – like Jack and his allies – who were fighting for their
own security in the present and those – like Quashee – who fought to
maintain the free and independent status won through the guerrilla wars
waged by their ancestors.

Indeed, this theme does feature in Burdett's *Life of Mansong*, in which
Jack leads plantation slaves into rebellion before taking up the position
of outlaw. The rebels succeed in burning Crawford Town, a European
settlement in the novel – although the historical Crawford Town was a
maroon settlement (Craton 1982, 94) – and withstand an initial attempt
by maroons to suppress them, but are defeated by a second contingent of
five hundred maroons who 'made a great slaughter,' leading to their defeat, after which only Jack is prepared to continue fighting (32–3).

---

[22]   The different versions of the melodrama text have this statement at different
points. In Murray (2002) it is at I.vi and is a response to the news that Jack has
captured Orford. In *Obi or, Three Fingered Jack* (nd) it is at I.ii, before Orford's
capture and, significantly, before the slaves learn of the Government's proclama-
tion of the reward of freedom.

Burdett's *Life of Mansong* thus displaces the difficult relationship between plantation slaves and free maroons. The other versions of the Jack
story overlook this relationship, evacuating the theme of maroon-
plantation slave conflict. In becoming a British story told about Jamaica,
rather than a Jamaican story, Three-Fingered Jack lost sight of the complex relationships and strategic difficulties among different segments of
those struggling and negotiating with plantocratic power, substituting a
more straightforward vision of social relations in which there were only
two sides to choose from: with Jack, or with the social order of slavery
and the plantation.

### III

Having simplified the narrative in this way, which side did the rewritings
under examination support? Would these texts, read and performed in
the context of debates about the slave trade and slavery respectively,
have been interpreted as supporting abolitionist and emancipationist arguments? Did they lead to an extended critique of slavery, or to a recuperation of the plantation regime? A number of scholars have recently
suggested that they contributed to a developing critique of the slave trade
and slavery. Srinivas Aravamudan emphasizes Earle's radical use of the
revolutionary rhetoric of the rights of man within an overall context of
'sentimentalist abolitionism' (2005, 50). Certainly, Earle's version is by
far the most directly hostile to slavery of the four under consideration.
Alone amongst them, it adopts an explicitly abolitionist position. This is
communicated right from the title page, which includes an extract from
an antislavery sonnet from Robert Southey's *Poems Concerning the Slave
Trade*.[23]

Moreover, the narrative sympathy of *Obi* is clearly with Jack. Earle
presents Jack heroically, as noble, and as the defender of the rights of
man. The narrator repeatedly defends him, implying at times that he
does so against criticism: 'Say what you will, he is a noble fellow' (112).
Jack's father Makro is also presented as brave and noble: he dies rather
than 'own a cursed European for my master' (92) and adopts the egalitarian Christian view that 'I never can own a superior but my Creator' (90).
In producing emotional support for an insurgent and outlaw former slave
and his intransigently oppositional enslaved father, Earle justifies rebellion,

---

[23]   The complete sonnet is reprinted in Kitson and Lee (1999), 4:244.

something that goes beyond the usual radicalism of calls for the abolition of the slave trade. In the context of the Haitian and French revolutions and the backlash against them in Britain, this was a daring position to take.

In other ways, Earle adopts a conventional critique of slavery, emphasizing the cruelties of slavery and the slave trade, its dependence on torture and in particular its destruction of family life. Amri's narrative emphasizes the pain of her separation from Makro after they are tricked into slavery: 'surely, cried I, they have not deprived me of the only comfort their cruelty could leave me, or is he dead?' (86). Although it turns out that they are on board the same ship, Makro dies before they reach land. He refuses to eat and then receives the inevitably deadly punishment of five hundred lashes. There are other scenes of extreme violence. Both Amri and her father Feruarue are tortured on the rack; Earle describes the latter's experience in some detail. Feruarue is then executed and his body burnt.

As well as the description of the physical and emotional suffering the slave trade produces for Amri, Earle emphasizes its destructive impact on Africa. A footnote to a description of a coffle of enslaved people heading for the coast explains that 'Wars in Africa are much encouraged by the Europeans, and particularly the Dutch and English' (83). A later explanation of another character's enslavement also emphasizes the trade's encouragement of wars among African polities: 'these white robbers would excite us to war against each other' (137), Jack's friend Mahali explains. In this Earle rehearses common anti-slave-trade arguments made by British abolitionists of the period. The intentions of the novel are explicitly abolitionist and implicitly, in their justification of rebellion, emancipationist.

Nevertheless, the novel in certain ways undercuts its own antislavery concerns. It is significant that Jack's hostility to the plantation regime is primarily motivated by his hatred of and desire to wreak revenge on Captain Harrop, the villain and the white man responsible for tricking his parents into slavery in Africa after they had rescued him from a shipwreck. By enormous coincidence, Jack eventually ends up enslaved on Harrop's Jamaican plantation, enabling him to exact his revenge by kidnapping Harrop. Life on the plantation itself is presented sketchily; Harrop's cruel and treacherous character is demonstrated by his cruel treatment of a young white heiress, Harriet Mornton, whom he tricks into marriage, rather than through his behaviour towards slaves. Earle's wider critique of slavery is confounded by being played out within the generic conventions of the sentimental novel, which focus attention on the evil personality of Harrop as an individual, rather than slavery as a system.

William Burdett's novel has less explicit political intentions; its purpose is to entertain and it makes relatively little effort to intervene in the debate over slavery and the slave trade. There is no explicit condemnation of or support for slavery or the slave trade, but there is considerable sympathy for Jack as an opponent of slavery, at least in the first half of the book. In the opening paragraph we learn of Jack's heroism and intelligence: he is 'of a bold and martial appearance', and has 'steadiness of manners, and firm intrepidity of ... mind' (Burdett 1800, 5). Later editions expanded on this: the tenth edition, for instance, ends by declaring Jack 'a man, perhaps, of as genuine courage as ever existed' (Burdett nd, 38). The African scenes in particular demonstrate Jack's courage and military skill. Jack in Jamaica is also briefly presented heroically. In one of many unacknowledged quotes from Benjamin Moseley, Burdett tells us that Jack 'rose above Spartacus' (Burdett 1800, 34), suggesting approval for slave rebellion. Yet Burdett's tone shifts after this point, increasingly presenting Jack in negative terms: he 'prowl[s] for fresh prey' at one point (48–9). Nevertheless, readers would already have formed a view of him as a positive figure. In presenting Jack as admirable, Burdett invites sympathy with his acts of resistance, implicitly endorsing enslaved people's antislavery activity.

In other ways, however, Burdett's text sidesteps the possibility of critiquing the slave trade and slavery. His account of Jack's enslavement relates entirely to warfare among African groups and does not discuss the role of European slave traders. Burdett passes over Jack's experience of the middle passage very quickly, surrendering the possibility of a description of its conditions. He pays very little attention to Jack's experience in Jamaica before his escape from slavery. Although we learn that Jack is 'branded on the breast' and 'repeatedly received the lash ... on his bare shoulders' (16), Burdett does not attempt to convey the experience of these physical violations; instead they are used to emphasize Jack's resolute hostility to 'the European race' and his desire for revenge.

At times, Burdett goes beyond restraint in not critiquing slavery to positively endorsing it. In particular, the novel subscribes to the view that, if properly managed, slavery was an acceptable system. Rosa's father, Mr Chapman, epitomises this vision of the good master. His slaves 'appeared all happy' and his plantation was an economic success. Burdett's narrator explains this by 'the willingness with which the negroes laboured for so good a master' and goes on to 'assert, from experience, that if every planter in Jamaica were to follow his human example, it would not only tend to increase their own private wealth, but the good of this country at large' (41–42). This statement puts Burdett firmly in the camp of the proslavery ameliorationists who aimed to protect slavery against abolitionist attack by reforming the system from within and asking slaveholders to adopt 'humane' procedures while retaining their human property.

Burdett's *Life of Mansong* thus cannot be convincingly claimed as either pro or antislavery. In its refusal to adopt an explicit political position it perhaps reveals the largely unseen 'middle ground' in the slavery debates; the view held by those who did not explicitly support slavery but preferred to turn a blind eye to its continuing cruelties.

Compared to Earle or even Burdett, the antislavery implications of the stage versions of *Obi* are slight. They do, nevertheless, exist. The opening song of the pantomime includes a lament that refers to the destruction of family life by the slave trade: 'poor Negro sold … Poor Negro child and father part'. (The melodrama also includes this song, but cuts out the verse including these words.) The melodrama meanwhile includes several speeches in which Jack/Karfa denounces the destruction of his family at the hands of enslavement, on the basis of which Alan Richardson describes the play as one of the more radical representations of slavery of the period (Richardson 1997, 181–2). Jack's encounter with Rosa in both pantomime and melodrama also shows him relatively positively: he could hurt her, but chooses not to – even if he exercises this reticence only in order to attempt to enslave her.

The most persuasive case for an antislavery reading of the stage versions of *Obi* comes from examining their transformation in performance. Jeffrey Cox argues that their overall conservative implications would have been altered on stage by the centrality of the role of Jack in both pantomime and melodrama (Cox 2002, para. 7–8). His point is reinforced by the comment of a reviewer of the pantomime that Jack 'is the best fellow in the whole groupe, and actually falls victim of his own humanity' (Dutton 1801, 28). Jack was always played by the company's leading actor, and would have been at the centre of the audiences' attention, perhaps leading them to see his struggle positively. This is most likely in the performances of the melodrama in which Ira Aldridge, who was renowned for his advocacy of racial justice, played Jack (Waters 2003).

Nevertheless, it seems unlikely that the power even of Aldridge could have drowned out the many elements of the stage version that clearly endorsed anti-abolitionist arguments. In both pantomime and melodrama,

the overall political position taken up could be described as the plantation pastoral, in which enslaved people are happy with their lot so long
as slaveowners are 'kind'. 'Poor Negro Woman', the song quoted above
that critiques the slave trade's impact on black families, continues with
an endorsement of slavery so long as the master is good: 'But if white man
kind massa be/ He heal the wound in negro's heart' (Fawcett 2002, 1.i).
In both pantomime and melodrama, its chorus is sung by the plantation
slaves who declare, 'When buckra man kind, then Negro heart merry.'

Repeatedly, the plays demonstrate the organic and natural hierarchy
of the plantation community. This would have been visually the case
through the movement of the actors emphasizing the slaves' willing sub-
servience and submission to the master. Jack is the exceptional slave who
fails to accept the master's authority, and must be cast out. Ormond explains that 'Heaven knows I pitied the unfortunates, and strove by kindness and humanity to mitigate their cruel lot. With Karfa (for so was he
then named,) alone, my efforts failed; each day but added to his ferocity;
crime followed crime, until the villain dared to attempt the honour of my
wife' (Murray 2002, I.i). Indeed, Jack's existence as a threatening outsider works to unite the overseer, slaves, and master. They share their fear
of Jack and his powers of obeah; the only difference is that the whites are
able to confront Jack while the black characters, with the exception of
Quashee and Sam, cower pathetically in fear of him. Jack himself is a
thorough-going villain. The pantomime presents his violent activity as
completely unexplained; the audience is expected to feel no sympathy
with or understanding of them. This is moderated slightly in the melodrama, through Jack's antislavery speech, but this comes after several
scenes which present Jack purely as a frightening, threatening figure. Taken
as a whole, it is unlikely that these performances aided either the campaign for the abolition of the slave trade in the 1800s or the emancipationist struggle in the 1830s.

The ending, in which Jack is defeated, is the most difficult aspect of
these texts for any reading which sees them as antislavery in implication.
Jack's defeat is not presented as cause for mourning; rather, it is in every
version the occasion for celebration. In the melodrama, Jack's death is
celebrated by 'shouts of the soldiers and Negroes' (II.vi). In the pantomime it is followed by a spectacular parade scene involving the entire
cast, with members carrying triangles, streamers, green leaves, illuminated
lanterns, bells and much else, and singing of Jack's defeat (II.viii).

With the exception of the melodrama, all the retellers of Jack's story
drew on Benjamin Moseley's key innovation, which was to turn Jack's

defeat into a parable of the power of Christianity over African religion. According to Moseley, Quashee got himself 'christianed' before setting out on the expedition to fight Jack, adopting the name James Reeder. Quashee's attempt to use the power of Christianity pays off: when he meets Jack and tells him of his new status, 'Jack was cowed; for, he had prophesied, that white Obi would get the better of him' (Moseley 2005, 167). Despite his previous defeat of Quashee in battle, Jack is now unable to fight successfully, and is quickly overpowered by Quashee/Reeder and his allies Sam and the unnamed 'little boy' (who becomes Tucky in some later versions of the story).[24]

Burdett, and the pantomime stuck closely with this sequence of events. Burdett directly quotes several paragraphs from Moseley at this point, without acknowledgement and with little alteration. In the pantomime when Quashee tells Jack he has been christened, '*Jack* is daunted, and lets his gun fall' (II.vi). In both of these versions, Jack's death at the hands of 'white obi' affirms both the power of Christianity and the reclaiming of the established order.

Earle's *Obi* uses the same plot, but struggles with it. While most of the book's action progresses at a leisurely pace, with considerable detail and digression, the denouement of Quashee's conversion, his revelation to Jack of his Christianity, Jack's fear and death is rushed over in a few flatly written pages. The book as a whole is much longer than Moseley's version, but this aspect of the story hardly expands on Moseley's narrative. Earle perhaps felt that, given his presentation of the novel as a true story and a memorial to a historical Jack, a 'bold and daring defender of the Rights of Man' (68), he could not depart substantially from the recorded fact of Jack's death, or even from Moseley's invented confrontation in which Jack reveals his fear of Reeder's 'white Obi'. But his discomfort with this aspect of the narrative is revealed through his lack of engagement with it. Despite his presentation of Jack as 'as great a man as ever graced the annals of history, basely murdered by the hirelings of Government' Earle continues by conceding that 'No doubt in the end Jack died deservedly – had he died like a man' (Earle 2005, 157). Earle backs away

---

[24]   According to Bilby (2005, 291–200), contemporary Jamaican maroon oral tradition includes many accounts of their ancestors' use of superior obeah to defeat runaway slaves, including those who were themselves obeahmen. In this context, we might read Moseley's reference to 'white obi' as a transformation of a maroon story in which maroons use Christian rather than African-oriented spiritual power. Moseley effectively makes Christianity a type of obeah.

from a full endorsement of slave insurgency, and presents white obi as more powerful than black.

The fact that all three early retellings of Three-Finger Jack turn ultimately on the question of the relative power of Christianity and obeah produces contradictory effects. On one level it demonstrates the impressive power of Christianity over obeah. Obeah is exotic sorcery; Christianity is more powerful. In this it taps into a wider set of concerns among advocates of a reformed system of slavery for whom conversion to Christianity was a central way of ensuring the accommodation of enslaved people to the regime of slavery. And yet in using Christianity to defeat obeah, the difference between the two – between 'religion' on the one hand and 'superstition' on the other – is eroded. Quashee is baptised for purely instrumental reasons: to access power, not because of faith or conversion. In this sense, Christianity becomes simply another form of 'superstition,' albeit one that is more powerful than obeah. Jack's uncontradicted reference to Christianity as 'white obi,' which features in both Earle and Burdett, reinforces this sense, making obeah and Christianity interchangeable.

Alone of the major adaptations, the melodrama *Obi* does not include the 'white obi' theme. Quashee kills Jack, but does not convert to Christianity first. Perhaps this was related to the new context brought about by the 1823 Demerara rebellion and continued by the Jamaican rebellion of 1831–32. Both of these rebellions drew on Afro-Christianity for their mobilising power; in both, proslavery forces blamed missionaries for leading enslaved people into rebellions (Turner 1982; Viotti da Costa 1994). In light of these rebellions, the adoption of Christianity by enslaved people became a far more contested phenomenon. It could no longer be assumed that when enslaved people such as Quashee became 'christianed' they would automatically use their new religion to defend slavery.

The cumulative impact of the cultural figure of Three-Finger Jack was not to produce a coherent argument regarding the slave trade or slavery. Rather, representations of Jack could be adapted and adopted by those on all sides of the slavery debates. Nevertheless, the easiest fit was with a gradualist and ameliorationist viewpoint; potentially hostile to the slave trade, but not emancipationist. Criticisms made by the prose and stage versions of Three-Fingered Jack could be reconciled with the continuation of slavery. Indeed, these texts, especially the pantomime and Burdett versions, could fit quite easily with the reforming planter school of thought outlined by propagandists like William Beckford (1788) and later Thomas

Roughley (1823) and Alexander Barclay (1826). These polemicists addressed themselves to both their fellow-slaveholders and to a wider British public, arguing that a reformed system of slavery could be and was being produced, and that this system obviated the critiques of abolitionists.

This moderately reformist position was a relatively easy one to uphold at the very start of the nineteenth century, prior to the abolition of the slave trade. At this point, the abolition of slavery itself was not really in question, and all sides in Britain looked towards the gradual improvement of the system. Supporters of slavery hoped that this would see off hostility. Opponents expected it to lead to slavery's gradual abolition, as slaveholders adopted wage labor systems as their source of new laborers dried up.

Things had shifted dramatically by the time of the staging of the melodrama *Obi* in 1830. By then, the debate had polarized as it became increasingly clear that slaveholders would not as a group implement the kinds of reforms envisaged by some of their most prominent advisors. In response, antislavery campaigners called for immediate and outright abolition of slavery. Large-scale slave rebellions placed slavery under increasing scrutiny. In this context, the melodrama *Obi* has to be seen as a much more clearly conservative play. Even with Ira Aldridge in the title role of 'an openly rebellious ex-slave' who is allowed to 'point up the contradiction underlying European claims to be civilizing and Christianizing Africa by means of a barbaric and un-Christian practice' (Richardson 1997, 181), the overall thrust is towards the destruction of the rebel, who is described by the benevolent master Ormond as a 'savage', a 'monster', and a 'wretch' (Murray 2002, I.i). As the debate around slavery polarized over the course of the nineteenth century, the ambiguous narratives of the earlier period became increasingly difficult to sustain.

## Works Cited

Aravamudan, Srinivas, 2005. 'Introduction'. In Srinivas Aravamudan, ed., *Obi, or The History of Three-Fingered Jack by William Earle*. Peterborough, Ontario: Broadview Editions, 7–51.

Arnold, Samuel, 1996. *Obi; or Three-Finger'd Jack: originally published by John Longman, Clementi's Company, London, 1800, Music for London entertainment, 1660–1800. Ser.D Pantomime, Ballet & Social Dance; v.4*. Ed. Robert Hoskins and Eileen Southern. London: Stainer & Bell.

Barclay, Alexander, 1826. *A Practical View of the Present State of Slavery in the West Indies. Containing More Particularly an Account of the Actual Condition of the Negroes in Jamaica*. London: Smith, Elder & Co.

Beckford, William, 1788. *Remarks upon the Situation of Negroes in Jamaica, Impartially Made, from a Local Experience of Nearly Thirteen Years in that Island*. London: T. and J. Egerton.

Bilby, Kenneth M., 2005. *True-Born Maroons*. Gainesville: University Press of Florida.

Botkin, Frances R., 2004. 'Questioning the "Necessary Order of Things": Maria Edgeworth's "The Grateful Negro", Plantation Slavery, and the Abolition of the Slave Trade', in Brycchan Carey, Markman Ellis and Sara Salih, eds, *Discourses of Slavery and Abolition: Britain and its Colonies, 1760–1838*. Basingstoke: Palgrave Macmillan, 194–208.

Boulukos, George E., 1999. 'Maria Edgeworth's "Grateful Negro" and the Sentimental Argument for Slavery', *Eighteenth-Century Life* 23 (1):12–29.

Brunton, Deborah, 2004. 'Moseley, Benjamin (1742–1819)', in *Oxford Dictionary of National Biography* (Oxford University Press), [accessed 29 June 2006]. Available from http://www.oxforddnb.com/view/article/19387

Burdett, William, 1800. *Life and exploits of Mansong, commonly called Three-finger'd Jack, the terror of Jamaica: with a particular account of the Obi; being the only true one of that celebrated and fascinating mischief so prevalent in the West Indies*. Sommers Town, London: A. Neil.

Burdett, William, 1801. *The life and exploits of Three-finger'd Jack, the terror of Jamaica. With a particular account of the Obi; being the only true one of that celebrated and fascinating mischief, so prevalent in the West Indies*. 4th edn, with additions, edn. Sommers Town, London: A. Neil.

Burdett, William, nd. *A New and Tenth Edition of the Life and Exploits of That Daring Robber, Three-Finger'd Jack, a Rebellious Slave, Who Was Brought from Africa, and Shortly Became the Terror of Jamaica, Including a Full and Accurate Description of That Fascinating Charm, Called Obi, Practised, with Such Mischievious Consequences, by the African Negroes in the West Indies*. London: A. Neill.

Carey, Brycchan, 2005. *British Abolitionism and the Rhetoric of Sensibility: Writing, Sentiment, and Slavery, 1760–1807*. Basingstoke: Palgrave Macmillan.

Cox, Jeffrey N., 2002. 'Theatrical Forms, Ideological Conflicts, and the Staging of Obi' in Charles Rzepka, ed. *Obi* (Romantic Circles Praxis Series), [accessed 18 July 2006]. Available from http://www.rc.umd.edu/praxis/obi/cox/cox.html

Craton, Michael, 1982. *Testing the Chains: Resistance to Slavery in the British West Indies*. Ithaca: Cornell University Press.

Cundall, Frank, 1930. 'Three-Fingered Jack, The Terror of Jamaica', *West India Committee Circular* 45: 9–10, 36–7, 55–6.

Drescher, Seymour, 1977. *Econocide: British Slavery in the Era of Abolition*. Pittsburgh: University of Pittsburgh Press.

Drescher, Seymour, 2002. *The Mighty Experiment: Free Labor versus Slavery in British Emancipation*. Oxford: Oxford University Press.

Dutton, Thomas, 1801. *The Dramatic Censor; or Monthly Epitome of Taste, Fashion and Manners*. Vol. 3. London: J. Roach and Chapple.

Earle, William, 1800. *Obi: or, The history of three-fingered Jack: in a series of letters from a resident in Jamaica to his friend in England*. London: Earle and Hemet.

Earle, William, 2005. *Obi, or The History of Three-Fingered Jack*. Edited by Srinivas Aravamudan. Peterborough, Ontario: Broadview. Original edn, 1800.

Edwards, Bryan, 1793. *The History, Civil and Commercial, of the British Colonies in the West Indies*. 2 vols. London: John Stockdale.

Ellis, Markman, 1996. *The Politics of Sensibility: Race, Gender and Commerce in the Sentimental Novel*. Cambridge: Cambridge University Press.

Eyre, Lawrence Alan, 1973. 'Jack Mansong: Bloodshed or Brotherhood?' *Jamaica Journal* 7 (4): 9–14.

Fawcett, John, 1800. Obi; or Three Finger'd Jack. A story told by action interspersed with songs, recitative, etc. Larpent Collection, microcard of manuscript in Huntington Library.

Fawcett, John, 2002. 'Obi, or, Three-Finger'd Jack! a serio-pantomime, in two acts' in Charles Rzepka, ed., *Obi* (Romantic Circles Praxis Series), [accessed 18 July 2006]. Available from http://www.rc.umd.edu/praxis/obi/

Felsenstein, Frank, ed., 1999. *English Trader, Indian Maid: Representing Gender, Race, and Slavery in the New World: An Inkle and Yarico Reader*. Baltimore: Johns Hopkins University Press.

Guha, Ranajit, 1983. 'The Prose of Counter-Insurgency' in Ranajit Guha, ed., *Subaltern Studies II: Writings on South Asian History and Society*. Delhi: Oxford University Press, 1–42.

Hill, Erroll, 1992. *The Jamaican Stage, 1655–1900: Profile of a Colonial Theatre*. Amherst: University of Massachussetts Press.

Hobsbawm, Eric, 2001. *Bandits*. London: Abacus. Original edn, 1969.

Hoskins, Robert, and Eileen Southern, 1996. 'Introduction', ed., *Obi; or Three-Finger'd Jack: originally published by John Longman, Clementi's Company, London, 1800*. London: Stainer & Bell, xi–xxix.

Joseph, Gilbert M., 1990. 'On the Trail of Latin American Bandits: A Reexamination of Peasant Resistance', *Latin American Research Review* 25 (3): 7–53.

Kitson, Peter J. and Deborah Lee, eds., 1999. *Slavery, Abolition and Emancipation: Writings in the British Romantic Period. Vol 4: Verse*, edited by Alan Richardson. London: Pickering and Chatto, 1999.

Lee, Debbie, 2002. 'Grave Dirt, Dried Toads, and the Blood of a Black Cat: How Aldridge Worked His Charms' in Charles Rzepka, ed. *Obi* (Romantic Circles Praxis Series), [accessed 18 July 2006]. Available from http://www.rc.umd.edu/praxis/obi/lee/lee.html

Midgley, Clare, 1992. *Women Against Slavery: The British Campaigns, 1780–1870*. London: Routledge.

Moody, Jane, 2000. *Illegitimate Theatre in London, 1770–1840*. Cambridge: Cambridge University Press.

Moseley, Benjamin, 1799. *A Treatise on Sugar*. London.

Moseley, Benjamin, 2005. 'A Treatise on Sugar (extract)' in Srinivas Aravamudan, ed., *Obi, or the History of Three-Fingered Jack, by William Earle*. Peterborough, Ontario: Broadview, 160–8.

Murray, William Henry Wood, 2002. 'Obi; or, Three-Finger'd Jack. A Melo-drama in Two Acts'. In Charles Rzepka, ed. *Obi* (Romantic Circles Praxis Series), [accessed 18 July 2006]. Available from http://www.rc.umd.edu/praxis/obi/

*Obi or, Three Fingered Jack. a Popular Melo-drama in two acts (as performed at Drury Lane Theatre)*. nd. London: Penny Pictorial Plays.

Oldfield, J. R., 1998. *Popular Politics and British Anti-Slavery: The Mobilisation of Public Opinion Against the Slave Trade 1787–1807*. London: Frank Cass. Original edn, 1995.

Park, Mungo, 2000. *Travels in the Interior Districts of Africa*. Ed. Kate Ferguson Masters. Durham: Duke University Press. Original edn, 1799.

Richardson, Alan, 1997. 'Romantic Voodoo: Obeah and British Culture, 1797–1807' in Margarite Fernández Olmos and Lizabeth Paravisini-Gelbert, ed., *Sacred Possessions: Vodou, Santería, Obeah, and the Caribbean*. New Brunswick, New Jersey: Rutgers University Press.

Roughley, Thomas, 1823. *The Jamaica Planter's Guide; Or, A System for Planting and Managing a Sugar Estate*. London: Longman, Hurst, Rees, Orme, and Brown.

Rzepka, Charles, 2002a. 'Introduction: Obi, Aldridge and Abolition' in Charles Rzepka, ed., *Obi* (Romantic Circles Praxis Series), [accessed 18 July 2006]. Available from http://www.rc.umd.edu/praxis.obi/rzepka/intro.html

Rzepka, Charles, 2002b. 'Obi Now'. In Charles Rzepka, ed., *Obi* (Romantic Circles Praxis Series), [accessed 18 July 2006]. Available from http://www.rc.umd.edu/praxis/obi/

Sypher, Wylie, 1942. *Guinea's Captive Kings: British Antislavery Literature of the XVIIIth Century*. Chapel Hill: University of North Carolina Press.

Turner, Mary, 1982. *Slaves and Missionaries: The Disintegration of Jamaican Slave Society, 1787–1834*. Urbana: University of Illinois Press.

Viotti da Costa, Emilia, 1994. *Crowns of Glory, Tears of Blood: The Demerara Slave Rebellion of 1823*. New York: Oxford University Press.

Warner, Michael, Natasha Hurley, Luis Iglesias, Sonia Di Loreto, Jeffrey Scraba, and Sandra Young, 2001. 'A Soliloquy "Lately Spoken at the African Theatre": Race and the Public Sphere in New York City, 1821', *American Literature* 73 (1): 1–46.

Waters, Hazel, 2003. 'Ira Aldridge and the Battlefield of Race', *Race and Class* 45 (1): 1–30.

# Putting down Rebellion: Witnessing the Body of the Condemned in Abolition-era Narratives

## SARA SALIH

On the island I accepted that I should never learn how Friday lost his tongue, as I accepted that I should never know how the apes crossed the sea. But what we can accept in life we cannot accept in history. To tell my story and be silent on Friday's tongue is no better than offering a book for sale with pages in it quietly left empty. Yet the only tongue that can tell Friday's secret is the tongue he has lost! (Coetzee 1986, 67)

### I

FRIDAY'S SILENCE poses a dilemma for Coetzee's Susan Barton. Not to talk about Friday's tongue is to produce an unacceptably incomplete historical commodity, but the history of the tongue is *in* the tongue that has been detached from a body rendered aphasic, how, Susan will never know. And by talking about what she cannot talk about (since it is no longer there), Susan *is* in fact bearing unwitting witness to the speaking silence at the centre of her narrative. "'The story of Friday's tongue is a story unable to be told, or unable to be told by me,'" Susan admits: "'many stories can be told of Friday's tongue, but the true story is buried within Friday, who is mute. The true story will not be heard till by art we have found a means of giving voice to Friday'" (Coetzee 1986, 118).

Who can tell Friday's story? Is it possible for art to 'give voice' to the truth of slavery? And how might art be created from an organ that has been severed from a black man's body? Evidently, such questions did not trouble those among J. M. Coetzee's novelistic forebears whose texts featured a black presence, or an interlude in the Caribbean, or both, but contemporary readers may find themselves querying the ethics of narrativizing plantation slavery, and they may feel uneasy at being brought into textual contact with fictions of atrocity, even those written over two hundred years ago. We might declare with Austen's reader that what we are encountering is 'only a novel', but given the enormous archive of materials about the British slave trade and its abolition, and the fine, sometimes invisible line, between fictional and non-fictional materials in that archive, it would be foolhardy to toss these narratives from us so carelessly. I recognize that this does not address the question as to how (or even *whether*) we should read, interpret and write about fictional and non-fictional texts that repeatedly and insistently represent scenes of uprising, violence and brutalization in the Caribbean prior to and after abolition. Training their metaphorical long-range vision all the way from metropole to colony, these texts represent the act of witnessing the horrors of the slave trade via the medium of 'native informants,' in narratives-within-narratives that constitute a kind of simulated slave testimony, delivered to white interlocutors who are located at a safe remove from what is being described.

Readers who encounter these texts in 2007 are likely to be troubled by issues of appropriation, as well as objecting to generic, stereotypical portrayals of 'slaves,' and the routine deployment of punishment and execution as narrative devices.[1] In spite of the manifold risks involved in describing and analysing these representations, I would like to dwell on the narrativization of Caribbean slavery in a selection of British texts that were produced in the 'ameliorist' decades prior to the Abolition Act of 1807. The texts I am going to discuss were published between 1766 and 1804; they do not constitute a discrete archive or canon, and they are generically diverse, ranging across prose fiction, 'history,' anti-slavery polemic and poetry (although I will be focusing on the first of these). Again, notwithstanding the risks, I am going to confine my analyses to *white* representations of black bodies, and I do not intend to discuss the narrativization of slavery by black writers during this period. I am not suggesting that there is an invisible, textual 'colour line' between white-authored and black-authored texts produced during the same historical 'moment,' and I am indebted to commentators such as Felicity Nussbaum and Roxann Wheeler who have engaged in useful contrapuntal discussions of black- and white-authored texts published in this period. While recognizing the importance of such work, I am primarily concerned with the act of imagining and fictionalizing slavery *from a distance*, at second or third hand, not from any putative personal experience. As far as is known, none of the prose fiction writers whose work I discuss ever visited

---

[1]  While recognizing that the term 'slave' is problematic in its designation of a 'thing' rather than an individual, I shall retain its usage here, since the construction of the slave as thing is precisely the subject of this essay. Henceforth, 'slave' and 'negro' will be used without inverted commas. Of course, 'negro,' 'slave,' and 'African' are not synonymous, although they were frequently conflated in the period under discussion. For a discussion of slave/enslaved, see Campbell 2004.

the Caribbean; the sources on which they are likely to have relied were written by white men who were not slaves, but who did have some experience of slavery in the Caribbean. It may well be that authors such as Elizabeth Helme and Anna Maria Mackenzie knew of or had read (for example) Olaudah Equiano's *Interesting Narrative* or Ignatius Sancho's *Letters*, or the numerous accounts circulated by the Committee for Effecting the Abolition of the Slave Trade. But although many of the texts I discuss were possibly motivated by the manifest aim of ameliorating plantocratic practices in British Caribbean colonies, their latent content suggests a deeper preoccupation with the textual regulation, disciplining and punishment of insurrectionary black slave bodies.

To put it another way: I am suggesting that the repeated, almost obsessive, representation of insurrection and the punished black body constitutes a double 'putting down,' i.e. textual depiction as a form of textual quelling whereby the unruly black body is disciplined and delimited. The spectacle of black bodies that are put down (i.e. represented and/as punished) seems designed to reassure white readers, at the same time as eliciting a sympathetic tear and a throwing-up of hands at the iniquities of the slave trade. That these texts fulfil a regulatory function in their *execution* (literal, metaphorical) of the slave might seem an obvious enough point. John Bender posits that the novel and the penitentiary were narrative modes (or regimes) within which the subject is perceived and constructed (Bender 1987, 44). This idea, however, does not take into account the old-style, spectacular modes of power and domination that were still occurring in British colonies such as Jamaica, alongside more modern forms of punishment, nor does it reckon with the tricky question of the enslaved, the not-quite human entity who is simultaneously constituted as subject and object in British discourse (Paton 2004, 20).

The texts I will analyse detail legalized brutalities that were not enacted on English 'criminals' at the time (e.g. mutilation, branding, decapitation, quartering), and they vacillate between portraying the negro as a volitional subject and the negro as a slave-'thing,' a vacillation that also characterizes contemporary legal constructions of the enslaved. I argue that the slave as 'bare life' and *homo sacer* – an entity with no legal rights that can be killed by anyone at any time – is the site of an epistemological and erotic opportunity in these narratives, where the brutalized, dismembered black body is 'seen' and represented in an auto- or homo-erotic 'scene' of witnessing that is constitutive of the white spectator.[2] This scene is also a site of danger for the sympathetic, sentimental onlooker who is implicitly invited to imagine him/herself into the suffering black body. How these texts negotiate the discursive contradictions of *homo sacer*, the (in this context) black slave body that, neither subject nor object, must be discursively known, feared, and narratively contained, is one of the questions I will address in this essay.[3]

## II

> [*Homo sacer*] has been excluded from the religious community and from all political life; he cannot participate in the rites of his *gens* nor … can he perform any juridically valid act. What is more, his entire existence is reduced to a bare life stripped of every right by virtue of the fact that anyone can kill him without committing homicide; he can save himself only in perpetual flight or a foreign land. And yet he is in a continuous relationship with the power that banished him precisely insofar as he is at every instant exposed to an unconditioned threat of death … [N]o life, as exiles and bandits know well, is more 'political' than his. (Agamben 1998, 183–4)

As bare life, the slave is simultaneously inside and outside of power, banished by the law and yet endlessly imbricated in a relationship with the sovereign power that claims the slave's body as an item of property subject to the law. For Agamben, the political subject as bare life is initiated in the 1679 writ of *habeas corpus* (Agamben 1998, 123). This law was invoked in Granville Sharp's defence of James Somerset in 1772, resulting in Mansfield's judgment that in England at least, a master only had rights to a slave if he could prove that the captive in question had *in writing* willingly 'bound himself, without compulsion or illegal duress.' As a *corpus* recognized by English law, the African slave in England was entitled to the King's protection, although this did not mean that slaves were legally constituted as subjects (Blackstone 1825, 1: 127; Thomas 1997, 473; Walvin 1992, 14–15). 'The idea that slaves were property was as firmly accepted in the law of England as it was in that of the colonies,' and English respect for the subject was necessarily limited by a slave system that did not recognize slave subjectivity. When British

---

[2]   The fictional spectators/listeners in the texts under discussion are frequently men, but I am not assuming the *reader's* gender.
[3]   See Baucom 2005, 187 for Agamben's 'omission' of slavery in his analyses of *homo sacer*.

humanitarians argued that slaves *were* subjects, they advanced a theo-retical and practical innovation that gained only slow acceptance during the controversies over amelioration and emancipation. James Somerset and Grace were free when they came to England because there was no disciplinary apparatus enforcing slavery in England (Goveia 1970, 20, 21).

Even within the Caribbean, the legal construction of the slave as a chattel gave rise to some significant anomalies: for example, if a white person wilfully killed a slave, the act was not recognized as homicide or murder, although it was usually regarded in theory (not always in prac-tice) as a criminal offence of a lesser order, punishable by a fairly low fine. On the other hand, if an enslaved person struck or insulted a white per-son, s/he was subject to horrific penalties of whipping, mutilation or death. The law provided that if the white person were in any way hurt or blood drawn, then severer punishments could be inflicted. In order to enact these punishments, the law had to recognize the slave as a subject, since one cannot exactly punish a chattel – or indeed, accuse it of a crime, so that as Goveia observes, the law had to envisage the slave as something more than a 'thing' in such cases. The slave was not just 'property,' as the law tried to posit; he was a volitional human being with a capacity for resistance which must be restrained. Accordingly, any slave who raised problems of public order was granted a legal *persona* so that he could be dealt with as a special kind of property (Goveia 1970, 24, 25). 'Violence turns anybody subjected to it into a thing,' observes Simone Weil, but here the slave-thing is constituted as a subject so that violence may be visited upon 'it.'[4] This indeed is the slave as *homo sacer*, a person (or not?) excluded from political, religious and legal communities who can be killed but not murdered, and who cannot evade the juridical power that both banishes her and endlessly threatens her with death (Agamben 1998, 183).

The dilemma Goveia identifies in Caribbean slave law is routinely and explicitly addressed by prose fiction writers, whose arguments against plantocratic methods of punishment are based on the contention that slaves are sentient humans and not merely objects. A paradigmatic and much-discussed example occurs in Sarah Scott's *The History of Sir George Ellison*, where Ellison argues with his wife about the punishment of slaves on their Jamaican plantation. Firmly countering Mrs Ellison's assumption that negroes are 'the most despicable part of the creation,' Ellison insists

---

[4]   Quoted in Sontag 2003, 11.

that slaves are 'fellow creatures' and that 'the distinguishing marks of humanity [do not] lie in the complexion or turn of features' (Scott 1766, 13). When Ellison appeals to something other than the body in order to assert slave humanity, and when he insists that 'the present difference' between white and black people is 'merely adventitious, not natural,' he expresses what was to remain a cultural obsession with the black body, its capacities and differences, well into the nineteenth century and beyond (Scott 1766, 13). Scott's novel by no means assumes that debating the question of 'epidermal difference' (as Frantz Fanon would have it) is redundant.[5] The fact that Ellison and his wife have this discussion at all is a stark reminder that the issue was far from settled in the minds of contemporary readers. Ellison's assertions about negro spiritual equality are presumably intended to persuade a nominal reader as well as his wife, and although Mrs Ellison's views concerning racial difference and the use-value of negroes are refuted by Ellison's subsequent conduct of the plantation, the text allows for an initial degree of ambivalence regarding whether the negro was to be treated as feeling subject or punishable object.

This uncertainty also marks later prose fictional representations of slaves, where a similar movement from doubt to conviction is staged for readers who would not automatically assume that negroes are people. In Helme's *The Farmer of Inglewood Forest*, the heroine Agnes is terrified of Felix's dark complexion until he is 'desired' to tell his life story to while away the time. 'Ah,' Agnes exclaims when Felix concludes the first section of his narrative, 'I shall never more … look on Felix's face with dislike; I shall … forget his complexion' (Helme 1796, 2: 236). After Felix has finished his pathetic tale, Agnes murmurs, 'I would compound for all men's faces to be like Felix's, to make them equally virtuous' (Helme 1796, 249). As in Scott's novel, Felix's humanity must be insisted upon, proved to his interlocutors, who are fully convinced by the end of his narrative that his soul is by no means as black as his face. William Earle's *Obi* and Anna Maria Mackenzie's *Slavery; or, the Times*, similarly labour to assert the humanity of their negro protagonists. *Slavery*'s Adolphus Zimza is the offspring of a 'mixed race' union between the (dead) Englishwoman Leonora and Zimza Senior, a West African king. In the first letter of this epistolary novel, Zimza insists that 'Leonora [his mother] … loved the English, though her sensibility distinguished innate sincerity through the dark hue that shrouded Zimza's countenance.

[5]  See e.g. Wheeler 2000, 2–48.

Yes, *she* looked to the heart for that equality the Christians deny us, nor shrunk disgusted from the sable umbrage of an honest countenance' (Mackenzie 1792, 1:15).

The negro body, as seen or reported as seen by white protagonists, must be known and understood, with explanations adduced for its difference. "'I would give [this estate] for the extacy I felt at seeing the joy of the poor reprieved wretches,'" Ellison tells his wife in the course of his attempts to convince her that physical punishment is an unnecessary mode of discipline: "'Had you, my dear, been present when they threw themselves at my feet, embraced my knees, and lift[ed] up their streaming eyes to heaven ... you would have wept with me'" (Scott 1766, 11). Ellison's highly emotive account encapsulates the fictional acts of 'seeing' in which the reader must engage for the manifest aim of the text to be successful: if we, like Mrs Ellison, can imaginatively witness the scene that Ellison evokes, then we will 'see' him seeing the grateful negroes whose humanity-in-deference is proved through their physical gestures. At the same time, because the reader is *imaginatively* 'seeing,' the 'scene' itself is delimited, the (in this instance) grateful black bodies textually circumscribed by the narrative-within-a-narrative. As readers, we are exhorted to 'look,' in a manner that resembles the primal scene (as Homi Bhabha calls it) in which Frantz Fanon is involved on a train when a child sees him and calls out, "'Look! A Negro!'" (Fanon 1952, 112; Bhabha 1983, 45). Unlike the girl on the train who is terrified and fascinated by the black man's physically-present body, and unlike Agnes in *Farmer*, the reader of the prose fictions under discussion is situated at a safe textual remove from the enslaved people whose bodies are the focus of the narrative gaze. Further, although Fanon feels himself 'assailed' by the little girl's interpellative address, he is not, in fact, the subject who is being hailed. The 'Look!' is addressed to the girl's (presumably white) travelling companions who are summoned to a scene that Fanon experiences as an assault. Likewise, it is to a *white* readership that these prose fictional affirmations of black humanity are addressed.

'The visual field is not neutral to the question of race,' writes Judith Butler in her Fanonian account of the paranoid 'reading' of Rodney King's body within a homophobic and racially saturated episteme: 'it is itself a racial formation ... hegemonic and forceful' (Butler 1993, 207). If, as Butler argues, the 'seeing' of black bodies by white onlookers is circumscribed by the racist organization and disposition of the visible, then every act of 'seeing' is already a 'reading' in which the black body is produced as an object of fear. Butler's insistence that 'seeing' is a racially overdetermined hermeneutic act is highly resonant in the context of Abolition-era fictions in which readers are repeatedly invited to 'look' and 'see' the black body, either solo or en masse. 'We can only see what we look at,' writes John Berger : 'To look is an act of choice' (Berger 1972, 8). If we apply Berger's comment to a late eighteenth- and early nineteenth-century readership, substituting 'look at' for 'read about,' we may say that these fictions are inviting their readers to engage in imaginative acts of 'seeing' slavery and the slave body by reading about them. Thomas Clarkson engages precisely this technique in part III of *An Essay on the Slavery and Commerce of the Human Species, Particularly the African*, when he invites his reader to 'turn [her] eyes' to a textual scene on an unidentified West African coast where slaves are being forced to board an English slave ship. 'To place this in the clearest and most conspicuous point of view, we shall throw a considerable part of our information on this head into the form of a narrative,' writes Clarkson:

> we shall suppose ourselves, in short, on the continent of Africa, and relate a scene, which, from its agreement with unquestionable facts, might not unreasonably be presumed to have been presented to our view, had we really been there.
>
> And first, let us turn our eyes to the cloud of dust that is before us. It seems to advance rapidly, and, accompanied with dismal shrieks and yellings, to make the very air, that is above it, tremble as it rolls along. What can possibly be the cause? Let us inquire of that melancholy African, who seems to walk dejected near the shore; whose eyes are stedfastly fixed on the approaching object, and whose heart, if we can judge from the appearance of his countenance, must be greatly agitated                                                                                     ...
>
> [The slaves] came distinctly into sight. They appeared to advance in a long column, but in a very irregular manner. There were three only in the front, and these were chained together. The rest that followed seemed to be chained in pairs, but by pressing forward, to avoid the lash of the drivers, the breadth of the column began to be greatly extended, and ten or more were observed abreast. (Clarkson 1786, 117–19)

To convey the treatment of Africans by English receivers clearly and *conspicuously* (i.e. in a way that is clearly visible or striking to the eye), Clarkson deploys an ekphrastic narrative mode in which the reader is supposed to see what is being described. Unlike Sterne's Yorick, who, in the much-discussed 'The Captive' chapter of *A Sentimental Journey* cannot bring the 'affecting ... picture' of slavery 'near [him],' Clarkson appears to have no difficulty 'seeing' the newly enslaved people who emerge from the cloud of dust (Sterne 1768, 72). Where Yorick envisages a 'captive' so that he may narrow his imaginative vision from the unimaginable 'millions of my fellow creatures born to no inheritance but slavery,' (Sterne 1768, 72) Clarkson introduces a single 'unhappy African' who tells the story of the wretched slaves the reader 'sees' and 'hears.' As the melancholy African gives his detailed first-hand account of how the slaves were captured from their village, his interlocutor indulges his imagination by constructing identities for the kidnapped people who pass before him. Towards the end of the chapter, Clarkson's 'honest African' asks why his people are suffering in this way. Clarkson replies that if the slaves' cries and groans could travel from Africa to Britain they would pierce generous Englishmen's hearts and prompt them to 'sympathize with you in your distress.' (Clarkson 1786, 123, 127).

The textually 'enslaving' auto-erotic empathy that Marcus Wood notes in Sterne's 'Captive' are not altogether missing from Clarkson's brief foray into fictional narrative, where the melancholy African and the slaves-in-a-cloud are embodied – both 'seen' and 'heard' – for the express purpose of conveying 'The Slavery of the Africans in the European Colonies' (the title of this section) in embodied form to an English readership (Wood 2002, 16). 'Have you not heard me sigh, while we have been talking?' asks the intelligent African during his testimonial exegesis of the scene: 'Do you not see the tears that now trickle down my cheeks?' (Clarkson 1786, 125). Without his feeling, first-hand, 'conspicuous' explication, the scene might lose its power to move, and like Yorick, the reader might find that she is unable to imagine the enslaved people who suffer under the white man's lash. In Clarkson's account, the reader is implicitly asked to forget that she is imagining that she is seeing/hearing, to forget, as we cannot while reading 'The Captive,' the narrative frame that contains and defines this section of the text. What is apparently missing from the prison cell in *A Sentimental Journey* is the fantasy of a melancholy African to facilitate Yorick's visualization (he has to rely on a starling as prompt). Instead, Sterne's chapter provides an ironic comment on the limits of the sentimental imagination, even when one is in the correct 'frame' (Sterne 1768, 72). It is a lacuna that Clarkson attempts to fill by representing the bodies of the enslaved, and by 'giving voice' to an African who has had first-hand experience of slavery (although he does not appear to be enslaved himself and he is quick to declare that he is not a slaver; Clarkson 1786, 119). Through such a 'view,' to use Clarkson's word, will our sympathies be engaged.

This type of scene occurs with remarkable frequency in contemporary prose fictions, where intelligent, melancholy 'Africans' evoke the iniquities of slavery for their horrified white listeners. I have already mentioned Felix, the loyal ex-slave in *The Farmer of Inglewood Forest*, whose generic 'STORY' of capture, enslavement and liberty is bracketed off from the main body of this rather lurid novel. Similarly, in Robert Bage's *Man As He Is* (1792), Sir George Paradyne finds himself alone in a country house, with no interlocutors other than an 'old woman' and the servant, Benjamin Fidel or Benihango. Like Felix, Benihango used to be a slave, and since there is nothing else to do, and since '[t]he slave trade was at this time becoming a popular topic,' Sir George quizzes Benihango about his life prior to coming to England (Bage 1792, 4: 228, 229). Benihango's 'STORY' is separated from the rest of the narrative which follows a similar arc to Felix's (capture, enslavement, white brutality, freedom-in-servitude). Adolphus Zimza in Mackenzie's *Slavery* is not a slave, but his part-African heritage is presumably supposed to qualify him to bear epistolary witness to both cruel and judicious plantation practices in the Caribbean; he also gives a very brief first-hand account of the uprising in San Domingo.

Where Sterne's narrator signals his failure to conjure the captives imaginatively, these later prose-fiction writers offer their readers stories of once-enslaved Africans *supposedly told by the Africans themselves*. Not much imagination is required: as in Clarkson's account, all the reader must do is suspend her disbelief for the duration of the STORY, while remaining sympathetic to the brutalities of slavery as narrated by someone who has experienced or seen them. Help is also at hand for the reader who is unsure as to how to respond to such tales, since s/he need only adopt the fictional white interlocutors' expressions of dismay, outrage and pecuniary contrition. Such fictions supplement or assist the reader's sympathetic imagination through the interpolation of simulated slave narratives in which 'Africans' are called upon to bear witness. It is hardly surprising that prose writers would deploy such an authentication device, in an era when questions of 'truth' were centrally at issue for both supporters and opponents of the slave lobby. As Dwight A. McBride puts it, 'It takes a witness for the "truth" to be told' (McBride 2001, 95).

'The truth,' though, as many recent commentators and theorists have noted, is *not* being told, and can never be told even by 'witnesses.' The value of testimony lies in what it lacks. The 'true' witnesses, the 'complete' witnesses, are those who did not and could not bear witness (Agamben 1999, 34). These are the troublingly named *Musselmänner* or

'Moslems,' Primo Levi's 'the drowned' who died in the Nazi camps and who, in their untestifiability, mark what Agamben calls a 'moving threshold through which man passed into non-man' (Agamben 1999, 47). This might remind us of Clarkson's moving column of slaves unfolding to view and apparently extending infinitely into space. Even in this fictionalized account, the men who are about to cross the threshold into 'thing-dom' cannot testify and Clarkson's African has difficulty bearing witness for them as they pass by (Clarkson 1786, 120–1).

The case is quite starkly put by Marcus Wood who identifies 'the crime' of slavery testimony as the attempt to acquire, to re-inscribe, and thereby to efface the voices of slavery's victims: 'the dirtiest thing the Western imagination ever did, and it does it compulsively still, is to believe in the aesthetically healing powers of empathetic fiction ... The echoes, the reflections, the refrain which runs through slave narrative by black or white is finally that slavery is a tale that cannot be told' (Wood 2002, 35–6; see Baucom 2005, 193–4). But slavery is a tale that *has* been told over and over again, and the discourses of empathy, sympathy, and sentiment, along with tropes of imaginative seeing, are deployed in repeated acts of 'impossible witness' (McBride). We might decry these simulated slave testimonies as 'dirty' appropriations of absent subjects whose sufferings are aestheticized in 'bad,' 'self-righteous,' virtuously – indeed *violently* – sentimental novels. I am recalling James Baldwin's vehement denunciation of *Uncle Tom's Cabin* in particular, and sentimental discourse in general, in which 'the constriction or failure of perception ... [left] unanswered and unnoticed the only important question: what it was, after all, that moved [Stowe's] people to such deeds' (Baldwin 1995, 20). What was it indeed? Uncomfortable though it may be to do so, we must apply Baldwin's question to Stowe's 'hard-boiled' predecessors who are at least as unflinching in their cataloguing and textual pictorializing of slavery's violence.

### III

[A] general inclination to revolt appearing among all the Koromantyn Negroes in the island, it was thought necessary to make a few terrible examples of some of the most guilty. Of three who were clearly proved to be have been concerned in the murders committed at Ballard's Valley, one was condemned to be burnt, and the other two to be hung up alive in irons and left to perish in this dreadful situation. The wretch that was burnt was made to sit on the ground, and his body being chained to an iron stake, the fire was applied to his feet. He uttered

not a groan, and saw his legs reduced to ashes with the utmost firm-
ness and composure; after which, one of his arms by some means get-
ting loose, he snatched a brand from the fire that was consuming him,
and flung it in the face of the executioner. The two that were hung up
alive were indulged, at their own request, with a hearty meal immediately before they were suspended on the gibbet, which was erected in
the parade of the town of Kingston. From that time, until they expired, they never uttered the least complaint, except only of cold in
the night, but diverted themselves all day long in discourse with their
countrymen, who were permitted, very improperly, to surround the
gibbet. On the seventh day a notion prevailed among the spectators,
that one of them wished to communicate an important secret to his
master, my near relation; who being in St.Mary's, the commanding
officer sent for me. I endeavoured, by means of an interpreter, to let
him know that I was present; but I could not understand what he said
in return. I remember that both he and his fellow sufferer laughed
immoderately at something that occurred, – I know not what. The
next morning one of them silently expired, as did the other on the
morning of the ninth day. (Edwards 1793, 2: 65–6)

Bryan Edwards's otherwise exhaustive account of the aftermath of Tacky's
rebellion in Jamaica contains an unwitting instance of what Agamben
identifies as the language that no longer signifies. In order to bear witness, language must give way to a non-language, thus revealing the impossibility of bearing witness (Agamben 1999, 39). 'The language of testimony is a language that no longer signifies, and that, in not signifying,
advances into what is without language, to the point of taking on a different insignificance – that of the complete witness, that of he who by definition cannot bear witness' (Agamben 1999, 39). The 'complete witness'
in Edwards's account, is not Edwards himself, even though he claims to
have been present at the scene, but the condemned man suspended on
the gibbet whose words Edwards does not understand. By contrast, the
rebel who is burnt alive, according to Edwards, dies wordlessly after a
final, eloquent gesture of defiance.

Edwards appears to personify this silent burnt African in a set of 'Stanzas, Occasioned by the Death of ALICO, an African Slave, condemned
for Rebellion, in Jamaica, 1760,' a poem that was published in Jamaica
the year before the publication of the *History*.[6] Immediately beneath the
title, the reader is given the following semi-pictorial pointer:

---

[6]   Although Edwards' 'Stanzas' do not specify that Alico took part in Tacky's
Rebellion, the date and place are surely meant to signal this.

(☛ He is supposed to address himself to his wife at the place of execution.)

In contrast to the nameless rebel in Edwards's subsequent 'documentary' account, this condemned slave is given a name, and he addresses his wife in iambic tetrameters/trimeters. In the eighth stanza, he urges a 'Christian' (Edwards?) to 'glut thy ravish'd eyes' as 'the scorching flames arise/ And these poor limbs devour' (Edwards 1792, 38). Like many other 'African' figments of the white imagination, Alico feels no pain and he welcomes death as '*freedom to the slave!*' (Edwards 1792, 39).[7] The catalogue of violence (to cite Baldwin again) conveyed in the *History*'s unflinching, unsentimental anatomizing of the three men's deaths contrasts markedly with the curiously disembodied 'emoting' of the 'Stanzas.' In the latter, we are presumably supposed to occupy the affective position of the condemned man's wife, from where we may witness his spirit vacating the 'limbs' that are devoured by the flames. The rebels in the *History* are speechless or incomprehensible – resembling Agamben's 'complete witnesses' who are seen, heard but not understood – whereas in the 'Stanzas,' Alico (behind whom stands Edwards) waxes eloquent about his desire to die and the freedom he will attain on the shores of heaven. With historical hindsight, 'giving voice' to the slave, ventriloquizing his sufferings, and offering the reader the (inevitably eroticized?) viewpoint of his wife, certainly seems as problematic, or as criminal, Wood might say, as the calm, objective spectator's view of the scenes of punishment in the *History*. However, I want to dwell on the penal function of *both* descriptions, since it is a salient characteristic of accounts of punishment and execution in Caribbean slave society during the decades preceding Abolition.

If we place Edwards' two narratives of the post-uprising scenes of punishment in chronological sequence, we might say that he moves from constructing the negro-as-subject, to a 'factual,' externalized description in which the nonchalant, defiant slaves are presented to the reader as 'things.' It is possible to track a similar discursive move in contemporary prose fictions, where the negro is granted narrative subjecthood only to be reified and objectified at the story's end. As I detail this shift, it will be useful to recall that both Caribbean slave law and English law posit the negro as property or thing *and* as (punishable) subject. A similar fluctua-

---

[7]   The 'savage's' indifference to pain was evidently a contemporary preoccupation: see Smith 1790, 240–1, 333, and Wood 2000, 216.

tion occurs in Abolition-era prose fictions, in which sentimentality and penality do not appear to contradict each other. Just as the negro must be legally constituted as a subject in order to be punished, so in fictional texts, readers' sentimental responses are more likely to be engaged by a person than a mere thing. Subjecthood is narratively assigned to slave characters so that readers may sympathize with them, as they do with the sight of a 'brother on the rack' in Adam Smith's account of the sympathetic imagination. This affective response brings the reader into close emotional proximity with the sufferer (Smith 2002, 11–12). As Ian Baucom argues, within a Smithean sentimental framework, the sympathetic onlooker may invest in the suffering of another without abandoning the safety of her spectatorial position. The secure, scopic self is multiplied and ethically enriched through an imaginative encounter that Baucom calls 'plagiaristic sentimentality,' with the emphasis firmly placed on the spectator's disinterested response to suffering rather than on what is degraded or lost (Baucom 2005, 249, 250, 259, 263). This means that (to adapt Mary Louise Pratt) the material, economic and physical exploitation of the slave is 'mystified out of the picture' in the transracial sentimental scene of imagining (Pratt 1992, 97). Furthermore, when Smith's 'brother on the rack' is a *slave* brother, the reader who imagines her/himself into a suffering black body may be vulnerable to what Ann Laura Stoler calls 'cultural contagion,' or affective miscegenation (Stoler 1995, 191).

In the texts I am discussing, any potentially contaminating, miscegenetic empathy that is aroused by the spectacle of the slave body in pain is sealed off when the slave is re-consigned to 'bare life' through the representation of his (or her) brutalization. The prototype for this textual reification of the slave is the spectacular execution with which Behn's *Oroonoko* concludes, and subsequent prose fictions continue to present their readers with the sort of anatomized rebellious slaves we encountered in Edwards' *History*. In novels such as Earle's *Obi*, slave insurrection is no more than a narrative pretext for the depiction of punishment, which in turn provides both reader and narrator with a sentimental, spectatorial opportunity. But if the slave as *homo sacer* is situated on Agamben's moving threshold of the human and the non-human, then what precisely is the reader weeping over when she imaginatively witnesses the brutal putting down of the slave's body?

IV

He was cast for death, he was to be slung up by his waist, forty feet
from the ground, to a gallows, exposed to the sun's burning heat and
to those noxious insects of the West Indies that infect the body, even
to putridity, for three days, receiving no sustenance. On the fourth, he
was to be taken down, and the soles of his feet seared, and under the
arm-pits, then to receive five hundred lashes, have his heart and en-
trails burnt before him, to be quartered, and his quarters to be hung in
four several parts of the Island, to strike terror to the slaves.
   This sentence was heard with horror through all the plantations in
the Island, but Jack listened to it with a firm indifference … (Earle
1800, 113–14)

When Earle published his sentimentalized, fictionalized account of 'the
famous negro robber, *Three fingered* JACK, the terror of Jamaica in 1780
and 1781' (Moseley 1799, 173), Jamaica held the record for slave uprisings in the Caribbean. Even before the Haitian Revolution of 1791 to
1804, there were more rebellions in Jamaica than in all the other British
colonies combined. Given this context, it is little wonder that prose fictions of the period should repeatedly, almost obsessively, represent rebellion and its aftermath. Rebellions erupt in (among others) *The Recess*,
*The Farmer of Inglewood Forest*, *Slavery*, 'The Grateful Negro,' and *Obi*:
with the exception of Mackenzie's *Slavery*, all these fictional rebellions
occur in Jamaica. Aravamudan cites *Obi* as the only prose fiction of this
period in which a black rebel is unequivocally celebrated, his insurgency
justified through the narrative of a family revenge plot (Aravamudan
1999, xxii). And yet, the novel contains no more than a hasty gloss of
'the unheard-of cruelties' Jack supposedly visits on 'numbers of [white]
innocents [who] fell beneath his rapacious sword' (hardly a 'celebratory'
description; Earle 1800, 150), whereas the narrator dwells on the torture
and execution of insubordinate black slaves, including Jack himself, his
father, grandfather and mother.
   Other prose fictions of the period similarly elide rebellion or deploy it
instrumentally as a plot device. The heroine of Sophia Lee's *The Recess*
falls into a swoon when she sees the 'ferocious eyes, and bloody hands' of
a band of 'ferocious slaves' who are staging an uprising that, conveniently
enough, interrupts a forced marriage ceremony (Lee 1783–85, 112). Likewise Adolphus Zimza in *Slavery* breaks off in the middle of a letter he is
writing from San Domingo because of 'a tumult among the slaves!', and
his next letter does not provide any information as to the rebellion's

conduct or cause (Mackenzie 1792, 2: 97–8). Zimza's subsequent visit to the plantation of judicious Mr Cumberland in Martinique provides a re-assuring alternative to the turmoil in San Domingo, and he describes with approval a scene in which Mr Cumberland's grateful slaves promise to protect their master against potential rebels. Edgeworth's grateful negro prevents rebellion from erupting on good Mr Edwards' estate, although the latter's cruel neighbour Mr Jefferies is ruined and has to return to England. The rebellion itself is not described, but we are told that 'the Koromantyn yell of war' is heard on Jefferies' plantation on the night of the uprising (Edgeworth 1804, 322).

The willing, grateful slave who prevents rebellion is the narrative coun-terpart of the marauding rebel, and s/he features regularly in the fictions of this period. Thanks to his intervention (most grateful negroes are men), rebellion may be evoked but circumvented in narratives that display little or no interest in exploring the causes of these uprisings. In that sense at least, *Obi* is of a different order to the other fictions I have cited. George Stanford, the novel's epistolary narrator, gives some context for Jack's actions by describing the violence and betrayal suffered by his mother, father and grandfather. Indeed, the narrator seems somewhat *too* eager to provide details about Jack's father's 'mangled body,' his grandfather's tor-ture and incineration, his mother's death by burning, as well as Jack's eventual bloody demise, and the sentence that is passed, but not en-acted. Significantly, there is no collective uprising in the end, since Jack is deserted by his followers before he is arrested and taken to prison (Earle 1800, 92, 100, 147, 111–12).

'[I]n Jamaica, we have many Newgates, and many bold fellows con-fined in them' Stanford writes to his friend after he has narrated Jack's arrest, but three pages later, Jack has escaped after beating out the brains of a sentinel, and we hear no more of the Jamaican Newgate (Earle 1800, 112, 115).[8] *Obi* is not at all preoccupied with the representation of con-finement and/or non-corporal modes of penality, unlike a roughly con-temporary novel such as *Caleb Williams*, whose prison sequence is mod-elled on the exploits of the ingenious Jack Sheppard. By the time sen-tence was pronounced on Three Fingered Jack, Europe was four decades into what Foucault identifies as the 'great transformation' that occurred between 1760 and 1840, when the spectacle of the tortured, executed prisoner was replaced by the institution of non-corporal penality in an

---

[8]  Paton 2004, 19, 23 discusses the increase in Jamaican penal institutions be-tween 1770 and 1820.

epistemologico-juridical system that had as little physical contact as possible with the body of the condemned (Foucault 1975, 11, 23). 1760 is
the year of Tacky's uprising, the most serious Caribbean rebellion of the
period, still resonating forty years later in Earle's novel. Since we know
how Tacky's rebels were punished, it should be clear enough that Bender's
'penitentiary idea' or Foucault's non-corporal penality had not taken hold
in Jamaica by 1760, when slaves were still subject to the most horrifying
violence, whether they were condemned by the law or not (Craton 1982,
138; Ellis 1996, 92). Where, asks Marcus Wood 'is the slave's body in
Foucault's archaeology of torture?' Discerning a paradox in the co-existence of ritualized violence with the logical, abstract behavioural codes
that displaced the spectacle of physical punishment, Wood concludes
that the public spectacle of torture and the private discipline of the
panopticon are fused in Caribbean slave societies (Wood 2002, 228–30).
This is an entirely plausible inference, and so it is striking that none of
the prose fictions I am discussing displays any interest in private discipline, perhaps because the very notion of the 'private' is somewhat anoma-
lous given that the slave is legally constituted as property. If we were to
reframe Wood's paradox slightly, we might ask how narrativizations of
the violence taking place in Caribbean slave society coexist discursively
with metropolitan paradigms of sentiment and sympathy, paradigms whose
inaugural moment might also be located somewhere in the 1760s. Is it
too far-fetched to suggest that Foucault's 'gloomy festival of punishment'
saw its textual continuation in fictions and histories that persistently
narrated rebellion's aftermath in British Caribbean slave colonies, long
after that 'festival' had been replaced by other penal economies in the
metropole? (Foucault 1977, 8) In that case, the regulatory function I
have been assigning to these texts in their 'putting down' of the rebellious black body would certainly seem to constitute what Wood identifies as a pornographic mode of representation, so that the textual
anatomization and dismemberment of the slave body in works such as
Edwards' *History* or Earle's *Obi* fulfils an epistemologico-juridical function (narrative as a vicarious form of punishment), at the same time as
providing the reader with an affective source of pleasure (narrative as
homo- or auto-erotic; Wood 2000, 262; Wood 2002, 89–93).

The effusively sentimental responses of *Obi*'s epistolary narrator ex-
emplify this textual conflation of punishment and pleasure, a conflation
that resembles the legal vacillation between negro-as-subject and negro-
as-object. Stanford's outpourings acquire additional emotional weight if
he gushes over Jack as a 'MAN!' rather than merely as a fetish object, but

it is also clear that there is a strong narrative pull towards fetishizing Jack
and constituting him as a thing. Even the 'or' in the novel's title suggests
that Jack and his fetish object are interchangeable, and Stanford's repeated encomiums on Jack's courage, manliness, fearlessness and so on,
suggest that Jack is a sort of erotic obi for the narrator. Early in his epistolary correspondence, Stanford declares that he is haunted, perhaps even
obsessed by Jack: 'I can think of nothing else,' he writes in his first letter:
'there is not a *thing* called Jack, whether a smoke-jack, a boot-jack, or any
other jack, but acts as a spell upon my senses and sets me on the fret at
the bare mention of it' (Earle 1800, 69–70; original emphasis). This association of Jack with magical *things* is apparently quite compatible with
Stanford's insistence that Jack is a 'man' and not merely an item. Stanford
envisages the following argument with his fellow planters:

> 'Jack is a Negro,' say they [white Jamaicans]. 'Jack is a MAN,' say I.
> – 'He is a slave.'
> – 'MAN cannot be a slave to MAN.'
> – 'He is my property.' (Earle 1800, 70)

Thereafter, Stanford does not miss an opportunity to celebrate Jack's classical heroism and courage, his love for and loyalty towards his mother, his
justified rage at the oppressions he and his family and fellow slaves have
suffered. Jack has a 'Herculean gripe,' 'the soul of a hero,' a 'noble soul'
and a heart 'nobler … than ever inhabited the bosom of an European.'
'Jack was a Man!!' Stanford exclaims, 'Jack was a Hero!!'[9] '[H]umanity
was not estranged from the heart of the bold marauder,' he insists after
describing Jack's encounter with a poor widow, and earlier Stanford 'soil[s]'
(a revealing choice of verb) the page with the 'rich … tear of sensibility'
when he expatiates on Jack's capacity to feel. 'He was not hardened, for
he was awake to feeling. He would do no harm to woman, child or any
defenceless being. … the stream of consanguinity flowed warmly to his
heart' (Earle 1800, 100, 147, 119, 143, 118).

Given the narratorial insistence that Jack is a fearless but feeling MAN,
the manner of his eventual demise may well seem somewhat bathetic.
Having already chopped off two of Jack's fingers, James Reeder *alias*
Quashee, a 'christianized' maroon, is tempted by a bounty offering freedom to any slave who 'will kill the said Three-fingered Jack, and bring in
his head and hand wanting the two fingers' (Moseley 1799, 177; Earle

---

[9]   Cf. Moseley 1799, 174, 178 for Jack's classical qualities.

1800, 154–5). After a bloody struggle, Quashee/Reeder and two accomplices succeed in beating Jack's brains out with stones, after which 'they cut off Jack's head and three-fingered hand, and carried them to Morant Bay; they then put their trophies in a pail of rum, and carried them in triumph to Kingston and Spanish-town, and claimed the rewards offered' (Earle 1800, 157). At this point in the novel, Stanford's epistolary commentary more or less converges with Benjamin Moseley's factual account in A *Treatise Upon Sugar* (1799), to which *Obi's* narrator adds only a brief and somewhat obscure gloss on Jack's death: 'Thus died as great a man as ever graced the annals of history … No doubt in the end Jack died deservedly – had he died like a man. But who worked his passion to the pitch? Who drove him to the deeds of desperacy and cruelty? Oh, fie! fie!' (Earle, 1800, 157).

*Did* Jack 'die like a man'? Stanford implies that he did not, and the fall from hero to object certainly seems considerable. If we were simply to state the obvious, we might say that the execution with which the novel concludes (ripe though it is for psychoanalytic, sexual-symbolic interpretation) follows Moseley's non-fictional *Treatise* so closely because Earle does not wish to tamper with 'history.'[10] But in shifting from a sentimental, subjective mode of narration to a 'factual,' objective one (as Bryan Edwards does in his move from 'Stanzas' to *History*), Earle demotes Jack from Herculean eroticized hero into the 'thing' he always was, at least according to Jamaican slave law. In turn, this narrative demotion effectively seals off the homo-erotic, miscegenetic possibilities that have been opened up by Stanford's enthusiastic admiration for someone who is, after all, a slave, and therefore triply inappropriate as a love object.

Once again, we return to the slave as *homo sacer*, the barely human entity that can be killed at any time without the commission of homicide. And yet, once he is dead and dismembered, Jack's liminality and abjection exceed even *homo sacer's*. Adam Smith might think that it is possible for a sympathetic spectator to imagine herself into the body of a corpse, but there is no corpse at the end of *Obi*, and Jack's body parts have presumably been collected so that they may be displayed as a warning to other would-be rebels (Smith 1790, 16). Again, the prototype for Jack's execution is *Oroonoko*, where the dismembering of the hero-slave is narrated in even greater, more gruesome detail, and we might also recall Edwards' account of the uncomplaining rebels on the gibbet, their

---

[10]   The sentence of death quoted at the beginning of this section does not appear in Moseley's account.

companion's serenity in the flames. But in *Oroonoko* as in *Obi*, the slave's utter insentience in death has been preceded by the assertion of his heightened emotions and his sufferings under slavery. The concluding circumvention of the slave's bodily experience leaves an affective textual space for detailed descriptions of the white onlooker-narrator's distressed responses. It does not require much narrative manipulating to consign Jack (or Oroonoko) to his juridical place as a 'thing,' but it is crucial to these texts' regulatory function that there has been something to 'put down,' in both senses of the phrase. *Obi* assigns humanity to Jack only to display the removal of that humanity – indeed, of life itself – and power is consolidated in direct proportion to the extent of what has been crushed. To paraphrase Elaine Scarry, the novelist as executioner of the negro slave, and the white reader as witness of this execution, gain more world-ground not in spite of but because of the negro's sentience and emotional capacity, even as the slave's physical pain is elided so that the texts may do their brutal representational work (Scarry 1985, 37). Through such disciplinary textual means, the negro body is 'seen,' known and dismantled in white-authored texts.

## V

> The Admiral had given notice to the clergyman at Kingston, that we should attend the service; otherwise I would not have gone, for we were obliged to pass close by the pole, on which was stuck the head of the black man who was executed a few days ago. (Nugent 2002, 165)

What are *we* seeing, knowing and dismantling when, in an academic context, we discuss these narratives with two hundred years of hindsight? We have some sense at least, of the many tongues lost from the slavery archive, the quiet empty pages that will never be filled. Perhaps, like Susan Barton, we find it difficult to accept that fact, and so, as Marcus Wood puts it, we feed off the archive and transform its words, as if we weren't quite sure what to do with them – their weightiness and the sheer mass of them (Wood 2002, 4). Scholars who 'work on' slavery and abolition must, like Lady Nugent, pass close by textual scenes of punishment where we may, for example, witness the remains of an enslaved rebel who was executed for conspiracy. This too is an untold story (certainly, Lady Nugent doesn't narrate it) and it reveals, if nothing else, the impossibility of bearing witness to what is no longer there. But if we are not bearing witness or telling untold stories, then what are we doing, those of us who work within and not just 'on,' this expanding textual non-space that is filled with white-authored accounts of slavery, the enslaved, and the manifold techniques of power invented to subordinate, control and torment? Is it morally responsible to read, as I have done, 'fiction' alongside 'non-fiction,' as though Edwards' *History* were a novel and Earle's *Obi* a historical source? Am I repeating 'hateful speech' when I extensively cite and quote the punishments visited upon the enslaved, the harms done to their bodies, and the dismantling of those bodies?[11] Is this essay yet another catalogue of violence, however benign the impulse of its author? And are we any closer to understanding (following Baldwin) what moved people to such deeds?

These are weighty questions, and I do not have answers to them. I can only conclude with another, related set of questions, once again from Coetzee's Susan Barton, in order to signal the inevitable incompletion of my own particular act of academic non-witness within an archive where enslaved people are largely wordless, utterly bodiless, yet repeatedly spoken *for*, even as Susan tries and fails to speak for Friday.

'What is the truth of Friday?' asks Susan:

Friday has no command of words and therefore no defence against being reshaped day by day in conformity with the desires of others. I say he is a cannibal and he becomes a cannibal; I say he is a laundryman and he becomes a laundryman ... You will respond: he is neither cannibal nor laundryman, these are mere names, they do not touch his essence, he is a substantial body, he is himself, Friday is himself. But that is not so. No matter what he is to himself (is he anything to himself? – how can he tell us?) what he is to the world is what I make of him (Coetzee 1986, 122–3).

## Works Cited

Agamben, Giorgio, 1998. *Homo Sacer. Sovereign Power and Bare Life.* Trans. Daniel Heller-Roazen. Stanford: Stanford University Press.

Agamben, Giorgio, 1999. *Remnants of Auschwitz. The Witness and the Archive.* Trans. Daniel Heller-Roazen. New York: Zone Books.

Aravamudan, Srinivas, ed., 1999. *Slavery, Abolition and Emancipation: Writings in*

---

[11] But see Butler 1997, 102: 'There is no possibility of *not* repeating. The only question that remains is: How will that repetition occur, at what site, juridical or nonjuridical, and with what pain and promise?'

*the British Romantic Period*. General editors Peter J. Kitson and Debbie Lee. Volume 6, *Fiction*. London: Pickering and Chatto.

Bage, Robert, 1792. *Man As He Is. A Novel*. 4 vols. London, Minerva Press.

Baldwin, James, 1995. 'Everybody's Protest Novel.' In *Notes of a Native Son*. London: Penguin, 1949. pp.19–28.

Baucom, Ian, 2005. *Specters of the Atlantic. Finance Capital, Slavery and the Philosophy of History*. Durham: Duke University Press.

Bender, John, 1987. *Imagining the Penitentiary. Fiction and the Architecture of Mind in Eighteenth-Century England*. Chicago: Chicago University Press.

Berger, John, 1972. *Ways of Seeing*. London: Penguin and BBC Books.

Bhabha, Homi, 1983. 'The Other Question.' In Padmini Mongia, ed., *Contemporary Postcolonial Theory*. London: Arnold, 1996. pp. 37–54.

Blackstone, William, 1825. *Commentaries on the Laws of England*. 4 vols. 16th edn. London.

Butler, Judith, 1993. 'Endangered/Endangering: Schematic Racism and White Paranoia.' In *The Judith Butler Reader*, ed. with Sara Salih. Oxford: Blackwell, 2004. pp. 204–11.

Butler, Judith, 1997. *Excitable Speech. A Politics of the Performative*. New York: Routledge.

Campbell, John F., 2004. 'Textualizing Slavery: From "Slave" to "Enslaved People" in Caribbean Historiography.' In Sandra Courtman, ed., *Beyond the Blood the Beach and the Banana. New Perspectives in Caribbean Studies*. Kingston, Jamaica: Ian Randle Publishers. pp.34–45.

Clarkson, Thomas, 1786. *An Essay on the Slavery and Commerce of the Human Species, Particularly the African*. London.

Coetzee, J. M., 1986. *Foe*. London: Penguin.

Craton, Michael, 1982. *Testing the Chains. Resistance to Slavery in the British West Indies*. Ithaca: Cornell University Press.

Earle, William, 1800. *Obi, or the History of Three-Fingered Jack*. Ed. Srinivas Aravamudan, Peterborough, Ontario: Broadview, 2005.

Edgeworth, Maria, 1804. 'The Grateful Negro.' In *Popular Tales*. London.

Edwards, Bryan, 1792. *Poems, Written Chiefly in the West Indies*. Kingston, Jamaica.

Edwards, Bryan, 1793. *The History, Civil and Commercial, of the British Colonies in the West Indies*. 2 vols. Dublin.

Fanon, Frantz, 1952. *Black Skin, White Masks*. Trans. Charles Lam Markmann. London: Pluto Press, 1991.

Foucault, Michel, 1977. *Discipline and Punish. The Birth of the Prison*. Trans. Alan Sheridan. London: Penguin, 1975.

Goveia, Elsa, 1970. *The West Indian Slave Laws of the Eighteenth Century*. Barbados: Caribbean Universities Press.

Helme, Elizabeth, 1796. *The Farmer of Inglewood Forest; Or, An Affecting Portrait*. Manchester: J. Gleave, 1823.

Lee, Sophia, 1783–85. *The Recess*. London.

McBride, Dwight A., 2001. *Impossible Witnesses. Truth, Abolitionism and Slave Testimony*. New York: New York University Press.

Moseley, Benjamin, 1799. *A Treatise on Sugar*. London.

Nussbaum, Felicity, 2003. *The Limits of the Human. Fictions of Anomaly, Race and*

*Gender in the Long Eighteenth Century.* Cambridge: Cambridge University Press.

Paton, Diana, 2004. *No Bond but the Law. Punishment, Race and Gender in Jamaican State Formation, 1780–1870.* Durham: Duke University Press.

Pratt, Mary Louise, 1997. *Imperial Eyes. Travel Writing and Transculturation.* London: Routledge.

Rogozinski, Jan, 2000. *A Brief History of the Caribbean. From the Arawak and Carib to the Present.* New York: Penguin Books.

Scarry, Elaine, 1985. *The Body in Pain. The Making and Unmaking of the World.* New York: Oxford University Press.

Scott, Sarah, 1766. *The History of Sir George Ellison.* Ed. Betty Rizzo. Kentucky: Kentucky University Press, 1996.

Smith, Adam, 2002. *The Theory of Moral Sentiments.* Ed. Knud Haakonssen. Cambridge: Cambridge University Press, 1790.

Sontag, Susan, 2003. *Regarding the Pain of Others.* London: Penguin Books.

Sterne, Laurence, 1768. *A Sentimental Journey Through France and Italy By Mr. Yorick.* Oxford: Oxford University Press. Repr. 1988.

Stoler, Ann Laura, 1995. *Race and the Education of Desire. Foucault's History of Sexuality and the Colonial Order of Things.* Durham: Duke University Press.

Thomas, Hugh, 1997. *The Slave Trade. The History of the Atlantic Slave Trade: 1440–1870.* New York: Simon & Schuster.

Walvin, James, 1992. *Black Ivory. A History of British Slavery.* London: Harper Collins.

Weeden, Butler (trans.), 1800. *Zimao, the African.* Dublin: Gilbert and Hodges.

Wheeler, Roxann, 2000. *The Complexion of Race. Categories of Difference in Eighteenth-Century British Culture.* Philadelphia: University of Pennsylvania Press.

Wood, Marcus, 2000. *Blind Memory. Visual Representations of Slavery in England and the Caribbean 1780–1865.* Repr. New York: Routledge.

Wood, Marcus, 2002. *Slavery, Empathy and Pornography.* Oxford: Oxford University Press.

Wright, Philip, ed., 2002. *Lady Nugent's Journal of her Residence in Jamaica from 1801 to 1805.* Mona: University of the West Indies Press.

# The Horror of Hybridity: Enlightenment, Anti-slavery and Racial Disgust in Charlotte Smith's Story of Henrietta (1800)

## GEORGE BOULUKOS

CHARLOTTE SMITH'S *The Story of Henrietta*, volume 2 of *Letters of a Solitary Wanderer* (1800) is the most complex treatment of plantation slavery in the late eighteenth-century novel. Set in Jamaica, it was written for an audience keenly aware of the Haitian revolution and bracing for similar developments in British colonies (Craton 1982, 180–1). The mood of Henrietta's story, and its vision of the future of plantation slavery, is pessimistic, even gloomy. Although hopeful visions of 'amelioration' – the humanitarian reform of plantation slavery – were the norm in fictional accounts of the plantation colonies from the middle of the eighteenth century, Smith's novel breaks with this trend (Carey 2005, 46–72; Boulukos 2001; Ellis 1996). Her consideration of the possibility of fixing the problems of slavery through plantation reform is brief and discouraging. Most strikingly, Smith believes strongly in racial difference and makes it a centerpiece of her opposition to slavery. Published in 1800, her novel marks the transition from discomfort with the concept of race in the eighteenth century to ever more pronounced belief in racial difference in the nineteenth century.[1]

Smith's despair about amelioration is based on two factors that differentiate her from most other eighteenth-century novelists to engage with slavery. She suggests that the political climate in Jamaica has become so reactionary that even planters attempting to reform their own plantations would become social outcasts, finding their lives and liberty endangered. More crucially, she sees the depravity of the slaves themselves as a permanent obstacle to such reforms. Nonetheless, Smith draws on the rhetorical tradition of Montaigne's 'Of Cannibals,' turning around the

---

[1] For arguments dating the emergence of modern ideas of race to the end of the eighteenth century, see Wheeler 2000 and Wahrman 2004, and for an argument that race was more prominent in anti-slavery refutations than in pro-slavery apologetics see Kitson 2004. See also Fredrickson 1971 for the point that 'scientific' views of race were viewed skeptically even in the US nineteenth century.

planters' habit of referring to slaves as 'savages,' in order to force her readers to consider who the 'true' savages are (Ginzburg 1996). The brutality of plantation life is most evident in its desensitizing, anti-sentimental effects on individual planters' personalities and behavior; still, slaves themselves are represented as ignorant, frightening, and depraved.

*The Story of Henrietta* elaborates an attack on slavery, but one based on a racist view of African slavery's disgusting, hybridizing threat to European culture.[2] The corruption and degradation of European Creoles, not the abuse and suffering of their slaves, is Smith's strongest argument against the slave system.[3] Proleptic of Hegel's master-slave dialectic, Smith implies that the only way to access a differentiated view of the world – and thereby to gain the ability to sympathize with oppressed others – is to have been forced to recognize and reject a master's dominating will, to have been placed in the position of a powerless slave.[4] In the *Story of Henrietta*, this process becomes the process of 'enlightenment,' the method (in Kant's terminology) for leaving one's nonage behind and becoming able to think and act independently (Kant 1973).

Smith's 'Hegelian' view of Henrietta – that true maturity and empathy can only be attained through the psychological differentiation attained in the experience of oppression – can be read in reference to Richardson's *Clarissa*.[5] Indeed, *The Story of Henrietta* is one of many late-century adaptations of the basic *Clarissa* plot, as Henrietta defies the orders of her parents to marry a suitor chosen exclusively from 'interested'

---

[2]   Hence, Smith's view of 'hybridity,' although she does not use the term, anticipates the nineteenth-century debates about racial crossbreeding that gave rise to the term, as documented by Young 1995.

[3]   For an account of the concept of 'Creole degeneration,' see Wilson 2003, 154–5.

[4]   See Hegel 1977, 111–17; my interpretation draws on Kojève 1969, 3–30, 43–63; for a compatible interpretation with different emphases, see Hyppolite 1974, esp. 172–7. Hegel and his commentators emphasize the importance of 'work' and the object worked on to differentiating the slave, in addition to the process of the life or death struggle with the Master. For recent work connecting Hegel's 'master/slave dialectic' to the history of slavery in the eighteenth- and nineteenth-century Atlantic world, see Davis 1975, 558–64; Gilroy 1993, 50–63; and Buck-Morss 2000. Gikandi 1996 critiques Gilroy for preferring 'to read slavery through Hegel's allegory rather than its material contexts,' 146.

[5]   For a critique of attempts to read *Clarissa* as enacting later enlightenment philosophical ideas, see Hensley 2001.

motives (Schochet 1988, Fliegelman 1982). This plot reflects the cultural conflict brought about by the move to a system of marriage based on love (Coontz 2005). The tyranny of parents unreasonably dictating to their adult children became an important political metaphor, proving particularly useful to American colonists when they rebelled against the Crown.[6] It resonates with the move away from the 'patriarchalism' of the seventeenth century to new, Lockean models of independent, rational individuality. Christopher Hill argues that 'Clarissa's standards, high Puritan standards, were not of this world: they could be realized only in the after-life' (Hill 1958, 349). Charlotte Smith, however, does not place her heroine's victory in the next world. Although like Clarissa she puts herself in the hands of a male 'protector' who intends to rape her, Henrietta survives, virtue intact, to be reunited with her beloved, Denbigh. The lessons that she learns from her experience of oppression, unlike Clarissa's, are meant to be applied in this world.

Notably, neither Henrietta, nor the hero of another subplot, George Maynard, are able to use their 'enlightened' status, as survivors of oppression, to solve the pressing problem of slavery. Indeed, Smith represents plantation reform as unrealistic. But unlike Hector MacNeill in *The Memoirs of the Life and Travels of Charles Macpherson* (1800), she does not, initially, draw this conclusion from an assessment of slaves' capabilities; instead, she presents reform as politically impossible. The issue of reform emerges from the interpolated narrative of a hermit, George Maynard, who has left society to live in a cave. He tells Henrietta's beloved, Denbigh, the depressing story of his life in Europe. Maynard chooses to return to Jamaica, the land of his birth, after every person he cared for died, including two children, a wife, and a close friend; he is estranged from a second wife. When this friend dies, as a result of having pursued Maynard across the continent, in order to reclaim him for society, Maynard despairs: '*He* too died! He died, and left me alone in the world, which did not now contain one being interested for me, or for whom I felt any interest' (C. Smith 1996, 280).

However, the friend's death inadvertently reconnects Maynard to a large group in whom he has an 'interest' in the financial sense. Going through his friend's papers, he finds a cache of anti-slavery literature, which shocks George out of his complacency:

---

[6] For studies of American adaptations of *Clarissa*, see Fliegelman 1982, Tennenhouse 1998, and Layson 2003.

> Accustomed to consider these people as part of the estates to which they belonged, I had never properly reflected on this subject before; and when I now thought of it, I was amazed at the indifference with which I had looked on and been a party in oppression, from which all the sentiments of my heart revolted. (281)

Slavery benefits Maynard more as a convert to abolitionism, by giving him a spiritual purpose, and thus confirming his new state of enlightenment, his sentimental awakening, than it ever had when he remained an unreflective slaveholder. Maynard enthusiastically embraces his new sense of purpose:

> I found I had now an object which was not unworthy of engaging the thoughts of a reasonable being. As a considerable proprietor, I had I supposed the means of doing some good to this miserable race. (282)

However, despite Maynard's initial confidence about his ability to do good with his own possessions, he soon finds that he has failed to account for Jamaica's hysterical political climate. Indeed, he is as oblivious to the mentality and politics of his fellow slave owners as he had previously been to the oppression and suffering of his slaves:

> My endeavours at reformation were not only considered as the idle dreams of a visionary, but as being dangerous to the welfare of the island. ... I persevered, till the examples of lenity to and emancipation of the negroes became so much circumstances of fear, that there was, I understood, a resolution taken to confine me as a lunatic. (282–3)

But even such threats can not force Maynard to give up his efforts; after all, he is convinced of his rightness, and has lost all other compelling attachments to the world.

The political realities of George Maynard's situation finally force him to abandon his efforts, once he discovers that they were

> Worse than useless to the unhappy people whose condition it had been my purpose to ameliorate; for greater severities were often exercised on those in whose favor I had interfered, than if I had never pleaded for them the cause of humanity. (283–4)

In fact, this dilemma drives Maynard to 'retire wholly from the world' (284), taking measures to insure moderate treatment of the slaves on his plantations despite his absence. Here, when considered in the context of all other novelistic representations of plantation reform, Smith's account has the effect of a revelation – hers is the only compelling consideration of the actual problems presented by the political context in which reform must take place, an effect particularly notable in the tense and polarized atmosphere of the late-century abolition debate. Perhaps earlier novelists representing reform, such as Kimber, Scott and MacKenzie, were not unreasonable to suppose that ameliorationist reforms – especially ones that might result in increased profits – would be accepted and even emulated (Boulukos forthcoming). Only *Macpherson* among the other late-century novels suggests that reform might be unpopular with planters. Moore in *Zeluco* (1787) does suggest that ameliorative reforms are unlikely to solve the problems of slavery, although he does not see planter resistance as the reason. But in the time of reaction against anti-slavery mobilization, it is quite plausible that planters would view 'humanitarian' attempts at reform with suspicion if not malice, despite their public-relations efforts to claim 'amelioration' for themselves.

Smith, however, does not rely on the inherent plausibility of planters resenting reform to convince her reader. She embeds in her novel the familiar eighteenth-century theory that slavery itself shapes planter psychology. This theory, in turn, helps to buttress her suggestion that planters would react strongly against reform. Maynard's coming to an awareness of his 'guilt' in slavery is carefully developed; it is the second of two important revelations made possible by his move from Jamaica to England. On his arrival in England, he is as unsuited for English society as any spoiled, corrupted planter's son, particularly recalling Thomas Day's depiction of Tommy Merton in *Sandford and Merton* (Day 1977, 1–2). As Maynard explains, he was unable to respect others as a boy:

> From my having two young negroes to wait on my caprices, and to enact my horses, my dogs, or anything else I required, to indulge my indolence, and submit to my ill-humour, I really imagined myself to be a creature of a superior order, whom it was the business of all other creatures to venerate and to obey. (C. Smith 1996, 173)

This understanding of himself collapses, however, when he and his elder brother – who is Henrietta's father – are sent to England for education. Both boys find that their English school simply will not allow such a self-conception. The results for the two boys are dramatically different. The elder brother, frustrated that he has been transformed from a 'tyrant' to a 'slave,' beats and abuses his younger brother, George, as a way of reaffirming his 'master' status. George, with no one to domineer himself, is forced instead to reflect on the situation.[7] By the time of his narrative, he is grateful for this horrible experience, because, like the slave in Hegel's master-slave dialectic, he develops a true consciousness from it. In retrospect he remarks, 'but to this circumstance (for we are creatures of accident) I perhaps owe that abhorrence of tyranny and injustice which I have invariably felt through the rest of my life' (176). Again like Hegel's slave, he finds that the experience of having his life in doubt in the struggle with a master is ultimately liberating: having been rescued from his brother, he explains, 'no longer fearing for my *life*, I began to find that I had a *soul*; at least that I had feelings and affections worthy of aspiring to rank above the ferocious animals to whom I had hitherto been subjected' (176). This experience of enlightenment, however, does not immediately lead George Maynard to remember, or reconsider, his relationship to the slaves his family owns.

Nonetheless, the formative experience of this master-slave confrontation continues to mark the difference between the two brothers. While George Maynard, the younger brother, returns to Jamaica only in order to undertake a mission against slavery, his older brother prefers life in Jamaica:

> He was a man whose ideas had received all their colour from his situation. The only son of a very rich planter, he had never been in England since he left school at ten years old, and had conceived such an aversion from a place where he had been on the footing of equality with other boys, that he never desired to revisit Europe. (11)

In fact, when George returns to Jamaica to try to absolve his responsibility for slavery through becoming a reformer, his older brother is one of his most ferocious opponents, leading the effort to have him declared insane.

George Maynard's description of boys like his brother – planter's sons who are so accustomed to having absolute power over slaves that they can't control their brutality – as 'ferocious animals' resonates throughout the text, as does his 'aspiring to rank above' such brutal men. The idea that people should be considered in different 'ranks,' that some are 'animals' or 'brutes' while others are fully human would seem to be very close

---

[7]   Smith here responds to fictional accounts of the education of West Indian children out of their prejudices, such as Day's *Sandford and Merton*. On such fictions, see Trumpener 1997, 169.

to the idea of racial hierarchy, to the notions of a graded chain of differences between different peoples that could be used to justify slavery and
colonialism (Woodard 1999). But here, Maynard turns this rhetoric around
to claim that the masters really belong to the lower rank: they are actually the brute animals in human form. The reversal seems fairly simple,
perhaps following in the tradition of Montaigne's 'Of Cannibals' and Swift's
'A Modest Proposal.' It certainly recalls Montaigne's assessment of the
inhabitants of the New World: 'we may well call these people barbarians,
in respect to the rules of reason, but not in respect to ourselves, who
surpass them in every kind of barbarity.' (Montaigne 1958, 156).[8]

Indeed, Smith develops this rhetorical reversal throughout the novel.
George Maynard is not the only character to suggest that Jamaican planters
are themselves 'savages.' The Henrietta subplot seems a vehicle intended,
perhaps primarily, to strengthen the reader's sense that planters are themselves brutal, if not 'savages.' Henrietta initially professes 'an inability to
govern herself,' seeming to endorse the suggestion that 'after all, a young
woman should have no will of her own' (45), but she is nonetheless dis-
pleased to find that her father, whom she comes to Jamaica to meet for
the first time in her adult life after having been raised in Europe, is 'always accustomed to command, and to look on those about him rather as
machines who were to move only at his nod, than as beings who had wills
and inclinations of their own' (66). Indeed, she uses some of the same
terms as George Maynard to express her discontentment with the man
her father commands her to marry: he, one Sawkins, is described as 'an
animal' (66). Again using language that suggests she is drawing on images of 'savage' life, she describes the situation saying 'my father sacrifices
his daughter' (67). The term 'sacrifice' might seem a weak indication of
an implicit comparison between her father's behavior and that of 'savages' until Henrietta repeats the image in more vivid terms: when her
father is known to be bringing both Sawkins and a priest to force the
marriage on her, she expresses her distress by writing that 'preparations
are making for the wicked, the inhuman sacrifice' (100).

Henrietta suggests an equivalence between her father and the Africans that he holds as slaves more directly when she contemplates her
only apparent options. She can either go along with the 'sacrifice' or flee
to the woods, infested as they are with runaways and organized maroons:

---

[8]   For two very different recent accounts of the 'Noble Savage' trope in the
eighteenth century, see Ellingson 2001 and Muthu 2003.

'I hear again the gombay in the woods; I hear the strange yells of savage triumph, and I shudder to think there is no alternative' (101). That there is 'no alternative' for Henrietta – who chooses to risk the maroons to escape from her father – suggests that she feels that the threat of her father's brutality and disrespect for her will is balanced by the equal threat of the treatment to which the maroons might subject her.

But Smith's use of the rhetoric of reversal here clearly falls short of Montaigne's. Henrietta does not believe that her father is more brutal or savage than the 'savage' Africans of Jamaica; instead, the rhetorical force of her reversal is that she is willing to allow the equivalence between the maroons (and Africans generally) and her father.[9] Indeed, throughout her narrative, Henrietta appears appalled and disgusted by the people of African descent whom she encounters. Her first shocking encounter of this sort is with her own half-sisters, who become symbols of her father's degradation, a further sign of the descent into 'savagery' that makes him equivalent to his slaves:

> And for the persons who surround me, I would I could escape ever naming them! Do you know, Denbigh, that there are three young women here, living in the house, *of colour*, as they are called, who are I understand, my sisters by the half blood! (57)

These women are a source of great pain and embarrassment to Henrietta. They embody the hybridity that she finds particularly repulsive, but their European blood is the same as hers. Their existence may confirm her charges that her father has become a 'savage,' but they also make it far more difficult for Henrietta to differentiate herself from such 'savagery.'

Not only are they completely unaware of the European standards of judgment which makes their very existence an embarrassment, but her half-sisters insistently remind Henrietta of their hybrid status, between European and African culture, in their language, manners, and even their feminine appreciation of (presumably imported) 'finery':

---

[9]    Montaigne and Swift's use of cannibals can be seen as parallel to Smith's use of 'savages' here. By claiming that European outrages, metaphorically described in terms of cannibalism, are worse than the actual cannibalism of Amerindians, actual cannibalism ends up being reinforced rather than undermined as the standard of true degradation and brutality. Rawson 1992 argues that both Swift and Montaigne were aware of European 'anthropophagous' acts, but suppressed them so that Amerindian cannibals would seem to be absolutely different from Europeans.

They speak an odd sort of dialect, more resembling that of the negroes than the English spoken in England; and their odd manners, their love of finery, and curiosity about my clothes and ornaments, together with their total insensibility to their own situation, is, I own, very distressing to me. (57–8)

However, the social embarrassment these women cause Henrietta is not the only objection she has to them. She finds them physically unappealing, and appears worried that as Jamaican-born women, their inferior characteristics pose a real danger – like a danger of infection – to her. One of them is

Nearly as fair as I am; but she has the small eye, the prominent brow, and something particular in the form of the cheek, which is, I have understood, usual with creoles even who have not any of the negro blood in their veins. As I am a native of this island, perhaps I have the same cast of countenance without being conscious of it, and I will be woman enough to acknowledge that the supposition is not flattering. (58)

Beyond her social embarrassment, although 'woman enough' to admit it, Henrietta worries that as a Jamaican-born woman, the mulattas' inferior characteristics – both mental and physical – may extend to her. Like them, she may embody the illicit, repulsive combinations that symbolize the colonies so perfectly – and again like them, she may be completely oblivious to her own shocking characteristics.

How exactly white Creole women come to have such undesirable traits is unclear. Henrietta links the phenomenon to race, but race does not offer a complete explanation: 'even who have not any of the negro blood in their veins' can be affected. This suggests at once that Henrietta suspects such 'blood' as a possible cause, and yet has ruled it out as the exclusive explanation. The process seems to be akin to one of infection, in which 'Negro' characteristics can spread even to those without such blood through sustained contact. Here, Smith reflects common conceptions of 'Creole degeneration' which imagine European Creoles as being influenced to degenerate by both the tropical climate and by contact with their slaves.[10]

---

[10] In addition to invoking 'Creole degeneration,' Smith here conflates medical and climatological understandings of racial difference; see Wheeler 2000, 1–48, esp. 6; Curtin 1964, 58–87; and Bewell 1998.

Henrietta is disgusted not only by her fair half-sister's physical and cultural traits, and by her failure to be ashamed of the unspeakable things she represents to Henrietta, but also with her intellectual failings. The young woman is so mentally inferior – whatever the cause – as to be ineducable:

> I have attempted to instruct, when I could enough command my spirits to attend to any thing: but she is so ignorant, so much the creature either of origin or of habit, that I cannot make her comprehend the simplest instruction. (58–9)

Henrietta's blood relations are not the only people who disgust her. She describes all the African-descended people in the house in terms that similarly fail to distinguish between the cultural and biological causes of what she sees as their disgusting ignorance: 'I find the negroes have some strange superstition notions about them, as, indeed, they have some wild and absurd impression or other in regard to every object that surrounds them' (96). Even with 'mulattoes' and their children, she explains, education is no solution to the problem: 'what attempts have been made to give them other ideas, seem only to have made in their minds a sort of to me "darkness visible"'(98). The allusion to *Paradise Lost* at once casts the mental state of the Mulattoes as hellish, and establishes Henrietta's difference from them as an educated woman, despite her suggestion of her possible unconscious similarity to them. As in the case of the physical characteristics she dislikes, Henrietta, despite her facility with Milton, worries that she is being infected by the Mulattas' ignorance: 'the hideous phantasies of these poor uniformed savages affect my spirits with a sort of dread, which all conviction of their fallacy does not enable me to subdue.' (97)

Despite her worries about being degraded by association with Africans and 'the unfortunate children belonging to them and white parents' (97), Henrietta, in the terms of the text, manages to emerge from a self-imposed 'nonage,' that is, to meet at least the letter of Kant's definition of 'enlightenment,' while those 'unfortunate children' (i.e., mulattos) who 'worry' her are shown to be entirely ineducable.[11] Henrietta's decision to take control of her own life – and thus to emerge from her nonage in both

---

[11]   The term 'nonage' is central to Kant's definition of 'enlightenment' as rational maturity in the essay 'What Is Enlightenment?' (Kant 1973) Without specifically using the term 'Enlightenment,' Kant suggests that Africans are less able to achieve such maturity in *Physical Geography* (Kant 1977). For analysis of Kant's role in developing modern ideas of racial difference, see Bernasconi 2002 and Eze 1995.

senses – is like George Maynard's in anticipating Hegel's master-slave dialectic. She understands herself as the intended 'slave' of Sawkins (61), even describing her father as 'drawing up the bill of sale' (76). Henrietta refuses to accept this status, repeatedly promising not to obey, 'though I perish in attempting to avoid it' (67), and recalls to us the idea from Hegel of the slave who risks death for freedom. Doing so leads her to achieve enlightenment, both in the Kantian sense of shedding her 'self-imposed nonage,' and in the Hegelian sense of emerging from struggle with a new and higher consciousness.

Mrs Apthorp, the same woman who argues that 'after all, a young woman should have no will of her own' (45) helps convince Denbigh that Henrietta should leave England and seek approval of their marriage from her father in part due to her 'nonage.' While the term clearly is intended to refer to the technical sense of Henrietta's being underage, in her 'time of life before legal maturity' as Dr Johnson defines it (Johnson, 1996), nonetheless it is a compelling coincidence that the story also portrays her intellectual emergence from this state, as she is forced by circumstance to take her fate into her own hands.

The act that announces Henrietta's decision to take her new-found ability to use her reason to make her own decisions about the direction of her life – that is, her emergence from nonage in the Kantian sense of the 'inability to use one's own understanding without another's guidance' is a curious one, especially given my argument that she is disgusted by, and suspicious of, the African-descended people she encounters (Kant 1973, 384). She chooses to entrust herself to the physical (but not rational) guidance of one of her father's slaves, Amponah, when he offers to lead her away from her father's plantation. Amponah, before this point, has been an odd character in the text. He has stood out from other slaves and mulattos in the household as worthy of a certain degree of praise (or at least positive comment): she reports that she 'felt a sort of relief in seeing Amponah, my father's black servant, who attended my brother to England, and was almost a twelvemonth in my aunt's family. He now seemed rather an old acquaintance whom I was rejoiced to see, than an abject slave' (55). She also refers to him as 'the faithful Amponah, the only servant in whom I have any confidence' (76). Henrietta is careful to make sure that she hasn't left any doubt of her assessment of his intellectual gifts, or the real extent of her friendly feelings for Amponah:

> Alas, Denbigh! to what a situation is your unhappy friend reduced, when her only counsellor is a poor negro slave! and when she has no friendly bosom on which she can rely for more rational advice. (99)

Henrietta can imagine Amponah neither as a 'friend' nor as 'rational.' While Henrietta's implicit swipe at Amponah's rationality is consistent with the portrayal of African-descended people throughout the tale, it turns out to be borne out – along with her regret at not having another counselor – by the plot.

Amponah has, nonetheless been established as a disturbing figure, or at least a figure of disturbance. Not only does he appear on-stage immediately at any threat or disruption, but he himself is always represented as somehow disrupted; attending Henrietta during a storm, in an attempt to convince her to come to the safest part of the house, Amponah 'really seemed, poor fellow! to be quite bewildered and lost through the extreme fear that possessed him' (84); in a later face to face encounter, Henrietta reports, 'my uneasiness was considerably increased by the appearance of Amponah, who seemed to be in the greatest agitation and uneasiness' (296). But Amponah isn't a source of anxiety only for his oddly frantic behavior – he also disturbs Henrietta by being socially (or racially) transgressive. When he appears in her room, she remarks that

> The great distance which is in this country kept inviolable between the black people and their master's family, and the degraded light in which they are considered, made me shudder and recoil from a liberty even the occasion did not seem to warrant. (82–3)

Her remarks here are striking in her insistence on displacing her reaction to Amponah's presence from herself to the cultural habits of 'this country.' Earlier, she had been glad to see Amponah, because she remembered him as having been 'in my aunt's family' (55); despite calling attention to such cultural differences between England and Jamaica, Henrietta unquestioningly adopts the attitudes of the country where she now resides, and she does not entertain the possibility that he is merely returning to the behavior that was, possibly, the norm between them in England.[12] In any event, Amponah's transgression of local customs indicates to Henrietta that all is not right with his behavior.

Nonetheless, Henrietta later agrees to make Amponah her Lovelace. When she finds that her father will arrive imminently and force her to go forward with the wedding to Sawkins, she decides that she has more to fear from the brutality of her father than from the 'savagery' of Amponah

---

[12] For the sense in which a slave would be considered 'in' a family, see Tadmor 1996 and Williams 1983.

and the maroons whom she knows to be hidden in the nearby woods. In writing of this eventuality to Denbigh, Henrietta initially praises 'Amponah, on whose faith and attachment I had the greatest reliance, and who was I believed much more intelligent than the rest of the negroes, proposed to me to escape' (299). But, even given his apparent intelligence, why would Henrietta, having observed Amponah's odd, disturbing, even transgressive behavior, and having registered her skepticism about his rationality, nonetheless entrust herself to him? There are two reasons. The first is that she takes seriously the equivalence she has posited between her father and the Africans of the island. If they are literally equivalent, why not exchange the one who promises an immediate threat for the other? Furthermore, the proto-Hegelian psychology embedded in the book – as exemplified in Henrietta and George Maynard's narratives – suggests that precisely through their experience of oppression, the slaves are likely to have experienced a degree of enlightenment, an ability to respect others' wills. Indeed, Amponah has already offered Henrietta solidarity, in the form of 'honest indignation' at her treatment, in her resistance to her father and Sawkins (64).

However, in the event, Amponah more than justifies her uneasy feelings about him. It turns out that his plans for her are as disrespectful of her will, as 'savage,' if not more so, than her father's. Once they are alone, she reports, 'there was something in his manner that aggravated my apprehensions. I thought he no longer spoke with his accustomed respect. He spoke as if he felt that I was in his power' (301). Henrietta's response to her perception of a threat from Amponah is to try to maintain a physical distance from him – she finishes the above quotation by remarking 'I had declined taking his arm to assist me in walking' (301). Despite his seeming 'indignation' at her mistreatment, Amponah's oppression has not led to enlightenment. Her perception of a threat is borne out:

> I saw his eyes roll, and his features assume an expression which still haunts my dreams, when fearful visions of the past flit over my mind. He made a step or two towards me. I recoiled, and, almost on the brink of the precipice we had just passed, no idea but that of throwing myself into it occurred to me when he thus spoke:
> 'Missy, I tell you trute now – I love you. I no slave now; I my master and yours. Missy, there no difference now; you be my wife. I love you from a child! You live with me: nay, nay, no help for it; I take care of that.'
> Thus speaking, he approached me, and all the horrors to which I saw myself liable were but too certain. (303)

This turn in the plot serves several functions: for one thing, it restates, or recalculates the nuances of, the equivalence between Henrietta's father and the African descended slaves and 'savages' of the island. Just when Amponah seemed poised to prove that the so-called 'savages' are in fact more admirable, gentle and respectable, than the planters, he instead shows himself to be just as indifferent to Henrietta's will, and as intent on exploiting her sexually, as they are. However, there is a marked difference. Rather than behaving like Henrietta's father, who tries to use Henrietta in socially mediated exchange, Amponah gives in to his own sexual urges, urges that he seems unable to control. His confession of long-standing 'love' for Henrietta casts even his past behavior into a new light. His awkward nervousness was not due to circumstances, but now becomes clear as the sign of his struggle to control his desire for her.[13] Here, Smith already begins to hint at a concept of racial difference like that imbedded in Thomas Jefferson's *Notes on the State of Virginia*. Jefferson sees blacks as less thoughtful and more emotionally impulsive than whites: 'their existence appears to participate more of sensation than reflection.' He applies this specifically to love and sexuality, claiming that, 'They are more ardent after their female: but love seems with them to be more an eager desire, than a tender delicate mixture of sentiment and sensation', going on to offer a 'as a suspicion only' the suggestion that Blacks, 'inferior to the whites in the endowments of both body and mind,' exhibit meaningful racial difference from whites (Jefferson 1999, 146, 150–1). 'Black' men are more emotional, more natural, and more direct than 'white' men; this means that they are also less refined, more savage, less able to control and channel their sexual desires. Furthermore, Amponah wishes to impregnate Henrietta with a mulatto child, forcing her to perpetuate the miscegenation and hybridity she sees as so disturbing.

Rather than learning empathy from his experiences of oppression, Amponah merely wishes to become a master: 'I *my* master and yours.'

---

[13]   There is a striking parallel between Amponah's behavior and that of a character in Penelope Aubin's 1723 novel *Carlotta Du Pont* (79–89). Carlotta and her companions discover Isabinda, along with a black man and their mulatto son, on a remote island. According to Isabinda, she is the daughter of a Virginia planter; Domingo, one of her father's slaves, has kidnapped her, impregnated her against her will, and held her captive for two years. The striking difference from Henrietta's tale is that Isabinda loves her captor, and she and Domingo are not only accepted, but even encouraged to marry; this indicates a radical shift in notions of racial difference and a new emphasis on 'miscegenation' at the close of the century. Of course, both stories call to mind the relationship between Miranda and Caliban in Shakespeare's *The Tempest*.

Smith's narrative generalizes this point; Amponah is not the only African-descended man in the text with strong, unwelcome sexual desire for Henrietta. In fact, the maroons who rescue her from Amponah's clutches simply reenact his transgression; the chief's plans reveals that he does not understand his rescue of Henrietta as a rescue at all, but as the acquisition of a new member of his harem; she overhears him telling his compatriots that 'he had in the woods rescued a beautiful white woman from a negro, and had brought her to be added to the number of his wives' (307). He, like Amponah, is motivated not by any sympathy or concern for upholding a standard for the treatment of women, but by his own sexual desire. He is, paradoxically, treating Henrietta much as her own father treats her: she is a piece of property, a possession, a virtual slave, to be traded between men, or to be captured and taken by force from her latest master.

The paradox of Smith's seemingly Montaignean critique of the 'savagery' of the planters is that its force rests on the idea that the 'savages' themselves are deeply repulsive and horrible. Henrietta seems reluctant to grant the African-descended men in the text full humanity. In the phrasing of her remark that the '*General* ... appeared to have not only more authority but to be more humanized than the rest' (305), she suggests that the process of becoming human is one imposed on these men, and one in which few have made much progress. But this degrading, racialized vision of African-descended men also has a resonance for the planters themselves. In fact, in Smith's view, the very institution that corrupts the brutal planters – the institution of chattel slavery – makes them like the 'savages' they enslave. When Henrietta denounces her father for treating her like a slave, describing the marriage negotiations as 'drawing up the bill of sale' (77) and decrying 'this detested sale, which my father means to make of his unhappy child' (89), Smith seems at first blush merely to be giving further evidence of the way that slavery corrupts planters into tyrants who can deal with others, even their own children, as if they were slaves. But given Amponah's and 'the General's' behavior, there is also another resonance: by ignoring Henrietta's will and treating her as a slavish object of male sexual domination and exchanging, her father acts very much like Smith's African-descended characters. 'The General,' Amponah, and Henrietta's father are all alike in their expectation that Henrietta will discipline her sexuality in submission to their will, merely because they have the social and physical means to dominate her. There is a forceful and disturbing parallel here, in terms of which a master becomes more like his slaves by enslaving others not only in the complex sense of his becoming 'brutalized' as he brutalizes others, but also in the sense that slaves, if left to their own devices, would enslave others. This of course resonates with the oft-taken stance that exonerates Europeans from responsibility for their participation in the slave trade because Africans themselves controlled the slave trade in the interior of Africa.[14]

Like her 'half sisters,' then, the African men Henrietta encounters prove ineducable. While both Henrietta and George Maynard achieved enlightenment through subjection to her father's unlimited will for domination, African slaves demonstrate the gap between themselves and non-creolized white Europeans in their utter incapacity for enlightenment, despite their experience of oppression. Indeed, when slaves and ex-slaves in the novel gain power over Henrietta, they have none of the sympathy for her that she and her enlightened uncle have for them.[15] Their only desire is to enslave anyone who comes into their power, and they show their equivalence with Henrietta's father by ignoring her will and trying to dominate her sexually, inevitably threatening to rape her. The only way that the gap between races can be closed, then, is when white Creoles are 'degraded' to the level of the 'savage' Africans. Brutalization can produce enlightenment in whites, but only serves to confirm the inherent brutality of Africans.

Smith anticipates the course of Hegel's thought on Africans and slavery in her denial of their capacity for enlightenment perhaps more exactly

[14]   The issue is still alive in the historiography: Thomas's book *The Slave Trade*, for instance, lists the question 'why did many African rulers and peoples collaborate?' on the book-jacket as one of the three central questions the book will address. Although his account attempts to find balance, the phrasing of some of Thomas's observations on the relations between the Portuguese and the Congolese reflect the tendency to hold Africans primarily accountable: 'By 1526, King Afonso was complaining that the slave dealers, whom, of course, he initially had encouraged, were leaving his realm depopulated' and 'the kidnapping [was] being done by Congolese, not Portuguese, who only constituted the market' (Thomas 1997, 110). For brief discussions of slavery in Africa, see Kolchin 1993, 19–20 and Davidson 1980, 32. The planter Bryan Edwards used this to support the African slave trade, for instance, by claiming that a 'good mind' should feel some 'consolation,' because slaves in Africa 'are, by being sold to the Whites, removed to a situation infinitely more desirable, even in its worst state, than that of the best and most favoured slaves in their native countries' (Edwards 1793, II: 106). Equiano challenges this argument by discussing the mildness of the slaves' condition in Africa (Equiano 1995, 40).
[15]   Contrast this with the insistence on human similarity through the capacity to feel 'pain and misery' described by Carey as fundamental to sentimental rhetoric, (Carey 2005, 38 and passim).

than she does in her version of the master/slave dialectic. In the *Philosophy of History*, based on lectures begun in 1822, or fifteen years after *The Phenomenology of Spirit*, Hegel argues that Africans are incapable of achieving an advanced state of consciousness, or of placing a significant value on human life, because of the thoroughly material basis of their culture and religion.[16] Hegel, drawing on pro-slavery propaganda, hints that New World slavery may allow Africans entry into the dialectic that is unavailable to them in Africa:

> Negroes are enslaved by Europeans and sold to America. Bad as this may be, their lot in their own land is even worse, since there a slavery quite as absolute exists; for it is the essential principle of slavery, that man has not yet attained a consciousness of his freedom, and consequently sinks down to a mere Thing – and object of no value. (Hegel 1991, 96)

Hegel goes on to call slavery – apparently not including slavery within the purely materialistic culture of Africa – 'a phase of advance from the merely isolated sensual existence – a phase of education' (Hegel 1991, 99). Hegel's view of Africans here appears to be based on the pro-slavery travel writing of the British eighteenth century, focused on the history of Dahomey, that stemmed from the work of William Snelgrave, and was further developed by William Smith, Robert Norris and Archibald Dalzel. This group of writers – whose anecdotes were endlessly repeated in polemical pamphlets and even reference materials – were dedicated to the argument that the basic political condition of life in Guinea is one of slavery, enforced by the Kings of Dahomey, who had conquered vast swaths of the region early in the century (Boulukos, 2007). Snelgrave and his followers were also invested in associating Dahomey with atrocities typified by cannibalism. Like Hegel, Charlotte Smith appears to have been far more influenced by this pro-slavery view of West Africa than by the abolitionist counter-discourse of writers including Michel Adanson, Anthony Benezet, and James Stanfield who depicted West Africa as primitive but free and Edenic.

The complexities of Smith's mirroring – and differentiation – between the African-descended slaves of the island and their 'white' would-be masters finds a perfect emblem in the appearance of the maroons who

---

[16] For an argument about how Hegel's view of Africans, and Toussaint in particular, changed between *The Phenomenology of Spirit* and *The Philosophy of History*, see Buck-Morss 2000, 859–65.

capture, separately, both Henrietta and Denbigh. Denbigh is intrigued by the appearance of the maroons, without explaining exactly why:

> I shall never forget the group as they appeared beneath the bright light of the moon then at full. The strange dresses, where Indian na-kedness was oddly intermingled with military ornaments; their dark faces, and that peculiar look of ferocity which the eye of the negro rolling in its deep socket gives to the whole race of Africans, and which was, in one instance, rendered more so by the plumed helmet of an English soldier, whom the black had killed and stripped; in another by a sort of turban, from which waved the scarlet feathers of the mackaw; and by a third part of an old uniform, and a laced hat (119–120)[17]

For Denbigh, this vision is strikingly strange, as he emphasizes in the words 'oddly,' 'strange,' and 'peculiar.' The use of European clothing only heightens Denbigh's impression of the strangeness, the difference and the savagery of the Africans. The 'plumed helmet of an English soldier' and other hybrid clothing not only serve as symbol of the killing of their original possessors, but also serve to set off and emphasize the 'Negro' or 'African' racial characteristics, in this case 'that peculiar look of ferocity which the eye of the negro rolling in its deep socket gives to the whole race of Africans.' The markers of the maroons' presence in the contact zone, the cultural indicators of their participation in a Creole culture, only throw into relief, and thereby confirm, for Denbigh their essential character as Negro savages.[18]

Henrietta finds the hybrid costume of the woman who turns out to be the general's mother similarly compelling. Unlike Denbigh, who seems intrigued by the 'strangeness' of the play between the exotic and familiar, even if he is confident of its ultimate meaning, Henrietta's tone makes clear that she is strongly affected – and totally repulsed – by the idea of contact between the races, which never seems far from miscegenation in her account:

> I never beheld so hideous, so disgusting a creature; and such was the dread with which I was inspired as she hung over me, that I was once more on the point of losing my misery in insensibility … this negress was a fat and heavy creature …  and though there was an affectation

---

[17]  Thomas Thistlewood offers a comparable account in a very different tone; see Burnard 2004, 23.
[18]  For the concept of the 'contact zone,' see Pratt 1992, 6–7, 43–4, 53–5, and 64.

of European dress, she was half naked, and her frightful bosom loaded with finery was displayed most disgustingly. (309)

It is never entirely clear what about the sight of this particular woman causes Henrietta's 'dread.' The General's mother represents neither the sexual threat embodied in Amponah and the general himself, nor the direct challenge to Henrietta's identity posed by her half-sisters, and yet Henrietta reacts most strongly to her. Perhaps the very thought that Henrietta could find herself similarly between cultures and races, if the General follows through on his threats, is enough to overwhelm her.

In these two quotations, both Denbigh and Henrietta experience the maroons as disturbing due to their uncomfortable status between European and 'savage' African cultures. The cultural meeting ground of the maroons' clothing, presents undeniable evidence of the 'radical contemporaneity' of African, European, and indigenous cultures in late eighteenth-century Jamaica.[19] Indeed, this clothing, as much a sign of the inextricable, undeniable intermixing of Jamaica as Henrietta's half-sisters, the 'hybridity' of West Indian culture, is for Smith and Henrietta a sign of the peculiar horror of Jamaican culture under slavery. In fact, given the complexities of the equivalence Smith develops between the 'savagery' of African-descended people and planters in Jamaica, the 'hybridity' of the maroons' dress seems a perfect emblem for Smith's critique of the planters themselves. Despite the 'affectation of European dress,' the thin veneer of civilized culture in Jamaica proves nothing more than 'finery … displayed most disgustingly.' Participation in slavery, both through its corruption of the will and too much contact between 'races,' has left the planters morally (and culturally) 'naked' – or at least nakedly brutal.

The Maroons become travesties of white people through their mixed dress; planters travesty European civilization through their uncontrollably brutal behavior. For Smith, hybridity means degradation for whites, even when only Africans openly embrace it.[20] Smith does not attempt to

[19] This term is originally from Fabian 1983, xi, 1–35, and passim. For applications to the British eighteenth century, see Pratt 1992 and Brown 1993, esp. 33–4.

[20] This problem makes difficult readings of Smith as simply anti-slavery or as only incidentally racist. For a defense of Smith from such charges, see Fry 1996, 98–100 and Fry 2002. Ferguson notes that Smith was one of the first of the erstwhile abolitionists to 'adopt Bryan Edwards' racist analysis,' presenting *The Wanderings of Warwick* and *Letters of a Solitary Wanderer* as evidence (Ferguson 1992, 364, n. 34). Sypher cannot resolve the stand being taken by Smith in *Letters*: 'What does Mrs. Smith really intend? Probably only an exciting tale,' Sypher 1969, 292.

naturalize out of sight Jamaica's status as a 'contact zone' between African and British cultures. But for Henrietta, and apparently for Smith, the contact zone is an argument not for the recognition of African humanity but for the abandonment of slavery and the plantation system. Indeed, Smith's maroons are suggestive of the threat of slave rebellion, calling to mind images familiar to British readers from accounts of the Haitian revolution in their pillaging of plantations, their appropriation of European military organization and clothing, and not least in threatening white women with sexual violence.

Thus, the strongest argument against slavery in *The Letters of Henrietta* is that contact between races can only produce danger and degradation for whites. To illustrate this point, Smith offers images of the hybridity of Jamaican culture – Henrietta's mulatto sisters, the 'affectation of European dress' intermixed with African costumes employed by the maroons – as a source of unmitigated horror. This horror is symbolized in the hybrid costume of the Maroon 'negress' which not only repulses Henrietta, but even endangers her physically: 'I never beheld so hideous, so disgusting a creature; and such was the dread with which I was inspired as she hung over me, that I was once more on the point of losing my misery in insensibility.' Slavery may well be the appropriate lot in life for African savages, Smith suggests, but for white Europeans, keeping slaves is far too dangerous, threatening to degrade their culture into a hybrid horror, and indeed, to destroy utterly the possibility of virtuous and rational white womanhood. Because radical contemporaneity is unavoidable in the contact zone, Smith contends, any contact between the races is best avoided.

## Works Cited

Adanson, Michel, 1759. *A Voyage to Senegal, the Isle of Goree, and the River Gambia*. London: J. Nourse.

Aubin, Penelope, 1723. *The Life of Carlotta Du Pont*. London: Bettesworth.

Bernasconi, Robert, 2002. 'Kant as an Unfamiliar Source of Racism.' In *Philosophers on Race*. Ed. Julie K. Ward and Tommy L. Lott. Oxford: Blackwell. 145–66.

Bewell, Alan, 1999. *Romanticism and Colonial Disease*. Baltimore: Johns Hopkins University Press.

Boulukos, George, forthcoming. *The Grateful Slave: The Emergence of Race in Eighteenth-Century British and American Culture*. Cambridge: Cambridge University Press.

Boulukos, George, 2007. 'Olaudah Equiano and the Eighteenth-Century Debate on Africa.' *Eighteenth-Century Studies*. 40(2): 241–55.

Brown, Laura, 1993. *Ends of Empire: Women and Ideology in Early Eighteenth-Century Literature*. Ithaca: Cornell University Press.

Buck-Morss, Susan, 2000. 'Hegel and Haiti.' *Critical Inquiry* 26: 821–65.

Burnard, Trevor, 2004. *Mastery, Tyranny and Desire: Thomas Thistlewood and his Slaves in the Anglo-Jamaican World*. Chapel Hill: University of North Carolina Press.

Carey, Brycchan, 2005. *British Abolitionism and the Rhetoric of Sensibility: Writing, Sentiment and Slavery, 1760–1807*. New York: Palgrave.

Coontz, Stephanie, 2005. *Marriage, a History: From Obedience to Intimacy, or How Love Conquered Marriage*. New York: Viking.

Craton, Michael, 1982. *Testing the Chains: Resistance to Slavery in the British West Indies*. Ithaca: Cornell University Press.

Curtin, Philip D., 1964. *The Image of Africa: British Ideas and Action, 1780–1850*. Vol. 1. Madison: University of Wisconsin Press.

Dalzel, Archibald, 1967. *The History of Dahomey: An Inland Kingdom of Africa*. 1793. London: Cass.

Davidson, Basil, 1980. *The African Slave Trade*. Rev. Ed. Boston: Little, Brown.

Davis, David Brion, 1975. *The Problem of Slavery in the Age of Revolution, 1770–1828*. Ithaca: Cornell University Press.

Day, Thomas, 1977. *The History of Sandford and Merton*. 3 Vols. 1783–1789. Ed. Isaac Kramnick. New York: Garland.

Edwards, Bryan, 1793. *History, Civil and Commercial, of the British Colonies in the West Indies*. 2 Vols. London: J. Stockdale.

Ellingson, Ter, 2001. *The Myth of the Noble Savage*. Berkeley: University of California Press.

Ellis, Markman, 1996. '"Delight in Misery": Sentimentalism, Amelioration, and Slavery.' In *The Politics of Sensibility: Race, Gender and Commerce in the Sentimental Novel*. Cambridge: Cambridge University Press. 87–128.

Equiano, Olaudah, 1995. *The Interesting Narrative and Other Writings*. 1789. Ed. Vincent Carretta. New York: Penguin.

Eze, Emmanuel Chukwudi, 1995. 'The Color of Reason: The Idea of "Race" in Kant's Anthropology.' *Anthropology and the German Enlightenment: Perspectives on Humanity*. Ed. Katherine M. Faull. Lewisburg, PA: Bucknell University Press. 200–241.

Fabian, Johannes, 1983. *Time and the Other*. New York: Columbia University Press.

Ferguson, Moira, 1992. *Subject to Others: British Women Writers and Colonial Slavery, 1670–1834*. New York: Routledge.

Fliegelman, Jay, 1982. *Prodigals and Pilgrims: The American Revolution against Patriarchal Authority 1750–1800*. Cambridge: Cambridge University Press.

Fredrickson, George M., 1971. *The Black Image in the White Mind: The Debate on Afro-American Character and Destiny, 1817–1914*. New York: Harper.

Fry, Carrol L., 1996. *Charlotte Smith*. New York: Twayne.

Fry, Carrol L., 2002–3. '"Misery Is … the Certain Concomitant of Slavery": The British Anti-Slavery Movement in Charlotte Smith's Novels.' *Publications of the Missouri Philological Association* 27: 45–54.

Gikandi, Simon, 1996. 'In the Shadow of Hegel: Cultural Theory in an Age of Displacement.' *Research in African Literatures* 27.ii: 139–50.

Gilroy, Paul, 1993. *The Black Atlantic: Modernity and Double Consciousness*. Cambridge MA: Harvard University Press.

Ginzburg, Carlo, 1996. 'Making Things Strange: The Prehistory of a Literary Device.' *Representations* 56: 8–28.

Hegel, G. W. F, 1977. *The Phenomenology of Spirit*. Trans. A. V. Miller. New York: Oxford University Press.

Hegel, G. W. F, 1991. *The Philosophy of History*. Trans. J. Sibree. New York: Prometheus.

Hensley, David, 2002. 'Reading and Misreading Richardson as Kant.' In *Talking Forward, Talking Back: Critical Dialogues with the Enlightenment*. Ed. Kevin L. Cope and Rüdiger Ahrens. New York: AMS. 185–216.

Hill, Christopher, 1958. 'Clarissa Harlowe and her Times.' In *Puritanism and Revolution: Studies in Interpretation of the English Revolution of the Seventeenth Century*. London: Martin, Secker. 332–56.

Hyppolite, Jean, 1974. *Genesis and Structure of Hegel's Phenomenology of Spirit*. Trans. Samuel Cherniak and John Heckman. Evanston IL: Northwestern University Press.

Jefferson, Thomas, 1999. *Notes on the State of Virginia*. 1785. Ed. Frank Shuffleton. New York: Penguin.

Johnson, Samuel, 1996. 'Nonage.' In *A Dictionary of the English Language: The First and Fourth Editions on CD ROM*. Ed. Anne McDermott. Cambridge: Cambridge University Press.

Kant, Immanuel, 1973. 'What is Enlightenment?' Trans. Peter Gay. *The Enlightenment: A Comprehensive Anthology*. Ed. Peter Gay. New York: Simon and Schuster. 383–89.

Kant, Immanuel, 1997. *Physical Geography* (selections). Trans. K. M. Faull and E. C. Eze. *Race and the Enlightenment*. Ed. E. C. Eze. Oxford: Blackwell.

Kitson, Peter J., 2004. '"Candid Reflections": The Idea of Race in the Debate over Slavery and the Slave Trade in the Late Eighteenth and Early Nineteenth Centuries.' In *Discourses of Slavery and Abolition: Britain and its Colonies, 1760–1838*. Ed. Brycchan Carey, Markman Ellis and Sara Salih. New York: Palgrave.

Kojève, Alexander, 1969. *Introduction to the Reading of Hegel*. Ed. Allan Bloom. Trans. James H. Nichols, Jr. New York: Basic Books.

Kolchin, Peter, 1993. *American Slavery: 1619–1877*. New York: Hill and Wang.

Layson, Hana, 2003. 'Citizen Clarissa: The Civic Pedagogy of a Seduction Novel.' In 'Injured Innocence: Sexual Injury, Sentimentality, and Citizenship in the Early Republic.' Ph.D. Diss. University of Chicago. 55–88.

MacNeill, Hector, 1800. *Memoirs of the Life and Travels of the Late Charles Macpherson, Esq*. Edinburgh: Arch. Constable.

Montaigne, Michel de, 1958. 'Of Cannibals.' In *Complete Essays of Montaigne*. Trans. Donald Frame. Stanford: Stanford University Press. 150–159.

Moore, John, Dr., 1820. *Zeluco*, 1786. 2 Vols. *The British Novelists*. Ed. Mrs. Barbauld. Vols. 34–35. London: Rivington et al.

Muthu, Sankar, 2003. *Enlightenment Against Empire*. Princeton: Princeton University Press.

Norris, Robert, 1968. *Memoirs of the Reign of Bossa Ahadee, King of Dahomy*. 1789. London: Frank Cass.

Pratt, Mary Louise, 1992. *Imperial Eyes: Travel Writing and Transculturation*. New York: Routledge.

Rawson, Claude, 1992. '"Indians" and Irish: Montaigne, Swift, and the Cannibal Question.' *Modern Language Quarterly* 53.iii: 299–363.

Schochet, Gordon J., 1988. *The Authoritarian Family and Political Attitudes in 17th-Century England: Patriarchalism in Political Thought*. 1975. New Brunswick, NJ: Transaction.

Smith, Charlotte, 1996. *The Story of Henrietta*. Vol 2. of *Letters of a Solitary Wanderer*. 1800. Reprint ed. Poole NY: Woodstock.

Smith, William, 1967. *A New Voyage to Guinea*. 1744. London: Frank Cass.

Snelgrave, William, 1971. *New Account of Some Parts of Guinea and the Slave Trade*. 1734. London: Frank Cass.

Stanfield, James Field, 1788. *Observations on a Guinea Voyage*. London: J. Phillips.

Sypher, Wylie, 1969. *Guinea's Captive Kings: British Anti-Slavery Literature of the XVIIIth Century*. 1942. New York: Octagon.

Tadmor, Naomi, 1996. 'The Concept of the Household-Family in Eighteenth-Century England.' *Past & Present* 151: 111–41.

Tennenhouse, Leonard, 1998. 'The Americanization of Clarissa.' *The Yale Journal of Criticism* 11:1: 177–96.

Thomas, Hugh, 1997. *The Slave Trade*. New York: Simon & Schuster.

Trumpener, Katie, 1997. *Bardic Nationalism: The Romantic Novel and the British Empire*. Princeton: Princeton University Press.

Wahrman, Dror, 2004. *The Making of the Modern Self: Identity and Culture in Eighteenth-Century England*. New Haven: Yale University Press.

Wheeler, Roxann, 2000. *The Complexion of Race: Categories of Difference in Eighteenth-Century British Culture*. Philadelphia: University Pennsylvania Press.

Williams, Raymond, 1983. 'Family.' In *Keywords*. Rev. ed. New York: Oxford University Press. 131–4.

Wilson, Kathleen, 2003. *The Island Race: Englishness, Empire and Gender in the Eighteenth Century*. New York: Routledge.

Woodard, Helena, 1999. 'Reading Pope/Reasoning Race: Enlightenment Humanism and the Chain's Discursive Legacy.' In *African-British Writings in the Eighteenth Century: The Politics of Race and Reason*. Westport, CT: Greenwood. 1–29.

Young, Robert J. C., 1995. *Colonial Desire: Hybridity in Theory, Culture, and Race*. New York: Routledge.

# 'To Rivet and Record':
## Conversion and Collective Memory in *Equiano's* Interesting Narrative

### LINCOLN SHLENSKY

OLAUDAH Equiano's 1789 slave autobiography elicits considerable disagreement among contemporary critics.[1] Contention regarding his identity and his literary project in *The Interesting Narrative of the Life of Olaudah Equiano, or Gustavus Vassa, the African, Written by Himself* is underlain, in turn, by philosophical and historiographical questions of considerable import. The most conspicuous of these controversies have touched upon the question of the authenticity of Equiano's narrative account of his life. Scholars such as Vincent Carretta and S. E. Ogude, most influentially, question the veracity of Equiano's presentation of his African childhood, while over the years others, such as the prominent Equiano scholar Paul Edwards, Catherine Acholonu, and Adam Hochschild have presented evidence and arguments supporting Equiano's account of his origins (Acholonu 1987; Carretta 2005; Edwards 1969; Hochschild 2005; Ogude 1984). On a different but intersecting axis, William Andrews, Valerie Smith, and Chinosole focus on the ironic self-positioning implicit in Equiano's hybridity or DuBoisian 'twoness,' whereas critical dissenters, such as Tanya Caldwell and Katalin Orban suggest Equiano's attempt to achieve perfect assimilation into English culture must be taken more literally (Andrews 1982; Caldwell 1999; Chinosole 1982; Orban 1993; Smith 1987). These debates emphasize the difficulty of establishing whether Equiano's chronicle of his childhood experiences corresponds to actual events, or whether the early chapters of his narrative represent a purely rhetorical effort of self-fashioning. They also raise questions about the sincerity of his conversion to Christianity and his adoption of European identity. Such questions are essential to locating Equiano in his

[1] I would like to thank the Department of English and the conveners of the Humanities Colloquium at the University of South Alabama for giving me the opportunity to present my early research on this topic. I also thank Jacques Marchand and Brycchan Carey for their helpful comments on an earlier version of this paper.

historical context and understanding his autobiography's rhetorical strategies and its impact on eighteenth-century readers.

In the following discussion I ask what the focus on textual authenticity in Equiano's *Narrative* may foreclose, or overshadow, in terms of a critical methodology. I suggest that there is value in reading Equiano's text as an articulation of the problems of writing slave history and as an effort to elucidate the paradox of slave memory. Memory of any kind, according to the French sociologist Maurice Halbwachs, a disciple of Henri Bergson and Emile Durkheim, requires the support of a collective social framework that authorizes and organizes individual acts of remembrance (Halbwachs 1980).[2] Slave memory, a topic Halbwachs never considered, poses a specific problem within his general analysis of memory. The life of a slave entails an unrelenting isolation of the self, forcefully described by Equiano in his *Narrative* as the product of frequently disrupted social relationships. The social cohesion necessary to framing and maintaining memory within a collective context is thus radically absent for the ex-slave narrator. Just as importantly, Equiano's literary project has to grapple with the rhetorical task entailed in imagining – inventing, actually – a receptive audience for whose members, with very few exceptions, the experience of slavery remains fundamentally alien. Not only had the vast majority of his audience presumably never known slavery, but this readership could hardly imagine the difficulty involved in trying to narrate the phenomenology of an experience suffered as a traumatic break in the structures of collective experience that underpin memory itself. Equiano had the burden, therefore, not only of describing his experiences in the absence of a mutually sustained social construct with agreed points of reference, but also of narrating an account of group history where the collective subject itself – that is, the slave community of which he had been, and theoretically continued to be, a member – was missing or radically reduced. Giving narrative form to the task of narration itself, in the absence of the basic social structures of memory that make narrative legible, is the remarkable undertaking of Equiano's project that I believe deserves more of our critical attention.

Equiano furnishes a key to his analysis of the problem of memory in the chapter recounting his religious conversion. I contend that the

---

[2] Halbwachs's death in the Buchenwald concentration camp in 1945 provides a sombre coda to his work on the structures of collective memory and, although he would not have been familiar with Equiano's *Narrative*, suggests an associative connection to the human degradations that Equiano witnessed and experienced as a slave.

conversion episode in Equiano's *Narrative* offers his readers a way to relate to Equiano's past that is not dependent on a specific account of history but, rather, insists on presenting the difficulty, if not the impossibility, of representing history from the standpoint of those who, as Henry
Louis Gates Jr points out, are unrecognized by it (Gates 1988). I view the
conversion episode as a decoding and recoding of the drama Equiano
presents as the narrative trajectory of his life, whether historically accurate or partly fabricated. Like his account of his origins, Equiano's conversion begins with a description of a traumatic separation, describes his
development of selfhood as a confrontation with the imposing authority
of an Other, and rehearses the epistemological scepticism that he knows
from the outset will condition the public reception of his *Narrative*. By
re-presenting his life story allegorically in the conversion chapter, Equiano
downplays the significance of *The Interesting Narrative* as individual autobiography while offering instead a symbolically distilled and emblematic
account of the barriers to, and possibility of, creating a truly representative collective identity in the West.

The conversion scene does more, however, than symbolically restage
the basic elements of his biography in the service of imagining a more
inclusive nation. In decoding the latent structure of his narrative as an
account of a collective identity that does not yet exist, and whose cor-
roborating memory cannot be assured, the conversion scene also recodes
Equiano's literary project as the positing of an identity that is neither
British nor African, nor again a 'hybrid' combination of the two. Unable
simply to claim or invent a social position that resolves the epistemological contradictions encountered by an African former slave who accepts
the egalitarian premises of the English polity, Equiano's project serves
rather to inscribe and interrogate the vexed deficiency of eighteenth-
century social categories of identity in England and its colonies. Forced
by events that precipitate his conversion to acknowledge his irreconcil-
able social subordination, Equiano comes to recognize that as a freed
black slave he can never assume a fully 'British' political, and all the less
a cultural, identity. His conversion indicates this by reinscribing historical relations of domination and submission in an allegory of religious
faith that highlights the basic arbitrariness of the English legal system,
while subversively suggesting that Christianity is truest when it acknowledges its debt to a repressed Other that it defines as 'primitive.' This act
of allegorization functions to preserve slave experience latently as a problem of collective memory in the unruly literary and cultural conjunction
of picaresque adventure, spiritual autobiography, sentimental fiction, slave

narrative and abolitionist tract that Equiano constructs. Within this heterogeneous textual frame, the conversion episode offers a hermeneutical key to Equiano's efforts to conserve slave memory as a stabilizing anchor of identity whose value, paradoxically, lies in its potential to disrupt the assimilationist social project and uniformitarian cultural assumptions with which the author of *The Interesting Narrative* publicly identifies himself.

There has been evidence all along, in fact, that Equiano did not view memory as strictly the province of the individual. Scholars have long been aware that Equiano borrowed heavily from other sources in writing Chapters One and Two of his *Narrative*. Indeed, in Chapter One, Equiano explicitly acknowledges the work of Anthony Benezet, from whose popular abolitionist anthology of earlier historical writings on Africa, *Some Historical Account of Guinea*, Equiano draws (Benezet 1771). While he does not indicate in his footnotes the extent to which he borrows from Benezet, many scholars have been forgiving about his borrowings. Some have reasoned that, by virtue of his age at the time of the kidnapping and the trauma likely associated with it, he would not necessarily have retained very much specific memory of African customs, geography, or even of his own family. Until recently, most scholarly analysis accepted Equiano's claims about his childhood in Africa as authentic. Edwards's groundbreaking study of the *Narrative*, for example, asserted that only a West African, and not a native English speaker, would have created the rhymes that Equiano uses in his poem at the conclusion of Chapter Ten, the so-called 'conversion' chapter (Edwards 1969). Catherine Obianju Acholonu likewise analyzed Equiano's use of Igbo words and other anthropological clues in Chapters One and Two, and, albeit on the basis of questionable anecdotal evidence, traced Equiano's origins to the town of Isseke in present-day Nigeria (Acholonu 1987). Adam Hochschild has more recently argued that Equiano was probably telling the truth about his African childhood, because autobiographers who lie about their personal history typically tend to do so throughout their work. Hochschild cites the recent example of Binjamin Wilkomirski, whose autobiography is riddled throughout with fabrications about his experiences in a Nazi concentration camp. Most of the adulthood experiences that Equiano describes in the *Narrative*, by contrast, are well-documented, and so, Hochschild claims, he doesn't fit the typical profile of the fraudulent autobiographer (Hochschild 2005).

The complexity of Equiano's position – and his project – is heightened, however, by recent scholarship by Ogude and Carretta, each of whom claims, based on different evidence, that Equiano did not grow up in Africa or experience the horrors of the Middle Passage described in *The Interesting Narrative* (Carretta 2005; Ogude 1984). Carretta's evidence is most surprising: he discovered a ship manifesto from the period after Equiano's manumission in which he listed his place of birth as South Carolina rather than Africa, and a baptismal record from 9 February 1759 that seems to confirm this. Carretta also offers a detailed analysis of the likely sources and obvious errors in Equiano's putative first-hand description of his African birthplace, and he points out that Equiano had hardly ever mentioned his African provenance prior to the *Narrative*'s appearance.[3] There are any number of reasons why Equiano might have concealed his African origins during most of his life, ranging from habit, to the fear that by identifying himself as an African, purportedly less tractable than those born into slavery, he might have prejudiced his efforts to obtain employment. Carretta's evidence, however, while far from conclusive, convincingly raises doubts about Equiano's claims to have spent his childhood in Africa and to have personally experienced the agonies of the Middle Passage. The new evidence leaves unanswered, nevertheless, important questions about Equiano's conception of his own role in creating a sense of collective identity and memory among Africans subjected to slavery.

I want to use the problem of identity raised by these questions about Equiano's history and truthfulness as a starting point for reconsidering one chapter of his narrative. Chapter Ten, in which Equiano undergoes what is known as religious conversion, seems to me to contain many possible clues as to the use that Equiano makes of memory and the value that he places on history. Focusing on this chapter to investigate Equiano's attitude towards his own history is not an obvious choice. To begin with, the conversion episode in *The Interesting Narrative* was viewed by some of Equiano's contemporaries, who were otherwise sympathetic to his abolitionist views, as something of an embarrassing intrusion into an otherwise powerful historical account. Mary Wollstonecraft, for example, wrote a mixed review of *The Interesting Narrative*, which appeared, unsigned, soon after the book's publication. She found the first half of the *Narrative* to be 'very interesting' but was less than impressed with the chapters describing Equiano's experiences after manumission, where she felt the autobiography turned 'flat' and 'insignificant.' She added, archly, that

---

[3]   Carretta is careful to point out, however, that reasonable doubt does not amount to proof, and that the questions about Equiano's origins may never be resolved definitively. See Carretta 2005, 147–8, 312–20.

'[t]he long account of his religious sentiments and conversion to methodism, is rather tiresome' (Wollstonecraft 1789).[4]

Modern critics such as Ogude and Adam Potkay view Equiano's description of his conversion as fitting into the genre conventions of the spiritual autobiography that became popular in the eighteenth century (Ogude 1984; Potkay 1994). Ogude directs attention to the many elements of Daniel Defoe's fictionalized spiritual autobiography, *Robinson Crusoe* (1719), that Equiano appears to have appropriated, including the shipwrecked Crusoe's guilty self-reproaches and his adamant self-reliance, both of which are typical features of the spiritual autobiography. Mark Stein notes that the connections between Equiano's narrative and *Robinson Crusoe* were described as early as 1808 by the Abbé Henri-Baptiste Grégoire, a French abolitionist. Stein points out that both Crusoe and Equiano are afraid of being eaten – Crusoe by the native Americans who occasionally land on the island where he is shipwrecked, and Equiano by the English crew of the slave ship that takes him from Africa to the Americas. But Equiano's evocation of cannibalism is more subversive than Defoe's, Stein claims, because Equiano reverses the trope of anthropophagy by applying it to English whites as a means of critiquing Western stereotypes of Africa (Stein 2004, 103–5).[5] To Stein's catalogue of signifying differences between Defoe's text and *The Interesting Narrative*, I would add that Equiano does not seem to share Crusoe's tendency to be wracked by insistent flashes of returning memory. Again and again, as Crusoe is tested by North Sea storms, capture and enslavement by the Turks, arduous farming conditions in Brazil, and his eventual island ordeal, he recalls his English countryside home and his father's admonishments as the young Crusoe rashly set off on his misadventures. Equiano, by contrast, almost never mentions his African home or his family again after having recounted his kidnapping at the beginning of the *Narrative*. It might be tempting to ascribe this to Equiano's discomfort with a falsified African past, but an alternative account of this discrepancy is also plausible. In keeping with Halbwachs's theory, we can imagine that the relative absence

---

[4]  Richard Gough, in a June 1789 review in *Gentleman's Magazine*, adjudged as 'uninteresting' all of the experiences Equiano describes subsequent to his manumission.

[5]  Charlotte Sussman contributes to this discussion by arguing that Defoe's use of the cannibalism trope may be more subversive than it appears. She suggests that when, upon seeing the undigested remains of cannibalism on his island, Crusoe vomits, his disgust may be read as a symbolic rejection of the consumer practices that arise from eighteenth-century English colonialism. Sussman 200, 15.

of analeptic memory in Equiano's narrative simply inscribes in his text the epistemological problem of recollection that is implied by his isolation from a cohesive social structure. Equiano leaves the past behind him because, once the rhetorical purposes of evoking the past have been served in authenticating his autobiography and establishing the legitimacy of his African cultural origins, there is no place for recollection as such – that is, for the constitutive function of collective memory – in his narrative.

Before offering evidence for this latter account of the narrative lacunae in Equiano's text, there are some other explanations for Equiano's unexpected silence about the past that deserve consideration. Tanya Caldwell takes the radical view that, in writing *The Interesting Narrative*, Equiano labours to present himself not as an African but as a British man of black complexion. She argues that Equiano fashions himself as the ideal *homo economicus*, whose anti-slavery activism is always framed in terms of the burgeoning mercantile values of Britain which Equiano himself shares. It is a travesty of Equiano's aims in writing his narrative, she claims, to present him as an African, or even, in the popular terminology of postcolonialism, as a Western and African 'hybrid' figure, because, as he demonstrates in the *Narrative*, he no longer identifies with his African cultural background nor wishes to be identified with it by others. His decision to use the autobiographical mode, she insists, does not represent an effort to invent a new cultural identity position for himself. Autobiography allows him, rather, to assimilate into British culture, and indeed forces him to do so, because the autobiographical mode in Europe of the eighteenth century inevitably channels the life portrayed into an existing religious or social paradigm and thus would necessarily deny a figure like Equiano access to any conception of an 'authentic African self.' She cites Leo Damrosch's claim that in the eighteenth century there is no model of the independent autonomous individual and that 'the alternative to the established hierarchy is not independent persons but new and more dangerous combinations of persons.' In Caldwell's view, 'Equiano's *Narrative* both reflects and affirms this eighteenth-century perception of self, for rather than struggling for autonomy the narrator gradually and subtly eradicates that otherness which he saw as a threat to his own security and to his abolitionist argument' (Caldwell 1999, 265).[6]

---

[6]   Ignatius Sancho, whose collected letters were published posthumously in 1782, likewise has been viewed by a number of critics as thoroughly assimilated; for a review and refutation of such assessments of Sancho, see Ellis 2001.

How well does Caldwell's argument account for Equiano's silence about his childhood after Chapters One and Two? My reading of *The Interesting Narrative* suggests that there is good reason to question her sweeping conclusion that Equiano views himself as 'fundamentally white' and uses his narrative to 'establish the thoroughly European nature of his mind' (Caldwell 1999, 265–266). There are too many indications in Equiano's *Narrative* that he is burdened with the past and that he both consciously and unconsciously expresses the conflicts and contradictions of his social position in England. Equiano's very effort to make the case for a cultural likeness between himself and his fellow white British subjects, I would argue, may be understood as an expression of his recognition of the distance between their outlook on the world and his, their lived lives and his. I want to suggest another possibility: that Equiano suppresses the past after initial accounts of his childhood until the moment at which his ambivalence toward the past irresistibly returns to haunt him in the conversion episode. The conversion scene, I contend, is the anchor of his autobiography because it exhibits the haunting structure of memory with which Equiano must grapple in order to complete the process of self-invention that begins with his growing awareness of the social inadmissibility of slave identity. Equiano's conversion experience is manifestly a response to the pressures he experiences as a man neither fully accepted as British nor certain of his identity as a black former slave. By placing the conversion scene at the navel of his narrative, Equiano reveals to his readers the conflicting pressures he and other former slaves experience in defining themselves vis-à-vis a polity that is neither willing to assimilate them fully nor to tolerate their otherness. The conversion episode, in which Equiano asserts the validity of an intuitive and subjective relation to Holy Scripture, permits him to express veiled anger at the precarious legal and social status of free blacks in England without alienating his white audience. His narrative of conversion also suggests a possible parallel between his spiritual quest and his search for social status as a black man and former slave who calls England his home. Just as Equiano invents a new spiritual identity for himself based on atonement for sins he acknowledges in the abstract without ever fully describing, so too his autobiography's implicit purpose is to appropriate for slaves and ex-slaves an abstract and collective idea of Africanness that has been forged, paradoxically, out of the deracinating violence of the European slave trade.

The conversion episode unfolds as a striking sequence of events that precipitates Equiano's central spiritual crisis and culminates in the apocalyptic revelation that brings his religious travail to a close. Chapter Ten of his narrative, which recounts this conversion, is oddly heterogeneous in structure: the motive for Equiano's spiritual epiphany remains obscured behind a series of discomfiting incidents, including the kidnapping of one of his black friends, and his futile attempt to gain the friend's release. The chapter begins with Equiano's return to London after a disastrous voyage to the Arctic, leading to spiritual reflections that are interrupted, in turn, by a personally devastating realization of his own tenuous hold on freedom as a black former slave in England. Equiano had purchased his freedom and received his manumission papers in 1766, and promptly thereafter embarked on a series of journeys that included a harrowing shipwreck in the Bahamas in 1767 and the nearly fatal Arctic expedition in 1773. Upon his return to London, he begins 'seriously to reflect on the dangers I had escaped, particularly those of my last voyage, which made a lasting impression on my mind' (Equiano 2001, 134–5).[7] This comment about his enduring memory of the calamitous Arctic expedition echoes an earlier use of the same phrase to explain to his readers (or to ask their forbearance for) his having included details of his African childhood in the *Narrative*. Thus at the outset of Chapter Two, after having given a general description of his native town of Essaka in the kingdom of Benin, Equiano offers this apology for his lengthy description of Igbo ('Eboe') culture:

> I hope the reader will not think that I have trespassed on his patience in introducing myself to him with some account of the manners and customs of my country. They had been implanted in me with great care, *and made an impression on my mind*, which time could not erase, and which all adversity and variety of fortune I have since experienced served only to rivet and record; for, whether the love of one's country be real or imaginary, or a lesson of reason, or an instinct of nature, I shall look back with pleasure on the first scenes of my life, though that pleasure has been for the most part mingled with sorrow. (31–2, emphasis mine)

Equiano's apology for presenting an African forehistory is undoubtedly rhetorical, an echo of his similarly rhetorical apology, at the outset of the *Narrative*, for having had the audacity to write his autobiography at all. What is interesting about both comments on the mental 'impression' made by memory, however, is their acknowledgment that the impact of memory is not lessened but heightened by intervening experience and

---

[7]    Further citations from Equiano's *The Interesting Narrative* refer to this edition.

the imposition of an interpretive framework. Equiano reiterates this paradoxical quality of subsequent experiences to 'rivet and record' earlier memories when, tutored in the reading of the Bible by his friend Daniel Queen, he remarks on the similarity between Igbo culture and that of the Hebrews depicted in the Bible: 'I was wonderfully surprised to see the laws and rules of my country written almost exactly here; a circumstance which I believe tended to impress our manners and customs more deeply on my memory' (68). Thus at the outset of the conversion chapter, just as at the outset of the *Narrative* as a whole, Equiano recounts a traumatic experience – his kidnapping from Africa, on the one hand, and his nearly fatal Arctic expedition on the other – while pointing out that the events themselves are memorable because they are located within a narrative structure recognizable only in retrospect. Memory, Equiano's *Narrative* suggests, is never simply a matter of individual experience, but, as Halbwachs's theory later postulated, is the product of a discursive framework comprising specific cultural sanctions, whether prohibitive or permissive.[8]

Just as Equiano's early descriptions of Africa end in a traumatic departure, so too his memory of the harrowing Arctic journey results in a renunciation of the secular existence he has led up to that point. After commenting that the Arctic debacle has caused him to 'seek the Lord with full purpose of heart ere it was too late' (135), Equiano resolves to sail for Turkey, where he hopes to live among the more devout Muslims, 'never more to return to England' (137). He takes a position aboard the merchant ship *Anglicania*, and manages to get his friend and fellow freed slave John Annis hired aboard the ship as a galley cook. His good deed and his plans, however, go awry. Annis's former master, William Kirkpatrick, from whom, according to the *Narrative*, Annis had 'parted by consent,' shows up one morning at the dock with a boatload of men, who seize his erstwhile slave and carry him off. When the ship's captain refuses to intervene, Equiano realizes that the kidnapping of Annis is 'a combined piece of business,' that is, an illicit connivance.[9] In light of

---

[8]   Carretta points out that earlier writers, with whom Equiano was probably familiar, had remarked on the similarity between the customs of Africans and the traditions described in the Hebrew Bible. Carretta 2005, 313, 315. If it is true that Equiano fabricated his childhood memories, then his emphasis in these passages on the retrospective reconstruction of memory takes on added potential significance as self-referential justifications for Equiano's textual practices.
[9]   Brycchan Carey and Sara Salih, in the introduction to the volume they edited with Markman Ellis, and Carey in a separate article included in the same volume, discuss briefly the legal limbo African slaves found themselves in after

Annis's fate, Equiano understands that as a black man he is not then, and may never become, secure in his freedom. Equiano has already experienced the precariousness of his status as a freed slave in the wild American colonies where, even after being freed, he had been beaten, threatened with lynching and reenslavement, and forced against his will to serve on various merchant vessels. In England, on the other hand, since his formal manumission, he had never before experienced such an explicit threat to his freedom. He must thenceforth recognize the fragile grip on freedom and legal equality that any black person holds, even in England under the prevailing British constitutional provisions. But Equiano does not acknowledge the obvious lesson about the tenuousness of his situation, either to his readers, or apparently, to himself.

What Equiano does express instead ought to surprise us. Having just described the torture, re-enslavement and finally the death in chains of John Annis after his forcible return to the Caribbean island of St. Kitts, Equiano continues, without so much as a paragraph break:

> During this disagreeable business I was under strong conviction of sin, and thought that my state was worse than any man's; my mind was unaccountably disturbed; I often wished for death, though at the same time convinced I was altogether unprepared for that awful summons. Suffering much by villains in the late cause, and being much concerned about the state of my soul, these things (but particularly the latter) brought me very low; so that I became a burden to myself, and viewed all things around me as emptiness and vanity, which could give no satisfaction to a troubled conscience. (137)

For what supposed fault does Equiano feel guilty? He never explains. And why, just now, is he 'under strong conviction of sin,' seven years after his release from slavery but in the midst of an unhappy reminder that those like himself can never feel confident of their freedoms? I suggest that Equiano's melancholic dejection is a form of repression: having recognized that John Annis's situation could easily become his own, Equiano has to face his own insecurity as a freed black slave in England who can,

---

the 1772 Mansfield decision. Carretta also includes a discussion of the case. The ruling provided that slaves could not be forcibly deported from England by their masters, but it did not actually emancipate them; because escaped slaves on English soil were legally deemed emancipated, however, the ruling was perceived by many as the de facto abolition of slavery in England. Carey 2004, 82; Carey and Salih 2004, 2; Carretta 2005, 205–9.

at the whim of whites, be bundled back into slavery at any moment. He also has to acknowledge the distance between his idealist assumptions about the ability of a free black man to attain full subject status in England, on the one hand, and, on the other, the evident reality that he continues to lack the power and rights enjoyed by any white citizen. If Equiano recognizes that these contradictions remain a central unresolved problem for all British blacks of the eighteenth century, however, he never explicitly says so. Nor does he question his own commitment to working within the English political and economic system and to aiding in the dissemination of its ideas and culture, if not its actual dominion. Instead of anger or outrage, as a reader might expect, what Equiano feels is guilt and a wish for his own death.[10]

The events that precipitate Equiano's spiritual quest at the outset of the conversion chapter, then, produce in him a profound yet unspeakable awareness of the distance between the promise of full English subjecthood and the reality of his continuing subordination. Yet Equiano does not, or cannot, acknowledge that his strategy of accepting and working within the explicit rules of the colonial British system of slavery and manumission have not yielded durable freedom for him or other former slaves. To admit this would be to undermine his own efforts to sway English public opinion towards abolition by writing an autobiography that appeals to the sentiments and egalitarian ideals of English whites. Instead, Equiano continues to try to resolve the contradictions of his own identity and history in symbolic terms. In his religious practice, just as in his response to slavery, Equiano has tried to adhere to the letter of the law. But his law-abiding propensity now brings on a spiritual crisis: in the eyes of the Christianity that he knows, there is nothing he can do to

---

[10] Equiano elsewhere expresses indignation much more explicitly. In a 1788 letter to the *Public Advertiser*, he writes with thinly concealed rage in response to a pro-slavery pamphlet authored by James Tobin. Masking his fury behind religious piety, Equiano suggests that Tobin's comeuppance will be more painful than that meted out by the slave-driver's whip: 'How dreadful then will your fate be? The studied and torturing punishments, inhuman, as they are, of a barbarous planter, or a more barbarous overseer, will be tenderness compared to the provoked wrath of an angry but righteous God ... who will ... cast the oppressive white to that doleful place, where he will cry, but will cry in vain, for a drop of water!' Equiano 1789, 197. It is a mark of Equiano's adherence to his strategic aim of appealing to the broadest possible audience that *The Interesting Narrative* rarely admits to its author's wish, suggested in the above passage, not simply for justice but for retribution.

purge himself of the *a priori* taint of sin. Just as his most strenuous efforts to follow the law have not allowed him to gain full freedom in white England, his 'good works' never seem to be sufficient to assure his spiritual redemption for the Christian church.

The crisis reaches its climax on 6 October 1774, while Equiano is on a voyage to Spain. Reading from a passage in the Book of Acts, he writes, 'the Lord was pleased to break in upon my soul with his bright beams of heavenly light; and in an instant as it were, removing the veil, and letting light into a dark place, I saw clearly with the eye of faith' (143–4). In this apocalyptic moment (etymologically apocalyptic, as in the drawing away of a veil), Equiano's crisis is resolved. As he puts it, at this moment, 'the scriptures became an unsealed book' (144). He recognizes that he can never be redeemed in terms of the Law, under which he remains 'a condemned criminal,' and that, indeed, his very knowledge of the law makes him a criminal of sorts. That is how he interprets the paradoxical passage in Romans 7:9: 'the commandment came, sin revived, and I died.' Human beings, as he reads the biblical aphorism, became acquainted with sin by their over-literal adherence to God's commandments. Equiano now accepts, for the first time in his *Narrative*, that he cannot free himself in a worldly or even a spiritual sense. His own actions, or 'works,' are constitutively insufficient. Only, that is, by defining a new, metaphorical relation to the law, to mastery, and to submission, can the slave – or the sinner – be 'born again' (144) as a free man.

In re-entering a state of submission, Equiano reinforces the overall structure of the conversion as a symbolic reframing and mastering of the past. This is not merely an imaginary resolution of the crisis that allows him to validate his strategic accommodations within the English social system. For one thing, even if his conversion is sincere, as it seems to be, his retreat to a symbolic plane for resolution necessarily implies that his real existential situation remains conflicted. His preoccupation with symbolic mastery indicates that questions of domination, submission, and resistance persist, and suggests that a real resolution of these problems remains elusive. There is an inherent contradiction in Equiano's decision to accept Annis's capture and reenslavement as pre-ordained fate, when his writing and promotion of *The Interesting Narrative* so clearly attest to his active political engagement and his implied belief in the salience of human intervention. Apart from this logical contradiction, there are also signs that Equiano sees his rebirth into Christian community as a kind of return to his roots, or, Helen Thomas offers, as a creolizing merger of African spirituality and radical Protestant dissent (Thomas 2000, 226–54).

Equiano seems to provide strategic hints throughout the *Narrative* that his submission to divine authority in the conversion echoes a philosophical attitude with which he was already familiar because it is at the heart of his sense of Africanness. According to Equiano, the Igbo believe in a single divine 'Creator' who 'governs events, especially our deaths or captivity' (26). He claims to have been immersed in such beliefs throughout his captivity. 'I was from early years a predestinarian,' he writes in Chapter Six, '[and] I thought whatever fate had determined must ever come to pass' (88). One might say, then, that the conversion scene does not so much introduce a new way of regarding the world for Equiano as it gives a socially acceptable Christian gloss to ideas of predestination and providence that, according to the *Narrative*, he has held from the time of his youth.[11] In this sense, the conversion entails a reclaiming of the past as much as it heralds Equiano's first volitional entry into, and acceptance by, a community of equals.

Equiano's *Narrative*, after all, is not just a highly personal account of his experiences since his childhood abduction. It is also the chronicle of a man who has lived his life in a state of fundamental solitariness and even detachment, and whose personal spiritual quest is concomitantly a search for a collective identity. By his own account, since early childhood Equiano had not spent more than brief periods with anyone who knew him well, much less with someone to whom he was emotionally attached. His encounters with others, as he describes them in *The Interesting Narrative*, are notably marked by transience – hardly surprising while he is a slave and mariner – and by tragedy, concluding in a series of fatal misfortunes. Beginning in adolescence, Equiano loses contact with any person for whom he has developed an emotional attachment. In 1755, however, at the outset of his shipboard servitude to Captain Pascal, Equiano befriends a white youth, five years his senior, named Richard Baker, who 'shewed me a great deal of partiality and attention, and in return I grew extremely fond of him' (46). The relationship is one of both utility and feeling, for it is Dick, as he affectionately calls him, who helps to teach Equiano the cultural codes of merchant marine life aboard an English ship; but there is also an emotional basis of the relationship, attested by the fact that the two 'inseparable' companions often sleep together at night to comfort each

---

[11]  Equiano need not have been born in Africa, as he claims, to have grown up with African customs and language. It is even possible, Carretta claims, that were he born in the Carolinas, Equiano would have spoken mainly Igbo as a child.

other's fears.[12] Dick dies during a voyage to Greece, however, only two years later, a loss that Equiano admits 'I have never ceased to regret' (46). In 1762 when, according to the *Narrative*, he is seventeen years old, Equiano meets and befriends a 41-year-old white man named Daniel Queen who 'soon became very much attached to me, and took very great pains to instruct me in many things.' Equiano remarks that Queen 'was like a father to me; and … I almost loved him with the affection of a son' (68). Shortly afterwards, to Equiano's great distress, he is sold away once again, never again to see or hear of Queen. His experiences of black companionship are even less consummate; Equiano never mentions in the *Narrative* an intimate relation or lasting emotional bond with another slave or free black, and even his friendship with Annis, never fleshed out as a meaningful relationship, is cruelly disrupted.[13]

Equiano does describe one encounter with an African that indicates his wish to experience intimate friendship, and the difficulty he has in doing so. Soon after Pascal brings him to England, Equiano mentions (but does not explicate) a friendly encounter between himself and a black 'boy' he meets on the Isle of Wight, where Pascal's ship is stationed.

> While I was here [on the island], I met with a trifling incident, which surprised me agreeably. I was one day in a field belonging to a gentleman who had a black boy about my own size; this boy having observed me from his master's house, was transported at the sight of one of his own countrymen, and ran to meet me with the utmost haste. I not knowing what he was about turned a little out of his way at first, but to no purpose: he soon came close to me and caught hold of me in his arms as if I had been his brother, though we had never seen each other before. After we had talked together for some time he took me to see his master's houses, where I was treated very kindly. This benevolent boy and I were very happy in frequently seeing each other till about the month of March 1761, when our ship had orders to fit out again for another expedition … I longed to engage in new adventures and fresh wonders. (62)

---

[12]  'Although this dear youth had many slaves of his own, yet he and I have gone through many sufferings together on shipboard; and we have many nights lain in each other's bosoms when we were in great distress.' Equiano 1789, 46.

[13]  Equiano may have had other close friends whom he doesn't mention in the *Narrative*, of course. The image he presents of himself, however, is that of a person who has had to invent himself without benefit of intimate and sustained social relationships.

If the event is so 'trifling,' why does Equiano bother to describe it in some detail or register his surprise? Why does he remember it at a remove of so many years, and in what way does it contribute to his *Narrative*? He does not offer an explanation. One has the sense in reading this passage, however, that Equiano remembers and writes about the boy's effusiveness towards him because, as with Dick and Daniel Queen, his encounter with this young African reflects Equiano's desperate search for companionship, love, but most of all a sense of identification and communion with other Africans. Equiano's memory of being embraced by the unnamed black boy, chronologically the first of these three companionly encounters, suggests an idea that would be unsurprising were it not utterly unarticulated in his *Narrative*: that even years after his supposed abduction from Africa, or in any case after his separation from his natural kin, he still feels an acute loss of community combined with a sense of personal loneliness and isolation. Paradoxically, it is in the conversion chapter, ostensibly at the height of an inwardly turned and self-reflective mystical encounter, that Equiano attempts to achieve a resolution of his isolation by reenacting, and apparently bringing to a different culmination, the experience of separation from his (perhaps merely allegorical) African origins.

Equiano's entry into the English Methodist community that he eventually joins has about it, therefore, a sense of a return to, and even a symbolic reformulation of, the past. Gates has written about the archetypal 'talking book' scene in *The Interesting Narrative*, in which the young Equiano discovers, in a comic episode, that books do not 'talk' to their readers, but rather that their lexical signs must be interpreted by a cultural insider already knowledgeable about the culture's signifying codes. According to Gates, Equiano is subtly indicating in this scene that an African slave has no place in European culture: that his subjectivity is denied altogether because the culture's signs do not 'speak' of him or to him (Gates 1988, 152–8). In the conversion chapter, there is a parallel scene that Gates does not discuss, in which a Methodist minister invites Equiano to an evangelical 'lovefeast.' In confusion, he supposes that he is to attend a sumptuous banquet, but his error is soon made clear to him, and the comedic quality of the scene is conveyed to his readers. He arrives at the chapel to find it full of people who are neither eating nor drinking. They are singing, praying, testifying, and, to Equiano's greatest astonishment, 'seem to be altogether certain of their calling and election of God' (139). After bread and water are distributed, Equiano compares the congregants at the feast to 'the primitive Christians, who loved each other and broke bread' together (139). His use of the term 'primitive Christians' to describe the group is probably suggested to him by the Methodists themselves, but it is nevertheless in this context an intriguing reversal of a trope – primitiveness – whose progressivist logic comes to define Africa and Africanness for Europeans beginning in the Enlightenment period.

As in Equiano's earlier conflation of the practices of the Igbo with those of the ancient Jews, in this scene, too, Equiano reaches backwards for a model of community that he cannot find at the time of his writing. Because Equiano has never been involved in an established church and his knowledge of Christianity is largely self-taught, he himself has only passing familiarity with the doctrinal formalities of institutional Christianity in eighteenth-century England. By emphasizing the 'soul feast' as a kind of return to an originary Christian identity, Equiano is in a sense identifying the Methodists' rituals with his own predominantly textual (that is, biblical) relation to Christianity and reclaiming thereby so-called 'primitive' cultural practices. His participation in the feast is a form of cultural recuperation, therefore, that permits Equiano to posit a link between Western Christian practices and the African cultural inheritance he claims.[14] In entering into the Methodist community, Equiano finds a way to return – symbolically, at least – to the idea of Africa as the repressed Other upon which European identity is founded. Such a transvaluation of Christianity permits Equiano to signify implicitly that the only way 'back' to African origins is through a symbolic reframing of European cultural and religious codes.

In this sense, the conversion entails a reclaiming of the past as much as it heralds Equiano's first volitional entry into, and acceptance by, a community of equals. The whole drama of his life is rehearsed and refigured in the conversion, including, it seems, his white readership's unrelenting disbelief in his writing abilities and in the veracity of his story. Equiano describes a paradigmatic moment of such scepticism in the aftermath of his apocalyptic revelation. Emerging from his ship cabin after he has experienced the powerful sequence of revelatory visions, he tries to tell his shipmates about what he has experienced. '[A]las,' he laments, 'who could understand me or believe my report!' (145). His exclamatory

---

[14]  Sussman does not consider this episode in Equiano's text, but to extend her logic about cannibalism and consumer protest, this scene might also be interpreted as Equiano's rejection of the metaphorical anthropophagy implied by consumerist materialism, in favor of abolitionist (or anti-colonial) asceticism.

comment suggests the extent to which he recognizes that his religious conversion recapitulates the structure of his *Narrative* itself. Both his narrative and the conversion scene contained within it are liable to be dismissed by an audience for whom the concern with literal authenticity forecloses allegorical readings and other nonliteral forms of symbolization that posit a community of readers with a shared set of cultural references. In evoking and revising his past, the conversion scene thus also codes and decodes his present. Equiano's framing of his conversion as an allegory of memory and repression is his inventive response to the unresolved contradiction of slavery that haunts the egalitarian ideals of eighteenth-century England. The refusal of most of his Christian audience to accept the radically equitable implications of Equiano's reading of biblical source texts, however, foils the universalism that underlies his allegory and resituates Equiano as a subversive thinker and social actor.

When Equiano exasperatedly concedes, after trying to convey his revelation to the rest of the ship's crew, that 'I became a barbarian to them in talking of the love of Christ' (145), he is therefore choosing his words carefully.[15] The epithet 'barbarian,' his use of which is puzzling in this context, may be read as Equiano's suggestion that he has returned, in a sense, to an 'African' identity that is collectively shared precisely insofar as it is recognized as an historical construct. Equiano does indeed become a barbarian, one who speaks in a voice whose universal recognizability resides in the unremitting outsiderhood his text locates. His desire to be admitted as a member of a society that unself-consciously defines itself in opposition to its racial Others seems inevitably to contradict his attempt to preserve a collective slave memory of oppression and resistance. That is one reason why *The Interesting Narrative* ought to remain of interest to contemporary readers: Equiano's elaborate act of self-invention is also, just as importantly, a compelling allegory of collective identity that imagines a society in which irreducible difference becomes a basic premise of social equality.

[15]  Equiano may be indirectly citing 1 Corinthians 14:11: 'Therefore if I know not the meaning of the voice, I shall be unto him that speaketh a barbarian, and he that speaketh shall be a barbarian unto me.'

*Works Cited*

Acholonu, Catherine Obianju, 1987. 'The Home of Olaudah Equiano – a Linguistic and Anthropological Search.' *The Journal of Commonwealth Studies* 22 (1): 5–16.

Andrews, William L., 1982. 'The First Fifty Years of the Slave Narrative, 1760–1810.' In *The Art of the Slave Narrative: Original Essays in Criticism and Theory*, ed. John Sekora and Darwin T. Turner. Macomb, IL: Western Illinois University.

Benezet, Anthony, 1771. *Some Historical Account of Guinea: Its Situation, Produce, and the General Disposition of Its Inhabitants with an Inquiry into the Rise and Progress of the Slave-Trade, Its Nature and Lamentable Effects.* Philadelphia: Crukshank.

Caldwell, Tanya, 1999. 'Talking Too Much English: Languages of Economy and Politics in Equiano's *The Interesting Narrative*.' *Early American Literature* 34: 263–282.

Carey, Brycchan, 2004. '"The Hellish Means of Killing and Kidnapping:" Ignatius Sancho and the Campaign against the "Abominable Traffic for Slaves".' In *Discourses of Slavery and Abolition: Britain and its Colonies, 1760–1838*, ed. Brycchan Carey, Markman Ellis and Sara Salih. Basingstoke and New York: Palgrave Macmillan.

Carey, Brycchan, and Sara Salih, 2004. 'Introduction.' In *Discourses of Slavery and Abolition: Britain and its Colonies, 1760–1838*, ed. Brycchan Carey, Markman Ellis and Sara Salih. Basingstoke and New York: Palgrave Macmillan.

Carretta, Vincent, 2005. *Equiano, the African: Biography of a Self-Made Man.* Athens, GA: University of Georgia Press.

Chinosole, 1982. 'Tryin' to Get Over: Narrative Posture in Equiano's Autobiography.' In *The Art of Slave Narrative: Original Essays in Criticism and Theory*, ed. John Sekora and Darwin T. Turner. Macomb, IL: Western Illinois University.

Edwards, Paul, 1969. 'Introduction.' In *The Life of Olaudah Equiano, or Gustavus Vassa, the African*, ed. Paul Edwards. London: Dawsons of Pall Mall.

Ellis, Markman, 2001. 'Ignatius Sancho's Letters: Sentimental Libertinism and the Politics of Form.' In *Genius in Bondage: Literature of the Early Black Atlantic*, ed. Vincent Carretta and Philip Gould. Lexington: University Press of Kentucky.

Equiano, Olaudah, 1789. *The Interesting Narrative of the Life of Olaudah Equiano, or Gustavus Vassa, the African, Written by Himself.* Edited by Werner Sollors. 1st edn. New York: Norton, 2001.

Gates, Henry Louis, 1988. *The Signifying Monkey: A Theory of Afro-American Literary Criticism.* Oxford: Oxford University Press.

Halbwachs, Maurice, 1980. *The Collective Memory.* Trans. Francis J. Ditter Jr and Vida Yazdi Ditter. New York: Harper & Row.

Hochschild, Adam, 2005. *Bury the Chains: Prophets and Rebels in the Fight to Free an Empire's Slaves.* Boston: Houghton Mifflin.

Ogude, S. E., 1984. 'Olaudah Equiano and the Tradition of Defoe.' *African Literature Today* 14: 77–92.

Orban, Katalin, 1993. 'Dominant and Submerged Discourses in *The Life of Olaudah*

*Equiano* (or Gustavus Vassa?).' *African American Review* 27 (4): 655–664.

Potkay, Adam, 1994. 'Olaudah Equiano and the Art of Spiritual Autobiography.' *Eighteenth-Century Studies* 27: 677–90.

Smith, Valerie, 1987. *Self-Discovery and Authority in Afro-American Narrative.* Cambridge, MA: Harvard University Press.

Stein, Mark, 2004. 'Who's Afraid of Cannibals? Some Uses of the Cannibalism Trope in Olaudah Equiano's *Interesting Narrative*.' In *Discourses of Slavery and Abolition: Britain and its Colonies, 1760–1838*, ed. Brycchan Carey, Markman Ellis and Sara Salih. Basingstoke and New York: Palgrave Macmillan.

Sussman, Charlotte, 2000. *Consuming Anxieties: Consumer Protest, Gender, and British Slavery, 1713–1833.* Stanford, CA: Stanford University Press.

Thomas, Helen, 2000. *Romanticism and Slave Narratives: Transatlantic Testimonies.* Cambridge and New York: Cambridge University Press.

Wollstonecraft, Mary, 1789. 'Review.' In *Analytical Review, or History of Literature, Domestic and Foreign*, ed. Joseph Johnson. London: J. Johnson.

# Henry Smeathman and the Natural Economy of Slavery

## DEIRDRE COLEMAN

Amid all the revolutions of the globe the economy of nature has been uniform, and her laws are the only things that have resisted the general movement. The rivers and the rocks, the seas and the continents have been changed in all their parts; but the laws which direct those changes, and the rules to which they are subject, have remained invariably the same.

(from John Playfair's *Illustrations of the Huttonian Theory*, 1802; used as epigraph to Charles Lyell's *Principles of Geology*, 3 vols, 1830–33)

IN THE EIGHTEENTH CENTURY, geologists like James Hutton, early discoverers of deep time in the earth's rocks and minerals, unsettled traditional views of a static and hierarchical universe, positing instead a revolutionary and contingent world, always in flux. Despite the acceptance of this new picture of a natural world subject to constant upheaval, there were many who, like John Playfair, still counterbalanced the revolutions of time and history with the stable, eternal present of the 'economy of nature.'

Carl Linnaeus's much translated and reprinted essay of 1749, 'The Oeconomy of Nature,' is the best place to start unpacking some of the rich associations of this optimistic concept within Christian natural theology.[1] Essentially, Linnaeus identifies in the interlocking processes of propagation, preservation, and destruction the wonderful order and wise disposition of nature. God has established a cyclical pattern whereby all species coexist peacefully, constituting an enduring community in which the destruction of one thing only ever serves for the generation of another (Linnaeus 1749, 57). Even the wildest beasts, such as 'the *hawk* kind among birds' are prevented from destroying whole species, being 'circumscribed within certain bounds' through either scarcity of numbers or through preying upon each other (Linnaeus 1749, 115). While it was

---

[1] See Linnæus 1749, 39–129. The theses defended by Linnaeus's students Biberg and Wilcke were written by Linnaeus; see Stafleu 1971, 143–5. An account of the essay's wide influence is given by Worster 1996, 33–5.

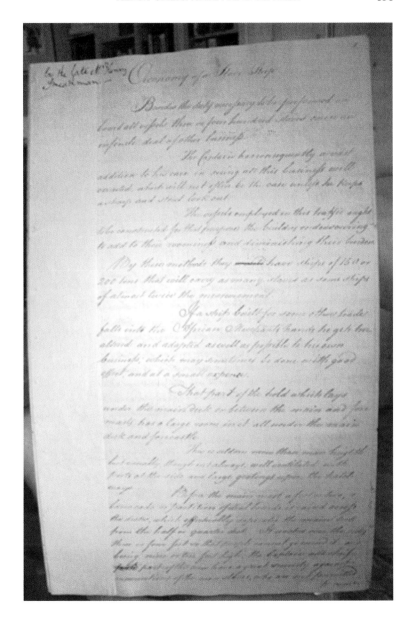

*Fig. 1.* The first page of Henry Smeathman's manuscript, 'Oeconomy of a Slave Ship'. The MS is a fair copy not in Smeathman's hand.

true that some animals appeared to be created 'only to be miserably butchered by others,' God's Providence aimed at sustaining 'a just proportion amongst all the species' (Linnaeus 1749, 119).

For Linnaeus, there was no other topic of 'such importance and dignity' as the economy of nature, employing 'almost all the powers of the mind.' In order to clinch this point at the conclusion of his essay, he appealed to the mystery and fascination of insects: 'time itself would fail before even the most acute human sagacity would be able to discover the amazing oeconomy, laws, and exquisite structure of the least insect, since as Pliny observes, nature no where appears more herself, than in her most minute works' (Linnaeus 1749, 125). That the mightiness of Linnaeus's theme should be best exemplified by the smallest of individual creatures is a theme to which he often returns, arguing in a later essay that insects exercised the greatest influence in the oeconomy of nature. Forming as they did the largest part of the animal kingdom, insects perfected nature's designs, 'preserving a due proportion amongst plants, consuming everything that is misplaced, superfluous, dead, or decayed in her productions; and lastly becoming nourishment to other animals' (Linnaeus 1773, 14–5).

Closely related to Linnaeus's concept of the 'economy of nature' is the less happy concept of the 'polity of nature' (or 'police of nature'). In his essay entitled *Politia Naturae*, Linnaeus explicitly invokes Hobbes's maxim of '*bellum omnium in omnes*' – the war of all against all (Linnaeus 1760b, 33).[2] Nature, he argues, is a tightly regulated state, wherein all species are assigned their different stations. Subordination, the preservation of species within their proper limits, the keeping up of an exact equilibrium ('due proportion') through restraint within limits, involving the curbing of both luxuriancy and destruction: these are the essay's ruling ecological themes. The translation of hierarchized regulation into the human political realm can be seen in Linnaeus's metaphors: the mosses are 'poor laborious *peasants*,' the grasses are the '*Yeomanry*,' the herbs are the '*Gentry*,' and the trees are the '*Nobility*' of the state (Linnaeus 1760c, 134–5). Man himself, 'nature's last and most distinguished servant,' has a key role to play in maintaining the balance of nature. After all, it is for his advantage and convenience that almost all things are subservient. Colossal

---

[2]    See Cap. I, § XII of Hobbes 1642, 96. F. J. Brand translated the *Politia Naturae* in 1781 but did so selectively, being annoyed that Linnaeus sometimes argued 'more like a Rhetorician than a Natural Historian'; see 'Dissertation III: On the Police of Nature,' in Linnæus 1760c; see 129–66 and especially 164–6.

whales in the ocean, ravenous predators such as lions and tigers: man must dominate all these in order to enjoy peace. He must also avoid being overwhelmed by the earth's abundance of plants, trees, fish, birds, and animals. But the natural law to which all living things are subject also rules over man, with contagious diseases raging to a greater degree in thickly populated regions, and war occurring where there is the greatest superfluity of people. Where the population increases too much, Linnaeus concludes, concord and the necessities of life decrease, and envy and malignance towards neighbours abound. Thus arises the '*war of all against all!*'(Hagberg 1952, 183; Linnaeus 1760b, 33).[3]

Despite his Hobbesian conclusion, Linnaeus worked hard to neutralize the spectacle of predators devouring their prey, the stronger always preying upon the weaker. One strategy of minimization was to emphasize that the greater often served the lesser. For instance, instead of vegetables being 'created for the food and uses of animals,' animals were created 'upon account of plants' (Linnaeus 1760c, 137). The vision of a universe subject to such regulation was determinedly a happy one. Blake's *The Book of Thel* captures the spirit of this world when Thel says enviously to the lily of the valley:

> Thy breath doth nourish the innocent lamb, he smells thy milky garments,
> He crops thy flowers. while thou sittest smiling in his face,
> Wiping his mild and meekin mouth from all contagious taints.
>                                                        (Blake 1982, 4)

There was, however, a spectre looming in the corner of Linnaeus's eye, namely species extinction. Ruled out in 'The Oeconomy of Nature' essay, the idea of extinction emerges strongly in *Politia Naturae*. Since, in the 'Great Family of Nature,' God 'has permitted nothing to be without sufficient reason,' there was good cause to fear any disruption to the workings of Nature's benign cycles of predation. For instance, 'if the species destined to prey upon any particular animal were to perish, the greatest calamities might result from it.' Such a calamity could already be seen in North America, Linnaeus writes, where human interference, namely shooting of the Quiscula (a large blackbird), had led to the total ruin of

---

[3]   The last two sentences of Cap. I read: 'Plerumque saltem aucta in uno loco multitudine, concordia rerumque copia minui, invidia atque in vicinos acerbitas invalescere videtur. Sic *Bellum omnium in omnes!*' (italics in original text). For the English translation of the paragraph, see Hagberg 1952, 183.

peas (Linnaeus 1760c, 161). A disturbance in the cycles of predation could also be seen in the human world, where man appeared as an animal whose rapacity, in William Smellie's words, 'has hardly any limitation' (Smellie 1790, I: 375). A couple of years before Smellie's book appeared, with its graphic picture of man waging war with his own kind, the idea of the extinction of the human species cropped up in the debates concerning the abolition of slavery. According to Thomas Clarkson, the Liverpool delegates giving evidence against the trade to the House of Commons calculated 'that if people were to die in the same proportion as slaves during their transportation, the whole human race would be extinct in the space of ten years' (Clarkson 1789, 31). Henry Beaufoy's Speech on the Bill for regulating the transportation of slaves from Africa made a similar calculation, stating that the destruction of the Negroes on the middle passage 'gives to the march of death seventeen times its usual speed,' and that 'if general but for *ten years* would depopulate the world' (Beaufoy 1789, 8). Such claims go far beyond Linnaeus's conclusion in *Politia Naturae* that pestilence and wars were Nature's way of curbing human populations.

The Hobbesian state of war at the heart of the polity of nature, slavery, and the centrality of insects to the grand vision underlying Linnaeus's 'economy of nature': all these are relevant to an important unpublished manuscript by the flycatcher Henry Smeathman, transcribed here for the first time.[4] Entitled 'Oeconomy of a Slave Ship,' the essay was written by Smeathman some time after arriving in Tobago in 1775, having travelled from Sierra Leone earlier that year in an 'old, rotten and crazy' ship called the *Elizabeth*. Leaking alarmingly, 'vastly crowded' with slaves, and the crew in a high state of preparedness for insurrection from below, the *Elizabeth* was a landlubber's nightmare.[5] Smeathman sent a fair copy of his essay to one of his patrons, the ornithologist Marmaduke Tunstall, and it is this copy which has survived (see fig. 1). Promising to send Tunstall a

---

[4]   I am grateful to the owner of this manuscript, Mr Michael Graves-Johnston, for permission to publish the essay and to quote from other Smeathman materials in his possession (for further details, contact Michael@gravesjohnston. demon.co.uk). For more on Smeathman's life, see Coleman 2005.

[5]   The ship which best fits Smeathman's description was built in Maryland in 1765. It left London 10 April 1775, captained by George Atcheson, embarked almost three hundred slaves, and was later condemned in Tobago as unseaworthy. For Smeathman's account of the voyage and the ship's fate, see his letter to Marmaduke Tunstall dated Tobago, 24 August 1775; for further details, see Identity Number 75405, in Eltis et al. 1999.

few exotic bird specimens in spirits on the next available fleet, Smeathman asked him in the meantime to accept the essay as a draft towards his 'Voyages and Travels,' the book which he hoped to publish on returning to England (Smeathman 1777, 3).[6]

This was not the first time Smeathman had shared with patrons eye-witness accounts of the slave system. Best known is his set-piece description of a fully slaved ship in the rains off the African coast, composed for Dru Drury and included in a letter to him of 1773.[7] Perched high up along with the captain in a specially barricadoed house affording a view over the whole deck below, Smeathman looks down from a vantage point well above the misery. His painting of the scene is a vivid one, with aesthetic effects emerging out of the horror. There is the gothic backdrop of the rain, thunder, and lightening, and a black, ironic humour about the busy-ness of suffering and dying:

> Alas! what a scene of misery and distress is a full slaved ship in the rains? The clanking of chains, the groans of the sick and the stench of the whole is scarce supportable … there was Mr. Berlin sick; a Captain too, both in the cabbin, delirious; two or three slaves thrown over board every day dying of fever, flux, measles, worms all together. All the day the chains rattling or the sound of the armourer rivetting some poor devil just arrived in galling heavy irons. The women slaves in one part beating rice in wooden mortars to cleanse it for cooking. Here the Doctor dressing sores, wounds & ulcers, or craming the men with medicines and another standing over them with a cat to make them swallow. Here they are hoisting casks, boxes & bales: the tackles creaking & the carpenter & coopers ha[mm]ering & opening. There an armourer rasping & filing and cleaning arms. Here the taylor takes a yard square for his shop board, and there the tonsor has got a fellow by the nose … The gangway is crouded with black & white sailors – belonging to boats & canoes along side. Here is fire & smoke, chopping, killing, skinning, scald[in]g, boiling, roasting, broiling, frying & scolding. (Smeathman [1772–5], 26–7.)[8]

Smeathman wrote many letters to Drury from the West African coast, all of which display a self-conscious literary style and a chummy homosocial

---

[6]   Letter to Marmaduke Tunstall dated Tobago, 28 May 1777. In private collection of Mr Michael Graves-Johnston.
[7]   This was first published in Fyfe 1964, 76–7, and subsequently in Coleman 2005, 50–2.
[8]   Letter to Dru Drury dated [Sierra Leone] 10 July 1773; reproduced in Coleman 2005, 50.

complicity concerning the highs and lows of living on the West African coast. Flycatching, slaving, sex, gardening, setting up house on the Banana Islands: these are just some of the topics covered in his letters. Although there is compassion for the suffering of the slaves brought on board, Smeathman's entomological eye is primarily trained on the superorganism of the slave ship, 'a large manufactory,' he called it, full of tradesmen cooperatively carrying out their specialist tasks. The ship's busy and productive economy stood as a welcome corrective to the constant irritant of living on the coast, namely the absence of 'oeconomy' or good household management amongst the local Africans. 'Though our stock of cattle is large', Smeathman wrote to Drury, 'our hous[e]keeping upon the whole is miserable. The truth is we have neither law, order or management, without which nothing can be done any where. "Order is heaven's first law."' (Smeathman [1772–5], 6.)[9] Indeed, so furious was Smeathman with the disorderly and 'lazy' Africans that his initial scruples concerning the slave trade evaporated, leading him to boast to Drury: 'I think it will be a meritorious act to send as many black gentry to our Plantations as I can' (Smeathman [1772–5], 13).[10] The backsliding is not so surprising given slavery's dominance of the coast's economy, and the difficulty of avoiding at least some complicity in the trade.

The manuscript appended here paints a very different slave ship from the one Smeathman had described to Drury two years earlier. After experiencing the middle passage crammed together with almost three hundred slaves on a small ship, and then seeing for himself the atrocities committed against Africans in the English colonies, the flycatcher appears to be reverting to the abolitionist sympathies with which he had originally set out for Africa in 1771, sentiments carefully taught him by his Quaker patron Dr John Fothergill. In one of the letters to Tunstall from Antigua, for instance, he refers to that 'infamous policy which degraded one species of human beings, to pamper the luxury of a few of the others' (Smeathman 1776, 5).[11] Notable here, however, is his ambivalent classification of Africans: while they are human beings, they nevertheless constitute a different 'species,' a word indicative of the shift to an increasing racialization of human variety in the later eighteenth century.[12] Similarly, when commenting upon transverse shackling on board

9   Letter to Dru Drury dated [Bananas] 22 August 1772.
10  Letter to Dru Drury dated [Bance Island] 10 May 1773.
11  Letter to Marmaduke Tunstall dated Antigua St. John, 17 June 1776.
12  See Kitson 2004.

the *Elizabeth*, where 'refractory or turbulent' slaves 'are joined right hand and right hand, and left foot and left foot', Smeathman excuses the severity as 'sometimes necessary and not so cruel, if we consider that it is seldom exacted but on fellows that were noted cut throats and great villians in their own Country.' This justification of enslavement as essentially no different from convict transportation, an argument first promoted by Edward Long in his *History of Jamaica* (1774), was to form a major part of the proslavery arsenal as abolitionism gained widespread support in the 1780s (Coleman 2005, 9–10).[13]

But the majority of the slaves on board, including many women and children, were clearly not criminals, and Smeathman's sympathy for them as suffering fellow humans is palpable, particularly in his sober, prosaic, and minute detailing of the slave ship's daily business. The slaves' degradation – the dispossession of their language, property, and identity – is made visible in the essay in very concrete forms, in their complete nakedness for reasons of hygiene and security, their food served up in mess tubs like 'Mash for a horse', and the dreadful conditions below decks where the men, chained together often without a common language, and covered in vomit, blood and excrement, sometimes killed each other in their bitter quarrels. Together with the horrors of slavery there was the pity – the inconsolable grief of the young children on board torn from their families, or the young women bartering sex with the seamen for their protection, and for a bit more space and food. There is also the droll irony of the female slaves' unwitting collusion in their own commodification, the women and girls stringing beads, a double-edged activity which 'amuses them and decorates them better for the market'. Finally, for Smeathman, there is the moving dignity of the slaves themselves, best seen in the customary 'respect to Age' which prevailed even in these terrible circumstances, and the 'great decorum' with which they ate their rations.

Notably, instead of the essay reading as the personal account of one particular voyage, 'Oeconomy of a Slave Ship' seeks greater authority by functioning at a generic, abstract level. For instance, we are not told the beginning and end point of this ship's journey; nor do we learn where in Africa the slaves have come from, or even from which part of the coast they were embarked. We also see nothing of what we know to have been the truth of this trade, that it was nasty, filthy and soaked in blood, as

---

[13]   For an excellent account of this argument in the later context of Botany Bay, see Christopher 2007.

unlike John Newton's self-serving description of 'a genteel employment'
as it is possible to imagine (Newton 1788, 95). Instead, Smeathman looks
on the scene before him with an entomologist's eye, detailing the ship's
absolutist government, the strict chain of command, the vertical stratifi-
cation of the ship's architecture and the narrowness of space, where the
female slaves on the *Elizabeth* literally get trampled underfoot on the half
and quarter decks. To this extent the essay resembles the description of
the slave ship composed for Drury. What is different is Smeathman's new
understanding that something has gone badly awry in the 'oeconomy' of
the slave ship where 'probably a fifth of the Negroes … die before the
ships reach the West Indies' and 'a much greater proportion' in less than
two years after arrival.[14] To this extent his use of the term 'oeconomy' is
ironic, for clearly there is no benign natural order underlying slavery.

   In addition to the terrible mortality, slave insurrections posed another
threat to the slave ship's 'oeconomy,' for a revolt from below could seriously damage the commercial profitability of an entire voyage. We know
from Newton's *Thoughts upon the African Slave Trade* (1788) that the fear
of insurrection was an ever-present one. Resentful of their confinement
and treatment, the slaves are received on board 'from the first as enemies
… One unguarded hour, or minute, is sufficient to give the slaves the
opportunity they are always waiting for' (Newton 1788, 102–3).[15] Shackled from the point of first loading, the slaves remained in fetters until the
ship came within sight of the West Indies. Where there were so many
blacks and so few whites, the appearance if not the reality of security was
all important. While still on the west African coast Newton records: 'This
day fixed 4 swivel blunderbusses in the barricado, which with the 2 car-
riage guns we put thro' at the Bonanoes, make a formidable appearance
upon the main deck, and will, I hope, be sufficient to intimidate the
slaves from any thoughts of an insurrection' (Newton 1750–54, 22). In

---

[14] According to Eltis et al. 1999, 54 of the 293 slaves embarked on the *Elizabeth*
died on the voyage.

[15] The idea of slavery as a state of war is familiar to us from Thomas Jefferson's
*Notes on the State of Virginia* (1784), which is totally pessimistic about the prospect of harmonious co-existence between blacks and whites, even after the abolition of slavery:

> Deep-rooted prejudices entertained by the whites; ten thousand recollections,
> by the blacks, of the injuries they have sustained; new provocations; the real
> distinctions which nature has made; and many other circumstances, will di-
> vide us into parties, and produce convulsions, which will probably never end
> but in the extermination of one or the other race. (Jefferson 1784, 138)

some ways the terrible order associated with the slave ship – captured
visually in the lower decks of the *Brooks* where the slaves lie in 'painful
rows with studious art comprest' (Stanfield 1789, 403) – projects an image of the only way in which the dangerous middle passage might be
safely conducted.

Marcus Wood has recently argued that there was a great incentive in
abolitionist writing to present the black slave as a passive, suffering victim, a figure of pathos given to despair and to suicide. There was even, he
suggests, a literary taboo over the representation of the rebellious slave
(Wood 2003, xl). Newton's published *Thoughts upon the African Slave
Trade* (1788) suggests that the topic was hardly taboo, although it is certainly true that some of the testimony heard before the House of Commons was squeamish, with several proslavery campaigners rubbishing the
evasiveness of abolitionist witnesses, some of whom referred euphemisti-
cally to 'accidents' on board ships when they were actually referring to
slave uprisings. Furthermore, the tendency for the topic of slave insurrection to veer off suddenly into slave suicide is striking. This can be seen in
Alexander Falconbridge's *Account of the Slave Trade on the Coast of Africa*
(1788), an abolitionist text which, on all other accounts, provides one of
the most graphic accounts of the horrors of the middle passage (Fyfe 2000,
214–15). Of course suicide was in some respects a form of insurrection, a
final refusal on the part of the slave to be enslaved, and like all forms of
slave rebellion, it was – if pre-empted – cruelly punished.

In writing of the middle passage, Smeathman does not touch upon
slave suicide but focuses instead on the ship's preparedness for a slave
insurrection, its readiness for an imminent outbreak of war between the
enslaved and their captors. The crew are every minute on their guard,
and the ship itself elaborately designed to forestall every avenue and opportunity for an uprising. The very idea of a balanced 'economy of nature,' driven by cosmic benevolence and a divine moral principle, has
disappeared. Like Newton, Smeathman writes of the necessity of keeping
up an appearance of security, for the Negroes are 'much over awed when
they see the crew always upon their guard, conducting things regularly,
and yet not seemingly afraid of them.' Insurrection is of course the very
opposite of equilibrium, the concept which lies so close to the heart of
Linnaeus's economy of nature. With his entomologist's eye, what
Smeathman perceives on board is not so much natural order as a 'most
strange scene of business and tumult.' The slaves may resemble the insects which had exemplified the mightiness of Linnaeus's theme, but in
the absence of liberty there can be no economy of nature. In the
imagination of one abolitionist poet, the slaves are regarded as:

Forming, like some ant-hill, a moving heap;
Tho' not, like its laborious tenants, free.

(Jamieson 1789, 398)

Finally, in terms of those conducting the slave ship's day to day 'business,' those who seek rest must do so, Smeathman writes, 'in spite of the rattling of irons, the cries of the squabblers, the groans of the sick, the clanking of the pumps, and the challenges of the watch: who every five or ten minutes put us in mind there is danger by calling out from one end of the ship to the other *alls well*.' The reassurance of *alls well* in the teeth of so much potential risk and violence captures the tension identified earlier in Linnaeus's writings, between the economy and the police of nature.

Smeathman liked to project himself in his letters as a 'speculative traveller,' a landlubber whose passion for butterflies, moths and fireflies took him to faraway places and landed him in all sorts of unexpected scrapes. 'There is nothing like travelling,' he wrote to Tunstall, 'it shows a man the world – as far as he can see in a dark night' (Smeathman 1766, 4; 1777, 2). Slavery was one of those dark nights, an experience which in some ways challenged the very power of articulation. That the flycatcher felt this difficulty can be seen in the peroration of his essay, where with 'a feeling heart' he somewhat grandly leaves his readers with nothing more than the echoed voice of some 'veteran dealer in black souls.'


[by the late Mr. Henry Smeathman]
Oeconomy of a Slave Ship

Besides the duty necessary to be performed on board all vessels three or four hundred slaves cause an infinite deal of other business.

The Captain has consequently a vast addition to his care in seeing all this business well executed, which will not often be the case unless he keeps a sharp and strict look out.

The vessels employed in this traffic ought to be constructed for that purpose the builders endeavouring to add to their roominess and diminishing their burden.

By these methods they have ships of 150 or 200 tons that will carry as many slaves as some ships of almost twice the measurement.

If a ship built for some other trade falls into the African Merchants hands he gets her altered and adapted as well as possible to his own business; which may sometimes be done with good effect, and at small expence.

That part of the hold which lays under the main deck or between the main and fore masts has a large room in it all under the main deck and forecastle.

This is seldom more than man heighth but usually, though not always, well ventilated with ports at the side and large gratings upon the hatch ways.

Before the main mast a foot or two, a barricado or partition of deal boards is raised across the decks, which effectually separates the main deck from the half or quarter deck. It reaches over the sides three or four feet so that people cannot go round it; and being nine or ten feet high, the Captain and cheif part of the crew have a great security against insurrections of the men slaves, who are not permitted to come [*page 2*] behind it or even look through it. There are two doors in this Barricado, always on the star board or right hand side. They are both together not so large as a common house door, and only permit one person to go through it at a time. The uppermost is only about the size of a small window where the Captain or any other person can stand and lean at ease to view the men upon the main deck. Buckets of provisions, and other necessary and useful things, can be delivered through it. The large door is immediately under the small one, and is opened, the latter being then shut, to let any of the crew pass. The whole partition is strong and the doors fasten on the afterside with strong bolts.

Before the Barricado the cheif mate takes his station, with sometimes the Boatswain or some other man to assist him. The cheif of his business is to examine the men night and morning to see that they have not cut or filed their irons or got loose, on which account they are not suffered to come up at pleasure, but are compelled to come singly or in pairs up a skuttle in the gratings, which will not admit of more at a time: being examined and the irons found fast and right, a long heavy chain called a main deck chain is reeved through the legs of a man who is single in leg irons, but between the men who are in pairs. The cheif part indeed are usually fettered in pairs in this manner. The two negroes being set upon the deck side by side; the two arms which are nearest as the right arm of the one and the left of the other are put into one pair of hand-cuffs. In the like manner the right leg of the one is joined to the left of the other in one pair of leg irons. So that they incommode each other as little as possible in such disagreable circumstances. But if they are refractory or turbulent they have sometimes not only stronger and heavier fetters but are joined right hand and right hand, and left foot and left foot, which must [*page 3*] needs embarrass them exceedingly, and leave little use of mischevious limbs. This severity is sometimes necessary and not so cruel, if we consider that it is seldom exacted but on fellows that were noted cut throats and great villians in their own Country; and still more rarely, unless they have been found plotting some roguery.

About 9 o'clock in the morning, when the sun has dried up the damp left after washing the decks, is usually the time when they are brought upon deck. The surgeon attending to examine whether they have been taken ill in the night, and to see how his patients are.

All the men being got up and as it were strung together in two chains, one on each side the deck, the ends of the chains are put through a small hole in the bottom of the barricado, and locked upon the quarter deck. The Surgeon begins to dress ulcerated and sore patients, and to give physick or drams as they may come in course. Under the main deck there is generally also a smaller room where the youths (termed by the Traders Men-Boys) and the boys sleep. Then the mate and Boatswain set to work to empty the tubs of filth to wash out and clean the rooms to smoak them with Tobacco, oakum and other antiseptic things; and sprinkle with vinegar &c.

Before or when the men begin to come upon deck, two *Sentries* mount guard upon a stage behind the Barricado at the top, with musquets and bayonets; where they over look the whole deck; and one at the door of the Barricado with a naked cutlass. This man officiates as porter to the door.

When anyone before the partition knocks, he opens the little door to know what he wants and passes the business aft. If the [*page 4*] person knocking wants to come aft, the Centinel shuts the small door and bolts it, and then opens the larger one, which is yet so little you must stoop to go through. Where there is a necessity for greater caution, the centinel does not open the little door, but opens a little loop hole close to the door, through which he can peep and demand who knocks.

All these precautions if not always necessary are yet proper. The negroes are much over awed when they see the crew always upon their guard, conducting things regularly, and yet not seemingly afraid of them.

It is seldom that any more people than the three before mentioned white men the Mate, Surgeon and Boatswain are suffered at a time before the Barricado, otherwise the men slaves might seize half the crew on the sudden, and soon become masters of the vessel.

Above all it is highly improper for the Captain to venture forward among the men, as they generally have an idea that demolishing him is three fourths of a victory. The Captain therefore only views them from the stage behind the Barricado, or through the little door, where he can enquire what they want in safety. His business is upon the Quarter Deck, from whence he looks down upon the half deck where the whole duty of the vessel passes under his eye.

Here is a most strange scene of business and tumult which will require much labour and perspicuity to describe justly.

The man who cheifly attracts our notice in this confused group, is the Cook; an officer of no small importance; who may [*page 5*] be said to make a great noise in the world; for he is sawing and splitting wood half the day, and with three or four or half a dozen black wenches, pounding, washing, and boiling rice in an immense large cauldron; besides which he has a *Cub house,* or little hutch, which contains a fire place, where he boils, roasts, broils, and fricassees after a fashion for the Captain's Table and the Crew. One would imagine that a kitchen for three or four hundred people ought to be a large roomy place.

The Cooks in this Trade are well off to find 10 or 12 feet square, and this only occasionally, in which to carry on their useful business. By the time that tea and toast have been dispatched in the cabbin, or soon after, the Cook gives notice that the victuals for the slaves are ready. These consist of Rice Horse Beans or peas as the ship can afford them and are varied as much as possible. To relish this insipid food they have salt and country pepper – the Cayenne pepper or Capsicum, and sometimes a little morsel of salt fish boiled with it, the quantity of half a pound or a pound to a mess of ten slaves, and if they have been able to procure enough they add a small quantity of Palm Oil, which is much superior in delicacy and flavour to butter or Olive oil, and a most wholesome corrective to vegetable diet. The Officers call out Messie Messie – on which the poor creatures form themselves into Messes of ten. A boy slave or two, then march round amongst them with a bucket of water and a small cann, and pour a little into the right hand of everyone as they sit, which they wash by moving their thumb and finger, without any assistance from their left hand, as it is never used in feeding, being employed when necessary in removing any dirt or filth and all such like occasions, and they take a little to wash their mouths.

This [*page 6*] done instead of a Towel they snap their fingers, and giving their hands a shake at the same time leave the wind to dry them, and rest them upon their knees, without making any use of them untill their victuals is served; which is done in tubs something less than a common pail, which gives it much the appearance of a Mash for a horse. The oldest Slave in the Mess[, ] for they are accustomed to pay great respect to Age, divides the little morsel of fish very equally amongst them.

This they generally lay on one side as a *bon bouche* as children hoard the raisins of plumb pudding, and dipping their hands into the tub with great decorum, take up about the quantity of a spoonful more or less, which turning and squeezing in their fingers till it is cool and compact they convey it to their mouths and eat with apparent satisfaction: exceeding happy if they find it holds out well and is not finished before their bellies are filled. This done their Mess Tubs are taken away, water is given them, as before, to wash, and generally as much as they choose to drink. During the Forenoon they are amused with singing and dancing. Tobacco is given to them to make into snuff, and if the weather is fine water is hoisted in upon deck to the men who are allowed to wash and splash very plentifully, and after that they are all fit to work to dance, some Arch boy or man being coaxed to sing them a country song and give them the step.

When dried they are sometimes served with Palm Oil of which they are exceeding fond to anoint themselves with. The women and girls are generally washing half the day, in a scaffold built on the side of the half deck on purpose for them to retire to; and the boys do the same on the forecastle. [*page 7*]

The officers and seamen having dined, the Captain treats the Slaves, he delivers by his Seamen a biscuit or two to each man, or stands on the Barricado and pitches them round, and they show their dexterity, catching like Monkeys. The Women have theirs likewise delivered to them aft of the Barricado, but the boys are drawn up on the Main deck and handfulls of broken biscuit thrown amongst them to scramble for, which produces a deal of mirth and amusement for the time, while the women are entertained in the same manner by the girls. After this a drum or an empty cask or a tub is introduced; while one beats, another sings, and all the rest dance and join in chorus, and those which signalise themselves most stand a chance for the best drams of Rum or Brandy sometimes of Bitters. Thus they are kept in spirits and exercised as much as possible, that they may have little time to reflect, and grow Mellancholy, or loose the functions of the body, and become diseased. Yet all these precautions often fail and upon an average probably a fifth of the Negroes bought by the white Traders in Guinea die before the ships reach the West Indies, after they arrive a much greater proportion die in less than two years; for a Planter who I can depend upon had only six slaves left out of forty five, which he had bought about nineteen months before.

[*In margin*] – After they have performed the exercises and pretty well rested about four in the afternoon their second meal is served in the same manner as that in the morning and before the sun[set] they are put down below to take their rest if they choose it thus finishing the multifarious day.

The women and girls sleep in a room, called the steerage, under the half deck behind the barricado; and in the day time [*page 8*] they sit about that and the quarter deck, as chance or choice disposes them; but so thick, that it is a matter of difficulty, sometimes, to get across the deck without treading on them. The cook would be much circumscribed in his department, if he was not as troublesome to such as encroach upon it, as they can be in impeding him. In a leaky ship as I have experienced in the *Elizabeth*, a pump or sometimes two on each side the main mast, working night and day afford abundance of amusement and subject for reflection to a speculative passenger. We are frequently disturbed in the night with the quarrelling of some of the savage slaves who bite and tear, and would kill one another if not quelled, notwithstanding the readiest interference, they sometimes come too late and have a dead man to bring up. As the women and girls sleep together we have generally the most disturbance from [them]; they are continually quarrelling; and the young and help-less, get many bitter and horrible beatings, which aggravated frequently by the reflection of having been torn from tender friends or relations, and the dreadful inconveniences they then suffer, renders them almost inconsolable, and their lamentable cries would affect the most obdurate heart with pity and compassion. The officers are obliged to coax and defend them, and usually take as many of the smallest and most helpless into the cabbin as they can stow in it. The handsome young women are generally under the protection of the Captain, officers, and passengers; and some times, every seaman has his Favourite, with whom he shares his hammock and his allowance.

Before the sun gets low enough to make the weather feel cool, the slaves are to be sent down, for they are all entirely naked, except the grown women, some few of whom, the favourites, are treated by their Gallants with a fathom of cloth to throw round them, and others are allowed a small strip a mere modesty piece [*page 9*] which hangs before them from a string which is tied round their waists. Sometimes it is long enough to go under their bodies, and reaches to the string behind where it is again tied.

The men the boys and the girls are not suffered to have a rag about them except a little bag in which they keep their pepper their salt and their allowance of Tobacco.

The men would have an opportunity of concealing knives and dangerous things, if they had any sort of cloaths, and the whole would get full of vermin and dirt.

If the women or girls have a few strings of beads round them, they are permitted: glass and polished stones cannot accumulate much dirt. Sometimes beads are given out to them to string according to their fancy; it amuses them and decorates them better for the market. Instead of a Table, a cushion, or a peg to work at, they tie one end of the string to their great toe, which is a substitute for a third hand on many occasions.

The signal being given, All hands muster, the women and children are soon driven to their apartments.

The Mate, Surgeon, and Boatswain and two or three stout hands attend at the hatch way forward; the chain is unlocked behind the Barricado and drawn forward; and the men taken off by ones and two's, as your cooks take large or small game off the spit, and examined that their irons are fast, that they are not chaffed by them, and that they do not carry any thing below with them that they may cut the irons, or enable them to do any mischief. One couple examined and gone down, another is taken off; all their complaints are heared, and such as are sick kept upon deck and put into the sick room, or boat, well covered with Sails and blankets, [page 10] and proper medicines and refreshments are or ought to be given them. The Hatches are made fast with iron barrs and locked, the Barricado doors are thrown open and the Captain and all hands walk forward and where they please to stretch their leggs. They then go to work[, ] draw water and wash the decks, very well, and before the watches are set, take in studding and stay sails, and such canvas as they think may embarrass them in case of a sudden change of weather. Supper is served; and that over, one after another they either take an evening walk, or skulk into their cots or hammocks, and seek for rest in spite of the rattling of irons, the cries of the squabblers, the groans of the sick, the clanking of the pumps, and the challenges of the watch; who every five or ten minutes put us in mind there is danger by calling out from one end of the ship to the other *alls well*. Sometimes the watch use the following method.

The officer upon the Quarter Deck calls out, *Look out a Midships there*, which one of the watch takes up on the main Deck and calls out, *Look out forward there*. The man on the forecastle returns, *Look out Aft there*. On which the whole watch answer together *Ay! Ay!* As these ways of challenging are always sung out with a tone peculiar to Seamen, it has rather a pleasing [air] of solemnity when four or five ships are laying near together in a Harbour, in a calm night, as the challenges are circulated from ship to ship, in tones and manner as different as the beings who utter them. Some wakeful Officer calls out, with an air of command; the sleepy seaman returns [*page 11*] it, as if he was all alive that the officer may not suspect him of nodding, the unhappy boy screams it out in a shrill treble, the sickly watches who languish under a variety of fatigue, hunger, disease, wet, beatings and other ill usage, pour out their *Alls well*, in a plaintive tenor that belies their tongue, and excites strong ideas of distress in a feeling heart; while some veteran dealer in black souls, roars out in a stentorial bass, that all the Bay resounds; and the trembling desart echoes back the rumbling growl.

## Works Cited

Beaufoy, Henry, 1789. *The Speech of Mr. Beaufoy, Tuesday, the 18th June, 1788, in a Committee of the Whole House, on a Bill for Regulating the Conveyance of Negroes from Africa to the West-Indies. To Which are added Observations on the Evidence adduced against the Bill.* London: Printed by J. Phillips.

Blake, William, 1982. *The Book of Thel*, in David V. Erdman, ed., *The Complete Poetry and Prose of William Blake*. Rev. edn. Berkeley and Los Angeles: University of California Press, 1789.

Christopher, Emma, 2007. "'The slave trade is merciful compared to [this]": Slave Traders, Convict Transportation and the Abolitionists,' in *Many Middle Passages*, ed. Marcus Rediker, Cassandra Pybus and Emma Christopher. Berkeley: University of California Press.

Clarkson, Thomas, 1789. *An Essay on the Comparative Efficiency of Regulation or Abolition, as applied to the Slave Trade: Shewing that the Latter only can remove the Evils to be found in that Commerce.* London: Printed by James Phillips.

Coleman, Deirdre, 2005. *Romantic Colonization and British Anti-slavery.* Cambridge: Cambridge University Press.

Eltis, David, Stephen D. Behrendt, David Richardson, and Herbert S. Klein, eds, 1999. *The Trans-Atlantic Slave Trade: A Database on CD-ROM.* Cambridge: Cambridge University Press.

Fyfe, Christopher, 1964. *Sierra Leone Inheritance.* London: Oxford University Press.

Fyfe, Christopher, ed., 2000. *Anna Maria Falconbridge, Narrative of Two Voyages to the River Sierra Leone, with Alexander Falconbridge, An Account of the Slave Trade on the coast of Africa.* Liverpool: Liverpool University Press.

Hagberg, Knut, 1952. *Carl Linnæus*, trans. Alan Blair. London: Jonathan Cape.

Hobbes, Thomas, 1642. *De Cive: The Latin Version, entitled in the first edition* Elementorum Philosophiæ Sectio Tertia De Cive, *and in later editions* Elementa Philosophica de Cive; *A Critical Edition*, ed. Howard Warrender. (The Clarendon Edition of the Philosophical Works of Thomas Hobbes; II.) Oxford: Clarendon Press, 1983.

Jamieson, John, 1789. *The Sorrows of Slavery, A Poem: Containing a faithful statement of facts respecting the African slave trade*, in *Amazing Grace: An Anthology of Poems about Slavery, 1660–1810*, ed. James G. Basker. Yale University Press, 2002.

Jefferson, Thomas, 1784. *Notes on the State of Virginia*, in *The Life and Writings of Thomas Jefferson*, ed. A. Koch and W. Peden. New York: Modern Library, 1993.

Kitson, Peter, 2004. '"Candid Reflections": The Idea of Race in the Debate over the Slave Trade and Slavery in the Late Eighteenth and Early Nineteenth Century,' in Brycchan Carey, Markman Ellis, and Sara Salih, eds, *Discourses of Slavery and Abolition: Britain and its Colonies, 1760–1938*. Basingstoke and New York: Palgrave Macmillan.

Linnaeus, Carl, 1749. 'The Œconomy of Nature. By Isaac J. Biberg,' in Benjamin Stillingfleet, *Miscellaneous Tracts relating to Natural History, Husbandry, and Physick: To which is added the Calendar of Flora by Benj. Stillingfleet*, 1759; 3rd edn., 32–129. London: Printed for J. Dodsley, Baker and Leigh, and T. Payne, 1775.

Linnaeus, Carl, 1760a. [*Politia Naturae.*] *Dissertatio academica de Politia naturae, quam consens. experient. Facult. Medic. in Reg. Academ. Upsaliensi, praeside viro nobilissimo atque experientissimo Dn. Doct. Carolo Linnaeo … publico examini submittit H. Christ. Daniel Wilcke, Stockholmiensis. In Audit. Car. Maj. Die XXIX. Martii, Anni MDCCLX*. Upsaliae.

Linnaeus, Carl, 1760b. *Politia Naturæ*, in *Caroli Linnæi, Amoenitates Academicæ; seu, Dissertationes Variæ, Physicæ, Medicæ, Botanicæ, Antehac feorsim editæ, niunc collectæ & auctæ, cum tabuli Æneis, Lugduni Batavorum, Apud. Wetstenium*, Vol. 6. Stockholm: Laurentius Salvius, 1764.

Linnaeus, Carl, 1760c. [*Politia Naturae.*] F. J. Brand (trans.), 'Dissertation III: On the Police of Nature,' in *Select Dissertations from the Amœnitates Academicæ: A Supplement to Mr. Stillingfleet's Tracts relating to Natural History*. London: G. Robinson and J. Robson, 1781.

Linnaeus, Carl, 1773. *Institutions of Entomology: Being a Translation of Linnaeus's Ordines et Genera Insectorum; or, Systematic Arrangement of Insects*, trans. Thomas Pattinson Yeats. London: R. Horsfield.

Long, Edward, 1774. *The History of Jamaica; or, General Survey of the Antient and Modern State of that Island*, 3 vols. London: T. Lowndes.

Lyell, Charles, 1830–3. *Principles of Geology: An Attempt to Explain the former Changes of the Earth's Surface, by Reference to Causes now in Operation*, 3 vols. London: John Murray.

Newton, John, 1750–4. *The Journal of a Slave Trader*, in *The Journal of a Slave Trader (John Newton), 1750–1754, with Newton's Thoughts upon the African Slave Trade*, ed. Bernard Martin and Mark Spurrell. London: Epworth Press, 1962.

Newton, John, 1788. *Thoughts upon the African Slave Trade*, in *The Journal of a Slave Trader (John Newton), 1750–1754, with Newton's Thoughts upon the African Slave Trade*, ed. Bernard Martin and Mark Spurrell. London: Epworth Press, 1962.

Sebald, W. G., 1999. *On the Natural History of Destruction; with essays on Alfred Andersch, Jean Amery and Peter Weiss*, trans. Anthea Bell. Harmondsworth: Penguin Books, 2004.

Smeathman, Henry, [1772–5]. 'Extracts from Mr Smeathman's Letters to Mr

Drury,' [contemporary copies], MS D.26, University Library, Uppsala.

Smeathman, Henry, [after 1775]. 'Oeconomy of a Slave-Ship.' [Contemporary manuscript copy; collection of Mr Michael Graves-Johnston, London.]

Smeathman, Henry, 1776. Henry Smeathman to Marmaduke Tunstall, Antigua St John, 17 June 1776. [Autograph; collection Mr Michael Graves-Johnston, London.]

Smeathman, Henry, 1777. Henry Smeathman to Marmaduke Tunstall, Tobago, 28 May 1777. [Autograph; collection Mr Michael Graves-Johnston, London.]

Smellie, William, 1790. *The Philosophy of Natural History*, 2 vols, Edinburgh, 1790 and 1799; repr., intro. Paul Wood. Bristol: Thoemmes Press, 2001.

Stafleu, Frans Antonie, 1971. *Linnaeus and the Linnaeans: The Spreading of their Ideas in Systematic Botany, 1735–1789*. (Regnum vegetabile; 79.) Utrecht: Oosthoek, for the International Association for Plant Taxonomy.

Stanfield, James Field, 1789. *The Guinea Voyage. A Poem. In Three Books*, in *Amazing Grace: An Anthology of Poems about Slavery*, ed. James G. Basker. Yale University Press, 2002.

Wood, Marcus, 2003. 'English and North American Slavery: Key Notes on Cultural and Historical Difference,' in Marcus Wood, ed., *The Poetry of Slavery: An Anglo-American Anthology, 1764–1865*. Oxford: Oxford University Press.

Worster, Donald, 1996. *Nature's Economy: A History of Ecological Ideas*. 2nd edn. Cambridge: Cambridge University Press.

# Slavery, Blackness and Islam: The Arabian Nights in the Eighteenth Century

FELICITY A. NUSSBAUM

## Slavery in the Orient

MODERNITY DID NOT form itself unilaterally or in isolation but through a complex circulation, translation, and interpenetration of texts. The abolition movement and orientalism – or more generally, imperialism – are frequently yoked together as two contemporaneous signs of modernity but seldom as objects of analysis. The year 2007 marks the anniversary of two seemingly disparate events. It commemorates the British Abolition Act of 1807, while it also comes roughly three hundred years after the French (1704–1717) and English (1706–1721) translations of the *Arabian Nights' Entertainments*. How, we might ask, does the British slave trade in the eighteenth century relate to the translation of oriental tales into the languages of the two major European imperialist forces? The subject of abolition is, in large part, the Negro from sub-Saharan Africa, while the subject of orientalism inhabits the East Indies, China, the Levant and the Barbary Coast. The two geographical regions serve different imaginative purposes for Europe: sub-Saharan Africa is most often represented as a lucrative source for slaves rather than as a threat to the polity of England and France, while the Islamic world, perceived as more potent even in decline, offered an alluring model of empire combined with a menacing eschatology. 'Apparently,' wrote Richard F. Burton in his 1885 preface to *The Arabian Nights*, 'England is ever forgetting that she is at present the greatest Mohammedan empire in the world' (Burton 2001, xxxvi).

Placing the anniversaries of British abolition and the publication of the *Nights* in juxtaposition creates an opportunity to consider the contradictions and parallels between oriental and black subjects, and between eighteenth-century attitudes toward imperialism and the antislavery movement. For example, recent investigations into Edmund Burke's political theory have suggested that he was an anti-imperialist in India and the Americas, but his views on the 'Negro question' – the status of slaves, abolition and racial equality – were less progressive. At the same time that Burke opposed British imperial goals in India, most famously during

the Warren Hastings trial, he apparently supported an 'expansionist' position in the Americas to civilize the savages of the West Indies and the
Americas. Others have pointed toward England's anti-slavery imperialism that established the freed slave colonies of Sierra Leone and Liberia
in part as a means to penetrate Africa and encourage trade. The abolitionist cause may also have been manipulated as an imperialist weapon
in the case of England's employing antislavery arguments as a ploy against
France in the West Indies to heighten their own opportunities for expansion. In addition, the East India Company joined forces with the antislavery lobby late in the century to improve profits in sugar (Kohn and
O'Neill 2006; Kitson 1999).

The history of manumission differs not only within Africa and the
Islamic world, but between France and England as well. France first abolished slavery in 1794, in part to appease England and to interrupt the
slave insurrection in the Antilles, but in 1802 Napoleon re-established it
at the request of his Mozambiquan wife. The law was not repealed until
1848, fifteen years after England's abolition of slavery. Britain pressured
Barbary Coast Muslims to abolish the enslavement of European Christians,
and they were finally successful in 1816.[1] Indian Ocean slavery ports remained active until well into the second half of the nineteenth century.

*The Arabian Nights*, raising critical questions regarding the circulation, translation and transformation of narrative across national boundaries, offers fables of empire while it interweaves stories of slavery and
blackness. While we most often identify slavery with the Atlantic trade,
slaves in *The Arabian Nights* inhabit a different history from plantation
slaves and do not fit easily into abolitionist discourse: they were more
frequently domestic or military; they experienced greater opportunity for
manumission; and though after 1807 the British put increased pressure
on the Islamic world to stop trading, their status was not affected by England and France declaring the end of the slave trade. The particular
characteristics of slavery within Africa and elsewhere varied significantly.[2]

Like creolization, métissage, mestizaje and hybridity, the black diaspora
– as Paul Gilroy has argued in his influential *The Black Atlantic: Modernity
and Double-Consciousness* – transcends the limitations of ethnic identity

[1]   Carretta 2005, 21 notes that Brazil ended slavery only about a century ago,
and Saudi Arabia finally in 1970.
[2]   For example, though Olaudah Equiano's own credibility regarding first-hand
knowledge of Africa has been seriously questioned, he described the conditions
in West Africa, where slaves were treated as near-equals and could even possess
slaves, as quite distinct from those in the West Indies (Equiano 1995, 39–40).

or the nation state. For Gilroy, the African slaves' experience of natal
displacement and transportation across the Atlantic Ocean unites them
in history, no matter what geographical territory or nation they derived
from. In creating the important concept of the Black Atlantic, Gilroy
limits the African diaspora principally to the Western hemisphere, but
the substantial trade in the Indo-Pacific demands extending the concept
well beyond the Atlantic. The traffic in slaves in the Muslim world began earlier and continued longer than Atlantic slavery (Bairoch 1993,
204). The African diaspora extended across the Red Sea (even into China)
and from North Africa (especially Libya) and East Africa (especially the
Indian Ocean port Kilwa) across the Indian and Pacific Oceans by way of
the North African Islamic slave trade that captured slaves, rivalling in
numbers the Black Atlantic market, to sell them for profit.[3] Islamic traders populated territories to the south, north and east.[4] The practice of taking black slaves to India from Ethiopia and other African territories probably begins in the eighth century (Segal 2001; Lewis 1990). Large numbers
of black Africans had a substantial presence in Italy, Spain and Portugal
during the fifteen and sixteenth centuries.[5] While eleven or twelve million Africans were sent to the Americas from the sixteenth through the
nineteenth centuries, Islamic slave traders conveyed another twelve million Africans across the Sahara desert, as well as the Indian and Pacific
Oceans. In the three sectors of trade in the eighteenth century, approxi-
mately 700,000 were transported across the Sahara, perhaps 200,000 from
the coast of the Red Sea and 400,000 from East Africa (Segal 2001, 55–
57). Black slaves were taken to the Islamic territory 'from West Africa
across the Sahara to Morocco and Tunisia, from Chad across the desert to
Libya, from East Africa down the Nile to Egypt, and across the Red Sea and
Indian Ocean to Arabia and the Persian Gulf' (R. Davis 2003, 9).

[3]  R. Davis 2003, XXV finds that slavery in the Mediterranean and the Atlantic
both date from as early as the final Spanish conquest of Granada in 1492 that
expelled Moors from southern Spain. Skeletons of Ghanaian slaves recently found
in Mexico derive from as early as the late sixteenth century (*Los Angeles Times* 4
Feb. 2006).
[4]  Segal 2001, 146 remarks, 'During the eighteenth century, Kilwa had become
East Africa's principal port for the export of slaves, drawn initially from south-
eastern Tanganyika and then increasingly from the region of Lake Nyasa'. Some
went to the Middle East and others to Zanzibar.
[5]  Rabb 2006, 12 shows that 'Africans made up as much as 10 per cent of the
population [in Iberian cities]; in the Algarve the proportion was probably even
higher. For outsiders, the African presence was so astonishing that it seemed to
be larger than it was; to one Flemish visitor to Lisbon in the 1530s, it seemed as
if the slave population outnumbered the Portuguese.'

The practices of slavery varied throughout Africa, and the linkage to skin colour, while much debated, is not secure. Bernard Lewis, for example, has claimed that 'for much of Islamic history ... there was no such virtually exclusive identification of slavery with blackness as came to exist in the Christian West with colonial expansion and Atlantic Trade' (Lewis 1990, 49).[6] The captivity and ransoming of Europeans visiting North Africa during the seventeenth and eighteenth centuries took place without regard to skin colour or religion, as Linda Colley, Robert C. Davis and Nabil Matar have documented.[7] David Brion Davis has argued that 'the continuing enslavement of Christians by Muslims and of Muslims by Christians actually conditioned both groups to accept the institution of slavery on a wider scale and thus prepared the way for the vast Atlantic slave system'(D.B. Davis 2001, 51). One crucial distinction between the Atlantic and Islamic trade was between employing slaves for commercial and domestic purposes (Segal 2001, 107). Both black and white Islamic slaves provided personal or household service, and their duties sometimes included sexual servicing for the men and, perhaps more clandestinely, for the women. Many served in the military and in the governments of Muslim rulers. Biographical accounts of specific Muslim slaves, Mandingoes and Fulani, who awaited exportation in Dahomey, Gorée and Sierra Leone can be found in historical documents (Fisher 2001, 31). The Ottomans held three million slaves, Nubians contracted to deliver hundreds of slaves each year to Iraq and Zanzibar became a crucial Arab-Persian Gulf post for conducting the slave trade. Malta, possessing perhaps 10,000 Muslim slaves in 1720, also served as a centre for trade with the North African ports of Tunis and Tripoli on the Mediterranean. Norman Robert Bennett notes that while Moroccan ruler Mulay Isma'il sought Negro slaves, his successor Sidi Muhammad (1757–90) disbanded the Negro slave armies and 'tawny nurseries' at the beginning of his reign and scattered large numbers of sub-Saharan Africans throughout Morocco (Bennett 1960). A formal declaration of emancipation by a Muslim ruler did not occur until 1846 when the bey of Tunis granted a deed of enfranchisement to black slaves.[8]

---

[6]   Among the growing number of studies of slavery in Africa are Fisher 2001; Manning 1990; Lovejoy 1983, reissued 2000; and Willis 1985.
[7]   According to R. Davis 2003, 26, Barbary ports offered an 'amalgam of Moorish, Berber, and sub-Saharan peoples.'
[8]   Lewis 1990, 79 indicates that 'The first Muslim ruler to order the emancipation of black slaves was the bey of Tunis, who in January 1846 decreed that a deed of enfranchisement should be given to every slave who desired it.'

Being Muslim made slavery somewhat problematic, especially in a person who was originally free, but it did not preclude slavery. Though some interpreted Muslim law as outlawing the enslavement of a fellow Muslim, the practice of freeing a convert to Islam was not consistently followed. In addition, because manumission could in some instances be earned after a specific number of years, the slaves' situation sometimes resembled that of indentured servants. Religious piety, the death of one's master or purchasing one's freedom were all possible opportunities for changing status. Slaves were also awarded as the spoils of war and enlisted in their owners' military campaigns; they served as highly valued luxury items, as gifts or currency. Similarly, Muslim rulers created, owned and distributed eunuchs as part of a royal monopoly that was only occasionally extended to the nobility and other elites (Fisher 2001, 292). In short, slavery and its legacy are not extraneous to the Orient but endemic to it.

## The Arabian Nights

*The Arabian Nights* (known as *Alf layla wa-layla* in some Arabic versions) in its European translations presents a rich text for speculating about the cultural work that its representations of slavery and blackness accomplish, from the first rumblings of ameliorist sentiments to the full-blown public debates about abolition that accompanied imperialist ambitions in India and elsewhere. As I have shown, colonial desires did not always go hand-in-hand with antislavery attitudes, nor did the abolition movement and racial equality always run parallel.[9] Interpreted in part as a description of Persia's imperial glory and thus stimulating comparisons between the nascent English and French empires and past empires, *The Arabian Nights* included tales that illustrated the achievement of sovereignty through violence, force, and magical events. Introducing both imperial power and slavery in an Eastern setting, the opening lines of the frame tale in the *Nights* recount 'the chronicles of the Susanians, the ancient kings of Persia, who extended their empire into the Indies, over all the islands therunto [*sic*] belonging, a great way beyond the Ganges and as far as China' (Mack 1995, 1). The Persian King Schahriar and his

---

[9]   Muthu 2003 seeks to recuperate the idea that in the late eighteenth century, as opposed to the nineteenth century, empire was not universally defended in Europe by thinkers such as Burke, Herder, and Kant.

brother Schahzenan divide the lands in their possession (the elder taking the larger portion) between them. Both rulers are infuriated when they learn of the adulterous liaisons of their wives with the men servants in the palace, and Scheherazade, Schahriar's daring new mistress, begins the cycle of tale telling in order to stave off her own murder. *The Arabian Nights* are, then, launched by the Persian kings' sexual jealousy of the black African slaves who cuckold them: imperial holdings are jeopardized by the philandering of their wives. Muslim women of a certain class in *The Arabian Nights* gain agency and exercise personal independence in consorting with racially differentiated men who are usually their social inferiors, but Scheherazade is the heroic exception in gathering power to herself instead through narration. In *The Arabian Nights*, Scheherazade weaves her magical tales night after night and ultimately turns the Sultan Schahrir into a lover of fiction and a reformed misogynist. In the conclusion to Galland's version, the power of Scheherazade's tales transforms the Sultan into believing that he had erred in killing his former wives, and he finally marries Scheherazade who apparently worries little about the Sultan's potential for suffering a relapse into his earlier murderous state of mind. In later versions, Scheherazade's having borne the sultan three children contributes to his change of heart.

This collection of tales told by Scheherazade to King Schahriar is made somewhat coherent because of its sometimes vaguely defined but relatively consistent Islamic religious practices and loyalties. Transcribed from many different languages and holding in conjunction multiple geographical locations, *The Arabian Nights* also reflects multiple temporalities at once, having been written, translated and interpreted over a thousand years. *The Nights* has had something of a revival of critical attention of late, sparked initially by Robert Mack's 1995 Oxford edition of the so-called Grub Street version, and closely followed by A.S. Byatt's 2001 edition of Richard Burton's 1885 translation. Known variously as *A Thousand and One Nights*, *The Arabian Nights*, and the *Arabian Nights Entertainment*, the tales defy clear description and simple generic classification since they are not only, or exactly, translations or interpretations but sometimes much altered or expanded. They represent a wide range of stories deriving from Persia in the ninth century, Baghdad in the mid-eighth century and Cairo in the twelfth to fourteenth centuries. 'How old are the *Arabian Nights*?' asks Robert Irwin. 'Should it be the Persian prototype, the *Hazar Afsaneh*? Or the ninth-century *Thousand Nights*, of which a few scrappy lines survive? Or *The Thousand and One Nights*, referred to in the twelfth century, but of which not even a few scrappy lines survive? Or the purely hypothetical thirteenth-century Syrian source manuscript? Or the Galland manuscript, which was written in either the fourteenth or the fifteenth century? Or the fuller version of the *Nights*, translated by Lane and Burton, which were filled out with all sorts of ancient and recent stories ... some time between the fifteenth and the early nineteenth centuries?' (Irwin 1994, 62). Many of the tales are thus at once nostalgic and modern, blending past and present in a temporal contact zone that often makes it difficult to know where one leaves off and the other begins. In the French and English translations there is similarly a blurred line between Arabic and European language sources in which the influence of cultures and religions are fused and blended with each other.

The many editions of the entire *Arabian Nights*, deriving from oral tradition as well as the multiple abridgements, extractions and revisions, reveal how much the purportedly unchanging Orient alters over the course of the eighteenth and nineteenth centuries. More than twenty different English editions appeared before the turn of the eighteenth century, and more than forty during the nineteenth. In addition to French and English versions, *The Arabian Nights* were published during the eighteenth and nineteenth centuries in Arabic, Bengali, Dutch, Danish, Greek, Hebrew, Italian, Polish, Spanish, Swedish, Turkish, Urdu and Yiddish. Galland, the first European translator of *The Nights*, learned Arabic, Persian, Turkish and Greek to cope with the linguistic palimpsest. Endlessly repeated, modified and rewoven, the tales were finally written down from various sources in French, some of them almost certainly through oral transmission, by Antoine Galland (1646–1715), beginning in 1704. A professor of Arabic, and an assistant to Barthélemy d'Herbelot whose massive project *Bibliothèque orientale* was published posthumously in 1697, Galland was employed by the French East India Company, and travelled the Mediterranean, living in Constantinople for a time (Mahdi 1995, 12–17).

*The Arabian Nights* are popular because of their marvellous elements in the midst of realism, the very qualities that attract us to the early novel. Along with the lesser known *Adventures of a Turkish Spy*, *The Arabian Nights* founded the genre of the Western oriental tale that greatly influenced the formation of the European novel; and they vied in popularity with Greek and Roman classics. Horace Walpole preferred *The Arabian Nights' Entertainments* to Virgil: 'Read Sindbad the sailors voyages, and you will be sick of Aeneas's,' he opined in June 1789 (1944, 9.20–21). That Walpole equated the Eastern tales with *The Aeneid* and even preferred *The Arabian Nights* demands a reassessment of their influence on the literature of the long eighteenth century that has been masterfully begun by scholars such as Ros Ballaster and Srinivas Aravamudan among others. Addison and Steele, Eliza Haywood, Jonathan Swift and Samuel Johnson found much to admire and imitate in the exotic tales, while James Beattie and Henry Fielding, among others, criticized them as too magical and implausible. Similarly, the objections of Bishop Atterbury, Lord Kames and Henry James Pye focused on the book's wild extravagance, disproportion, and amorality as the very antithesis of neoclassical tenets (Ali 1977). The Nights thus presented a popular alternative to classical precedents, and Coleridge and Wordsworth like other Romantic poets found the Tales to be a particularly fertile counterpoint to the more traditional legacy of the enlightenment. The Nights are filled with gripping narratives – memorable stories that appeal, like the Gothic, because of their irregularity, elements of the marvellous, and their dissimilarity from the neoclassical.

The appearance of Galland's twelve-volume Mille et une nuits in English translation (1704–17) constituted a significant cultural event.[10] Though his work was largely based on the fourteenth-century Syrian manuscript, his version strayed from translation into paraphrase and even invention as he rendered a spare original into a polished, lyrical and refined narrative that would appeal to a French aristocratic readership. Muhsin Mahdi writes that Galland 'felt free to abridge, omit, and change with impunity; remove repetitions at will; amplify the text or add explanations where he felt readers could benefit; and link the elements of a story and make it look more logical in the way it moved from one episode to another' (1995, 34). There is no systematic or authoritative Arabic edition in English translation until the nineteenth century (1811), and thus the European versions precede the Arabic versions. Comparison to the original Arabic suggests that Galland was in many instances 'creating an Arabic story himself out of a slender outline' (Knipp 1974, 44–54). Galland exaggerates, misinterprets and elaborates upon marvellous elements in his translation of the more colloquial and less stylized original tales that were probably originally intended for those at the bottom of the social scale, the poorest classes, perhaps one of the reasons that the tales are generally not highly regarded by Arabists (Shaw 1975, 62).

[10]  Volumes 1–4 were published in 1704, volumes 5–7 by 1706, volume 8 in 1709, volumes 9 and 10 in 1712, and 11–12 appeared posthumously in 1717. It is not known for certain when the English version was published, though 'possibly as early as 1706' (Shaw 1975, 62, 64).

If Galland, the French translator, was writing for an elite public, the Grub Street authors were seeming to aim at a more bourgeois public.[11] One sign of the remarkable popularity of *The Arabian Nights* was the thrice weekly serialization in 445 instalments over a three-year period in the *London News* (1723–26), and its subsequent publication in the Grub Street press (Mayo 1962, 59). The collection of tales was widely serialized, adapted and abridged. Pocketbooks were marketed to Ireland, Scotland and England through Dove's English Classics, and expurgated children's books proliferated to the extent that James Beattie remarked that most English young people knew the *Nights* intimately (Beattie 1783, 2.510). By 1800 there were eighty English versions including 'translations, pseudotranslations, and imitations' (Haddawy 1990, xx). Later translators included Edward Lane (1839–41), John Payne (1882–84) and most notably Richard Burton (1885–86) who also translated the *Kama Sutra*.

Throughout the century, discrete tales such as *Sinbad* or *Ali Baba* were extracted for publication in periodicals and other magazines. Ongoing printing of individual tales of the *Nights* was especially compatible with the burgeoning periodical publication that appealed to a middling class readership. The influence of *The Arabian Nights* was also felt in fictions such as Jonathan Swift's *Gulliver's Travels* as well as in putatively non-fictional writings like Mary Wortley Montagu's *Turkish Letters*. Lady Mary in fact owned a ten-volume set of the *Nights*, and her perceptions of Turkey bear unacknowledged resemblances. Clara Reeve in the late eighteenth century testifies to the enormous popularity of the *Nights* in England, to 'the great demand for this book' which 'raised a swarm of imitations' (Reeve 1785, 2.58). As Robert Mack has pointed out, there is considerable cross-pollination with the Odyssey, Chaucer, Shakespeare, Calderón de la Barca (*La vida es sueño*), Boccaccio and Ariosto.

The tension between an allegedly authentic portrait and a pseudo-Orient affords one of the reasons for the popularity of the tales in a century that spawned the European novel. The *Tales* offered a fictionalized and fantastic exoticism – a pseudo-Arabia and a pseudo-Islam as filtered through European languages. Paradoxically, the *Arabian Nights* became a touchstone for supposedly genuine knowledge about the Islamic East. In *The Progress of Romance*, Reeve remarked on the 'Authenticity' of the *Arabian Nights Entertainment*; and Henry Weber in his 1812 edition wrote that as a school boy he had read the tales as an 'authentic portrait of oriental nations' which afforded 'a perfect insight into the private habits,

---

[11]  See Hawari 1980, 151 for a discussion of Galland's interpretative gestures.

the domestic comforts and deprivations of the orientals' (Reeve 1785; Weber 1812, pp. ii–iii).[12] Drawing on the often remarked parallel to the classics as a source for comparative religions, Weber suggested that a school boy could learn the Mahometan faith from the *Nights* just as he learned the mythology of Greek and Romans. Perhaps as a result of the *Nights'* popularity, and as a rebuttal to its Islamic core, the Society for the Promotion of Christian Knowledge (SPCK) translated the New Testament, the Psalter, and *Catechetical Instructions* into Arabic in 1726, and orientalist scholar George Sale translated the Koran into English (Grant 1968, 97). In short, the *Arabian Nights* figures a pervasive Muslim identity transcending national boundaries that parallels and rivals Europe's Greek and Roman heritage. *The Arabian Nights* added an enchanting dimension of the inexplicable, the supernatural and the mysterious to the rational enlightenment; it offered an avenue into modernity through its opposite, and an alternative to a free, Christian and English identity. Its excess made England's luxury and its imperial trade seem to be positively modest in comparison, its cruelty as opposed to brutal Eastern despotism only incidental. It accustomed readers to slavery as commonplace even as it linked noblewomen with infidelity, lowly social status and blackness.

*Blackness in 'The Tales'*

Blackness and its embodiment are threats to English and French sovereignty that compete with the fear of Islam and the East. During the years when *The Arabian Nights* first appeared, Shaftesbury's principal concern in formulating the 'Moorish fantasy' that he believed dominated the English imagination, was that England's daughters would imitate Desdemona in succumbing to the enchantment and tales of seduction wrought by Othello, 'a Moorish hero, full-fraught with prodigy, a wondrous storyteller' (Cooper 1999). That Moorish hero encompasses both blackness and Islam in proportions that vary depending on the critical argument and context. In *The Arabian Nights* it is the Persian Scheherazade's tongue that convinces and entices rather than the Moor Othello's, but the sexual threat that blackness and interracial union evoke in Shaftesbury's

---

[12]   Clara Reeve writes, 'I have spoken largely of the *Arabian Nights Entertainment* as a work of Originality and Authenticity, and let me add of amusement. The great demand for this book, raised a swarm of imitations, most of which are of the French manufactory, as the *Persian Tales* – *Turkish Tales* – *Tartarian Tales* – *Chinese Tales* – *Peruvian Tales* – *Mogul Tales*, &c' (Reeve 1785, vol. 2.58).

formulation, asserted in 1711 as the serialized tales gained popularity, parallels that which the Persian kings experience in the *Nights'* frame tale. African man and Eastern woman share the power of narrative seduction.

The impetus for narrating *The Arabian Nights*, was the sultanesses' infidelity, exacerbated by the ruling brothers' anger at the racial and social difference between the royal Persians and the black African servants or slaves. Discussing the frame tale in its varied versions across three translations, Jennifer Thorn has argued that Richard Burton's late nineteenth-century fascination with interracial sex overwhelms even his misogyny, while Galland's earlier version emphasizes instead an exotic luxury and refined sensibility aimed primarily at aristocratic readers.[13] Thorn contends that Burton 'is obsessed with racial hierarchy' while 'Galland's "racism" is comprised in equal parts by the irrelevance of "blacks" and his unobtrusive assimilation to the status of "nonblacks" of the "Tartars, Persians, and Indians"'(Thorn 2002, 155). The racial thinking in Galland's version and its Grub Street imitation deserve further analysis, however, for the French translator retains in my view important distinctions between Arabs and Muslims, on the one hand, and Africans, blacks and slaves on the other. While it is certainly the case that Tartars and Persians are not figured as black (though Indians sometimes are), blacks are not so much irrelevant to Galland or the Grub Street version of *The Arabian Nights* as that the significance of complexion and geographical origin are inconsistently portrayed over the many tales.

In the French and English eighteenth-century translations, slavery is dictated by class relations as much as it is by more explicitly racial ones. In the sizzling passage that precipitates the tale's misogyny, Schazenan, departing for a visit to his brother, unexpectedly returns to his queen to bid her goodbye, discovers that she 'had taken one of the meanest officers of the household to her bed' ('qui ... avait reçu dans son lit un des derniers officiers de sa maison') (Galland 1965, 1. 24). The fact that Schazenan's wife engages with a common manservant heightens the insult to royalty, and he kills them both on the spot before embarking on his trip. Crazed by the realization of his wife's infidelity, he chances to see twenty women, ten of whom reveal themselves to be cross-dressed black men, who pair up and engage in sex in his brother's pleasure garden. 'Modesty,' we are told in the Grub Street edition, 'will not allow, nor is it

---

[13]   Thorn 2002, 164 also suggests that Burton reveals an affinity for patriarchal homosocial bonding and an antifamilial intensity that is missing in Galland.

necessary, to relate what passed between the blacks and the ladies' (Mack 1995, 4). In this reversal of conventional Islamic polygamy, the black men are not specifically identified as slaves or eunuchs, though it is clear they are subalterns, and they would likely have been servants in the sultan's household. They are accompanied by Schahriar's sultaness who summons a black man ('un autre noir') called Masoud, from a tree, and they merrily engage in sex. Masoud is not specified to be a servant or slave, but only a gleeful simian-like participant leaping from a tree to the orgy. The brothers – Schahriar, cuckolded by the black Masoud, and Shahzenan by a low domestic servant who is called 'black' in later editions – trick the sultaness into repeating her base act, and she too is murdered. The misogynous concern of the frame tale is the brothers' wives' adultery regardless of colour, though being cuckolded by a slave or a black man apparently increases the offence.

Though Galland's French translation and the English Grub Street version resemble each other closely in this regard, subsequent translations, including most especially Burton's late nineteenth-century version, become increasingly racially specific. While there is nothing in Galland about the sultaness's lover being a black or a slave or a cook in the introductory frame tale, subsequent translations rendered by Lane, Payne and Burton use these terms. The Grub Street version of the sultaness's infidelity with 'one of the meanest officers of the household' is rendered elsewhere as an adolescent working in the kitchen (Khawan, Arabic into French, 1965–67); but later becomes 'a male Negro slave' (Lane 1839–41), a black slave (Payne 1882–84; and Mardrus, Arabic into French, 1900–1904), 'a black cook of loathsome aspect and foul with kitchen grease and grime' (Burton 2001) and again simply a black slave in C. Knipp's own translation of the Calcutta II manuscript.[14] In short, the frame tale lends itself easily to being manipulated into this kind of racialization.

The associations of Africa and blackness with enchantment, metamorphosis, disguise and the threat of the unknown in *The Arabian Nights* are often highly conventional. Black genies, cannibals, eunuchs, savages, slaves, giants and dwarfs in the individual tales are villains, captors and captives who propel the narratives. As subhuman beings or humans metamorphosed into animals, they are also predictably linked with deformity or monstrous ugliness. In Sinbad's 'Fourth Voyage,' for example, cannibal

---

[14]   Knipp 1974, 52–3 provides sample texts, though he does not provide analysis.

blacks seize the voyagers and fatten them with herbs and rice in anticipation of their feast. In the 'Sixth Voyage' it is made clear that a Mahometan is *not* a black eunuch, and in 'The Story of the Barber's Fifth Brother,' a black eunuch slave enslaves a Muslim woman. In 'The Story told by the Taylor,' a barber falls in love with an alabaster white woman who is described as having been 'born in a country where all the natives are whites' in contrast to himself who 'resembles an Ethiopian; and … his soul is yet blacker and more horrible than his face' (Mack 1995, 261).

It is more surprising, however, that among the many stories in *The Arabian Nights* Scheherazade recounts, several are cleverly reminiscent of Schahriar's avenging his queen's exotic desires and validate his misogyny. Black men are not infrequently the competitive counterpoint to the Persian, Turkish, Tartar or Indian male as the object of sexual desire for the Eastern woman. In 'The History of the young King of the Black-Isles,' though blacks generally operate at the periphery of the individual tales, they leap to the centre. There the young king discovers his queen in flagrante with an Indian whom the queen identifies as 'my lovely black,' and whom the king calls 'that monster in nature' (Mack 1995, 63). When the king wounds the lover, the enchantress queen paralyzes the king and transforms his lower body into black marble. Provoking havoc in the kingdom, the adulterous wife demolishes the palace, the city and the four islands. In addition, she magically transforms the kingdom's subjects into four different coloured fishes (white, red, blue and yellow) representing Muslims, Persians, Christians and Jews respectively. In the *Nights* 'blacks' frequently form a distinct linguistic group whose language differs from the *lingua franca* and cannot be understood by Arabic speakers.[15] Coming to the rescue of the paralyzed king, a neighbouring sultan murders the black lover and impersonates him by 'counterfeiting the language of blacks' (Mack 1995, 62–4). He commands the queen to restore her husband and his kingdom to their natural form and finally murders the enchantress, slicing her in half. Political order and religious harmony are restored through the death of the powerful desiring woman and the black, and the sultan appoints the young king as his new heir. In 'The King of the Black-Isles' as in the frame tale, blackness provides a sexual and political threat

---

[15]  The problem of not understanding the language of blacks surfaces again in Sindbad's 'Sixth Voyage' where he finds himself among 'a great number of negroes,' only one of whom understands Arabic (Mack 1995, 170).

to Islam.[16] But among all the tales in *The Arabian Nights*, it is the popular 'Story of Aladdin; Or, the Wonderful Lamp' that offers the most fertile source for tracing the ambiguous meanings of 'African,' 'slave' and 'black' outside the Black Atlantic in connection to abolitionist and anti-imperialist views during the eighteenth century.

### 'The Story of Aladdin; Or, the Wonderful Lamp'

'The Tale of Aladdin; Or, the Wonderful Lamp,' deriving from oral tales repeated over several centuries, was a Syrian-French-English text first published in the first decades of the eighteenth century during the same period when England was granted the Asiento to supply Negroes to Spanish American colonies (1713). Finding that his translation of *The Arabian Nights* was commercially successful, Galland added to the collection his own 'authentic' tales that expanded or elaborated upon oral transmissions. The story of 'Aladdin' (Alâ al-Dîn) is one of the so-called 'orphan tales,' like the voyages of 'Sinbad the Sailor' and 'Ali Baba and the Forty Thieves,' in the sense of their having no written original in Arabic, Persian, Turkish or Sanskrit. Each of the orphan tales may have been a creation of Galland's own mind or, more likely, they were interpretations of tales that had been conveyed to him from notes or by word of mouth. 'Aladdin is not among the eleven basic stories of the original work,' as Husain Haddawy has noted, 'nor does it appear in any known Arabic manuscript or edition, save in two, both written in Paris, long after it had appeared in Galland's translation' (Haddawy 1990, xvii). Evolving into temporal and linguistic points of cultural contact, these three orphan tales are also, perhaps not coincidentally, the ones that were most frequently serialized, and which most attracted readers during the eighteenth century.

In March 1709 the Eastern traveler Paul Lucas introduced Antoine Galland to Hanna, a Syrian Maronite from Aleppo, to whom he refers variously as 'Hanna Hean, Jean-Baptiste, Jean Dipi, Dipy, and dippy, thus a namesake of Pierre Dipy or Dippy, his predecessor at the Collège Royal.' This Maronite spoke French, Provençal and Arabic (Mahdi 1995, 32–4).[17] On 3

---

[16] Mahdi 1995, 139 argues that these stories distinguish proper Islamic faith from the new forms of faddish religion which are dominated by women and the unfortunate.

[17] Galland delayed publishing 'Aladdin' until 1712 when the first part appeared in volume nine and the remainder in volume ten. Maronites are Arab Catholics from the Levant, who have their own hierarchy and liturgy (Syriac rather than Latin).

November 1710, over a year later, Galland makes a journal entry that he had begun to read 'Aladdin and the Magic Lamp' in Arabic (Mahdi 1995, 201 n. 71). The tale did not surface in Arabic until a manuscript written by Dom Denis Chavis, a Syrian Christian priest, appeared in 1787, but that text turned out to be a forgery in that it was merely a translation from Galland's version back into Arabic, a process that was repeated in the early nineteenth century in Paris.[18] There is no systematic or authoritative Arabic edition until the nineteenth century, and thus the European versions precede the Arabic versions. In short, the Aladdin tale is very likely an eighteenth-century European invention, or at the very least an adaptation or elaboration, of an 'Arabic' tale. Though the Arabic manuscript that the Maronite allegedly transcribed has disappeared, Galland remarks at the end of his version of 'Aladdin' that the story stood out from those the Sultan had heard before: it was 'toute différente de ce qui lui avait été raconté jusqu'alors' or 'quite different from that which had been told to him until then' (Galland 1965, 3. 177). Galland's version of Hanna's Arabic transcription of an oral tale in English translation is freely amended, less colloquial and more highly stylized, and Hawari suggests that the translation bears the characteristic signs of a skilled European novelist rather than an Arabic narrator (1980, 156).

*The Thousand and One Nights* are only loosely connected, principally through the device of references to the frame tale between stories, and they are not 'complete.' From all indications Galland, like the Grub Street translators who followed his lead, apparently sought to draw tighter connections among the stories, in part by adding an after-tale frame story of his own invention between Scheherazade and Schahriar at the conclusion of the 'Aladdin' tale (Mahdi 1995, 203 n. 77). This addition is particularly significant because it may arguably be regarded as marking the turning point in the Sultan's violent antipathy toward women. 'Aladdin' is one of the few tales that refers back to the introductory story, as if to underscore the connections among slavery, femininity and blackness in the frame and tale. 'Aladdin,' I am arguing, echoes the lesson of the frame tale with its anxiety about the miscegenated adultery between the Persian sultaness and African slave that originally sparked Schahriar's rage and resulted in Scheherazade's subsequent narration of the *Arabian Nights* tales.

[18]    Syrian Mikhail Sabbagh claimed to have copied it from a Baghdad manuscript in 1703. Payne and Burton used this translation, which surfaced in Paris in 1805 and 1808, as the basis of theirs (Haddawy 1990, xvii).

'Aladdin; Or The Wonderful Lamp' in its eighteenth-century version, untainted by the 1992 Walt Disney musical film, is a rags-to-riches story set in Muslim China (home of the Tartars), probably the Xinjiang province, North of Tibet, adjacent to Pakistan and the northern tip of India.[19] Though imaginative geography may not require accuracy of location, the golden age of Islam in this territory was the Ming Dynasty which ruled from 1368 to 1644. Aladdin, the son of a Chinese tailor called Mustapha and a cotton-spinning woman, rises to marry the princess of the land through the assistance of an African magician and the genies of the lamp and the ring. Aladdin is a kind of Muslim nabob who rationalizes the magical acquisition of precious goods. The tale justifies his seeking sovereignty while exploiting the captive genies' labour and ridding the world of troubling African strangers.

The tale's emphasis on the expansion of markets and commerce reinforces the argument that it may well have been composed – or at least modified – near the beginning of the eighteenth century. Other hints of a modern historical context include the young Aladdin being accused of 'libertinism' because he plays with blackguard boys, although he is reputed to be an isolate who has no friends. In addition, the African magician in the story is an avid physiognomist, a pseudo-science that found many enthusiasts in the period. Though a Muslim Tartar, as Aladdin comes of age he develops a remarkably Protestant and bourgeois work ethic typical of themes in the developing children's literature of the eighteenth century. Beginning as a hapless and lacklustre lad, he becomes a proper industrious merchant, conscious of time-discipline, and he learns the exchange value of small marketable goods.[20] Challenging inherited status, he makes clear that power and rank may be acquired regardless of the accident of birth – the familiar plot of many an eighteenth-century novel. He displays the ingenuity and perseverance typical of bourgeois heroes and stakes a claim for affective rather than arranged marriage in his unorthodox courtship of the princess. Ultimately he combines middling class

---

[19]  Conant 1966 xvi quotes Galland's definition of 'Oriental' in French: 'Under the name Oriental, I do not understand only Arabs and Persians, but also Turks and Tartars and almost all the people of Asia up to China including Muslims or pagans and idolators' (my translation). Robert Mack believes that the reference may be to the vast empire of Persia rather than modern-day China (Mack 1995, 894).

[20]  Though he does not mention *The Arabian Nights*, Isaac Kramnick writes the seminal article on the use of children's literature for bourgeois indoctrination in the eighteenth century (Kramnick 1983).

values with aristocratic privilege to emerge triumphant as the new sultan. 'Aladdin,' like the other orphan tales, unites moral instruction with the 'useless trumpery' of magical enchantment that Locke had cautioned against.[21] In short, the tale is a hybrid of ancient and modern, Christian and Muslim, Arab and European, Chinese and African.

In the story, the African magician, who purports to be Aladdin's uncle, travels to China – from the most extreme tip of Africa according to the French version – to find the burial place of a magic lamp (Haddawy 1990, xxxv).[22] Preying on Aladdin's destitution because of his father's recent death, the African magician offers extraordinary promises to the indolent boy who serves a kind of apprenticeship to him. The malevolent magician possesses special arcane knowledge useful to the young bourgeois; he imprisons him in a cavern and leaves him for dead along with the magic lamp and ring. A genie, the slave of the ring, magically appears to free him and to award him pearls, diamonds and rubies. Returning to the city, Aladdin becomes obsessed with Princess Badroulboudour, the 'full moon of full moons' (Mack 1995, 668), the beautiful brown daughter of the Sultan. The genie (whose 'hideous form' is much remarked upon) magically places Aladdin in her bedchamber, with a sabre separating the lovers to protect the princess's chastity. The Sultan demands an exorbitant bride price from Aladdin who sends a splendid procession of forty black and forty white slaves to carry gold to the ruler. With the help of the talisman lamp and its genie, Aladdin acquires everything that might propel the fantasies of an eighteenth-century tradesman, merchant or nabob to imperial aspirations – unimaginable wealth, the princess and the kingdom.

The evanescent genies miraculously appearing throughout the tales are dark mysterious beings who labour in behalf of their master, but whose necromantic activities are uncontrollable and unpredictable. Inventing these supernatural powers offers something of an explanation for the appearance of a stranger or an inexplicable happening. The goal of many of

---

[21]   Locke 1693, quoted in Kramnick 1983. In his preface to the *Nights*, Galland reinforces a claim for the moral purpose of the tales: 'If those who read these stories have but any inclination to profit by the examples of virtue and vice, which they will here find exhibited, they may reap an advantage by it, that is not to be reaped in other stories, which are more proper to corrupt than to reform our manner.' (Galland 1965, 1.2)

[22]   Interestingly, the map of the places mentioned in *The Arabian Nights* in Husain Haddawy's superb translation does not include Africa: Africa is literally off the map (Haddawy 1990, xxxv).

these tales is to evacuate the stranger of his might, whether servant or magician, possessor of extraordinary magical abilities or sexual prowess, and to eradicate him. After Aladdin's marriage, the scene shifts to the continent from which magic derives: 'Africa,' 'a country [sic] that delights the most in magic of any place in the whole world' (Mack 1995, 659), is both a source of mysterious knowledge necessary to gain wealth, and the threat to it. There the magician who has acted as an unwitting agent of Aladdin's class ascendancy conjures up visions of Aladdin in the desert sand. He deeply resents that Aladdin escaped the cavern and, with the help of the genie in the lamp, prospers. Riding to China on a Barbary horse, the African tricks the princess (who is still unaware of the lamp's magic powers) into exchanging the magic lamp for an ordinary one. The magician with the help of the genie, now in his command, transports the palace and the princess to Africa. When the Sultan discovers that the palace is missing, he arrests Aladdin and threatens to behead him; but the people threaten rebellion. Summoning the genie of the ring, Aladdin is himself magically wafted to Africa to engage the princess in a ruse to poison the magician. The African magician dies, the palace is transported back to China, and Aladdin rules the day. Aladdin cleverly gains dominion over the forces emanating from a fabulous Africa that gathers to it associations of the most arcane magic.

The peculiar ending to the original tale is often omitted from adaptations and abridgements. After the death of the African magician, his younger brother, a similarly malevolent force who is previously unmentioned, travels to China to regain the magic lamp. The brother exchanges clothes with Fatima, the pious reclusive miracle worker whom he encounters. He challenges her to make the resemblance between them more exact in changing his complexion: 'Colour my face as thine is, that I may be like thee.' Fatima takes 'a pencil, and dipping it in a certain liquor, rubbed it over his face, and assured him the colour would not change, and that his face was of the same dye as her own' (Mack 1995, 720). Though one might conjecture that she colours his skin with roucou, a reddish liquor deriving from chestnuts or walnuts, the fact that the exact colour, features, and geographical origins of the African magician and the virtuous Fatima remain ambiguous suggests that these were not the primary determining characteristics in either late seventeenth-century Syria or France. In eighteenth-century versions of the tale, the 'Chinese' Aladdin had at first believed that the African magician is his father's brother, his physiognomy and complexion apparently not registering sufficient difference to arouse Aladdin's suspicions of a ruse. Similarly, 'Africa' is not fully legible: when Aladdin and his princess are magically transported there, they have difficulty recognizing the land where they have been taken. The magician would have been different from a black slave, but as a hideous presence he embodies the ambivalence of the mysteriously powerful African Moor.[23]

Though no specific details of her origins are offered in the story, the name of Fatima 'the Radiant' was associated with the only child of Mohammed, born in Mecca; she was an exemplary daughter, wife and mother. One might assume that she was Arabian rather than sub-Saharan African; and consequently that in imitating her colouring, the younger brother may have lightened or ruddied his complexion rather than blackened it. In any case, he strangles Fatima and cross-dresses, turning from an African man into an Arabian woman. Thus, the two categories, Arab and African, are briefly yoked together as the wicked dark man is transformed into the most virtuous of women. Aladdin, recognizing the disguised brother in spite of the disguise, slays him. This killing of the cross-dressed and racially counterfeit African at the end of the Aladdin tale, I suggest, rather than encouraging cultural harmony through romance between African and Arab, offers its opposite: a warning against geographical, cultural and racial intermixture. Arab and African, man and woman, necromancer and Muslim holy woman are joined together in monstrous combination that threatens Aladdin's newly achieved status and the kingdom itself. Aladdin's continued prosperity, dependent on the death of the African brothers who had falsely claimed to be his relatives, is founded on luck, magic and a bed of sand. The hero's prosperity was originally dependent upon the wizardry of the African brothers, but their murders ensure that Aladdin can rise to become the new ruler of the sultan's empire and solidify his wellbeing. In sum, Africans or blacks, strangers within, pose a real if diffusely identified sexual, economic and political threat, but one that is obliterated through Aladdin's canny recognition of their supernatural trickery.

In the continuation of the frame story that Galland added after 'Aladdin,' Scheherazade reinforces the antagonism toward the African magician in accusing him of possessing a greed fed by 'the most horrid and detestable means' (Mack 1995, 725). She condemns the African brothers' revenge, and she sides with Aladdin, 'a person of mean birth,' whom she excuses from avarice because he had not actively sought his

---

[23]  Burton 2001, 576–7 elaborates on the original story in calling the magician both a 'Moorman' and a 'Maraccan' whose home is 'Sunset-land'.

unexpected wealth. She also voices a none-too-veiled moral applicable to her interlocutor, the Sultan Schahriar, in pointing to the folly of the sultan in 'Aladdin' who, in condemning the hero to death, risked civil disorder and the loss of his power. The sacrifice of a woman who is clearly religiously identified, and of the 'other' personified in the African magician and his brother, enables the triumph of the new imperial monarch.

The lesson of the tale and its frame story would seem to be that Moorish Africans will die if they attempt to assimilate into Muslim Chinese, Tartar, Arab or Persian culture, even though their wizardry brought extravagant rewards to Aladdin. Africans in the tales and especially in 'Aladdin' are in danger of dying if they attempt to transculturate or to pass into Arab or Chinese culture; and Islamic womanhood – even the most holy – is at risk when confronted with the African male. The hybrid African and Arab, man and woman, temporarily embodied as one transvestite being when the African magician's brother impersonates Fatima, presents an intolerable threat to Aladdin and the kingdom he has been granted through popularity rather than through inheritance.

At the conclusion of the *Arabian Nights*, Scheherazade agrees to marry the Sultan Schahriar whom she cures of his misogyny; but no character in any of the tales mounts a contest to racial thinking equivalent to Scheherazade's brave, learned and patriotic challenge to the sultan's murderous attitude toward women. This contradiction allows *The Nights* to become not only a handbook for European orientalist imperialism in the eighteenth century, but also a vehicle for allowing an ill-defined uneasiness about African power to evolve into Richard Burton's overtly hostile and highly eroticized rendering of black men and their relationships with lighter women in his late nineteenth-century translation. The black slaves and eunuchs in *The Arabian Nights*, often grouped in tens and twenties, like the genies inhabit a different history from plantation slaves and do not fit easily into black Atlantic or abolitionist discourse; but their representation travels the length of the eighteenth and nineteenth centuries before, during and after the acts of abolition and emancipation. The Arabian, Persian, Turkish and Indian characters of *The Arabian Nights* gather to themselves associations with despotic cruelty, exotic barbarism, and the awful sublime while *The Tales'* investment in the alterity of blacks, eunuchs and slaves – Africans all – intersects, competes with, and often exceeds these other groupings. *The Nights* in its many early versions, though it operates outside Black Atlantic circulation, offers significant traces of the beginnings of a modern black diasporic subject who is linked with and yet distinct from an Islamic and, most especially, an 'Oriental' one. The British Abolition Act of 1807, as significant as it is to world history, eliminated only some aspects of slavery, and *The Arabian Nights* reminded readers, for better and worse, that Europeans neither created nor ended all slavery.

## Works Cited

Ali, Muhin Jassim, 1977. 'The *Arabian Nights* in Eighteenth-Century English Criticism,' *Muslim World* 67 (1977): 12–32.

Aravamudan, Srinivas, 1999. 'In the Wake of the Novel: The Oriental Tale as National Allegory', *Novel* 33.1 (Fall 1999): 5–31.

Bairoch, Paul, 1993. *Economics and World History: Myths and Paradoxes*. Chicago: University of Chicago Press.

Ballaster, Ros, 2005. *Fabulous Orients: Fictions of the East in England 1662–1785*. Oxford: Oxford University Press.

Beattie, James, 1783. 'On Fable and Romance', in *Dissertations Moral and Critical, Philosophical and Critical Works*. 2 vols. London.

Bennett, Norman Robert, 1960. 'Christian and Negro Slavery in Eighteenth-Century North Africa', *The Journal of African History* 1.1 (1960): 65–82.

Bluett, Thomas, 1734. *Some Memoirs of the Life of Job, the Son of Solomon, the High Priest of Boonda in Africa; Who was a Slave about two Years in Maryland; and afterwards being brought to England, was set free, and sent to his native Land in the Year 1734*. London.

Burton, Sir Richard F., trans., 2001. Preface (15 August 1885) to *The Arabian Nights: Tales from a Thousand and One Nights*, intro. by A. S. Byatt. New York: Modern Library.

Carretta, Vincent, 2005. *Equiano the African: Biography of a Self-Made Man*. Athens, GA: University of Georgia Press.

Colley, Linda, 2002. *Captives: Britain, Empire, and the World, 1600–1850*. London: Vintage.

Conant, Martha, 1966. *The Oriental Tale in England in the Eighteenth Century*. New York: Octagon Books.

Cooper, Anthony Ashley, Third Earl of Shaftesbury, 1999. *Characteristics of Men, Manners, Opinions, Times* [1711], ed. Lawrence E. Klein. Cambridge: Cambridge University Press.

Cooper, Rev. Mr., [1791?]. *The Oriental Moralist, translated from the original and accompanied with suitable reflections adapted to each story*. London.

Davis, David Brion, 2001. 'Slavery – White, Black, Muslim, Christian', *New York Review of Books* (5 July 2001).

Davis, Robert C., 2003. *Christian Slaves, Muslim Masters: White Slavery in the Mediterranean, the Barbary Coast, and Italy, 1500–1800*. London: Palgrave.

Equiano, Olaudah, 1995. *The Interesting Narrative and Other Writings*, ed. Vincent Carretta. New York and London: Penguin.

Fisher, Humphrey J., 2001. *Slavery in the History of Muslim Black Africa*. London: Hurst and Company.

Galland, Antoine, 1965. *Les Mille et une nuits*. Intro. Jean Gaulmier. 3 vols. Paris:

Garnier-Flammarion.

Gilroy, Paul, 1993, reissued 2005. *The Black Atlantic: Modernity and Double-Consciousness*. Cambridge, MA: Harvard University Press.

Grant, Douglas, 1968. *The Fortunate Slave: An Illustration of African Slavery in the Early Eighteenth Century*. London: Oxford University Press.

Haddawy, Husain, trans., 1990. *The Arabian Nights, Based on the text of the Fourteenth-Century Syrian Manuscript ed. by Muhsin Mahdi*. New York: Everyman's Library, Alfred A. Knopf, NY.

Hawari, R., 1980. 'Antoine Galland's translation of the *Arabian Nights*', *Revue de littérature comparée* 54 (1980): 150–64.

Irwin, Robert, 1994. *The Arabian Nights: A Companion*. London: Allen Lane.

Khawan, René R. [1965–67]. *Les Milles et une nuits. Traduction nouv. et complète faite directement sur les manuscrits*. Paris: A. Michel.

Kitson, Peter, ed., 1999. *Slavery, Abolition and Emancipation: Writings in the British Romantic Period*. Vol. 2. London: Pickering and Chatto.

Knipp, C., 1974. 'The Arabian Nights in England: Galland's Translation and its Successors', *Journal of Arabic Literature* V (1974): 44–54.

Kohn, Margaret and Daniel I. O'Neill, 2006. 'A Tale of Two Indias: Burke and Mill on Empire and Slavery in the West Indies and America', *Political Theory* 34.2 (April 2006): 192–228.

Kramnick, Isaac, 1983. 'Children's Literature and Bourgeois Ideology: Observations of Culture and Industrial Capitalism in the Later Eighteenth Century', in *Studies in Eighteenth-Century Culture*. Ed. Harry C. Payne. Vol. 12. Madison: University of Wisconsin Press.

Lane, Edward William, trans. and ed., 1839–41. *The Thousand and One Nights, commonly called, in England, The Arabian Nights' Entertainments. A New Translation from the Arabic, with Copious Notes*. 3 vols. London: C. Knight.

Lewis, Bernard, 1990. *Race and Slavery in the Middle East: An Historical Inquiry*. New York: Oxford University Press.

Locke, John, 1693. *Some Thoughts concerning Education*. London.

Lovejoy, Paul, 1983, reissued 2000. *Transformations in Slavery: A History of Slavery in Africa*. Cambridge: Cambridge University Press.

Mack, Robert L., ed., 1995. *Arabian Nights' Entertainments*. Oxford: Oxford University Press.

Mahdi, Muhsin, ed., 1995. *The Thousand and One Nights*. Leiden: E. J. Brill.

Manning, Patrick, 1990. *Slavery and African Life: Occidental, Oriental, and African Slave Trades*. Cambridge: Cambridge University Press.

Mardrus, J. C., 1900–04. *Le Livre des mille nuits et une nuit: Traduction littérale et complète du texte arabe*. 16 vols. Paris: Editions de la Revue Blanche.

Mayo, Robert, 1962. *The English Novel in the Magazines, 1740–1815*. Evanston: Northwestern University Press.

Muthu, Sankar, 2003. *Enlightenment Against Empire*. Princeton, NJ: Princeton University Press.

Payne, John, trans., 1882–84. *The Book of the Thousand Nights and One Night: Now first completely done into English prose and verse, from the original Arabic*. 9 vols. London: Villon Society.

1791. *The Oriental Moralist; or, The beauties of the Arabian nights entertainments …* London.

Rabb, Theodore K., 2006. Review of *Black Africans in Renaissance Europe*, ed. T. F. Earle and K. J. P. Lowe. Cambridge: Cambridge University Press, 2005. *Times Literary Supplement* (4 April 2006): 12.

Reeve, Clara, 1785. *The Progress of Romance, through Times, Countries, and Manners … in a Course of Evening Conversations*. 2 vols. Colchester.

Segal, Ronald, 2001. *Islam's Black Slaves: The Other Black Diaspora*. New York: Farrar Straus and Giroux.

Shaw, Sheila, 1975. 'The Rape of Gulliver: Case Study of a Source', *PMLA* 90.1 (January 1975): 62–8.

Thorn, Jennifer, 2002. 'The Work of Writing Race: Galland, Burton, and the *Arabian Nights*', in *Monstrous Dreams of Reason: Body, Self, and Other in the Enlightenment*. Ed. Laura J. Rosenthal and Mita Choudhury. Lewisburg: Bucknell University Press.

Walpole, Horace, 1944. *Correspondence of Horace Walpole*. Ed. W.S. Lewis. Vol. 9 of 48 vols. New Haven: Yale University Press.

Weber, Henry, Esq., 1812. *Tales of the East: Comprising the Most Popular Romances of Oriental Origin: and the Best Imitations by European Authors with New Translations, and Additional Tales, Never Before Published. To which is Prefixed an Introductory Dissertation, Containing an Account of each Work, and of its Author, or Translator, by Henry Weber, Esq.* 3 vols. Edinburgh: John Ballantyne and Company.

Willis, John R., 1985. *Slaves and Slavery in Muslim Africa*. 2 vols. London and Totowa, NJ: Frank Cass.

# Slavery and Sensibility: A Historical Dilemma

## GERALD MacLEAN

SLAVERY REMAINS a hot topic. Legislation aimed at ending the trade in African slaves to the Americas, however successful in eventually stopping an enormously profitable trans-Atlantic commerce, has by no means eradicated an international division of labour that continues to depend upon trafficking in human lives, nor has it by any means erased the perception that some people were born to labour for the benefit of others. The dilemma I wish to examine here is this: while no historian imagines that making the past better understood can, in itself, compensate for or redress the errors of long ago, the very act of recovering and writing about such errors can have inadvertent consequences. When the topic under investigation is the history of the global slave trade, about which so much has been written yet so little fully understood, those consequences can be truly alarming. To illustrate this dilemma, I shall first examine a little-known captivity narrative from the mid-eighteenth century and then turn to a recent study of the transatlantic slave trade and its reception.

### Mrs Crisp, The Female Captive

Following the academic and commercial success of her *Captives*, Linda Colley is about to publish her next bestseller, *The Ordeal of Elizabeth Marsh: The World in a Life* (Colley profile, interview, 2005). This book promises to provide hitherto unknown details about the family background, adventures, global travels and mishaps in love, marriage and colonial business ventures of a woman whose life would have been extraordinary in any age. Here, I shall offer some rather formalistic comments about an extraordinary book, *The Female Captive*, which was written by Colley's heroine, Elizabeth Marsh. In 1769, it was published by subscription in two volumes in one by C. Bathurst of Fleet Street but then almost entirely ignored until 1934 when an abridgement appeared in *Blackwood's Magazine*.[1] In 2003, Khalid Bekkaoui of Sidi Mohammed ben Abdallah

---

[1]  Marsh 1934, 573–96. Colley 2003, 48 n. 31 reports two contemporary reviews. Sir William Musgrove's annotations to the British Library copy of Marsh's narrative were briefly noticed by 'Y. S. ' 1851: 423.

University in Fez published an edition based on the British Library copy that is thought to be the only remaining copy of the printed text. Since Bekkaoui's edition appeared, Felicity Nussbaum has discovered what is likely to be the original manuscript in the UCLA library and, in collaboration with Bekkaoui, is preparing an edition for Broadview Press.[2]

*The Female Captive: A Narrative of Facts Which happened in Barbary, in the Year 1756* (Crisp 1769) is the first authenticated captivity narrative written in English by a woman. It is also the first in this genre and language claiming to be written by a woman, though Bekkaoui notes that four spurious captivity narratives supposedly by European women were published in the United States between 1804 and 1830, between them running to over thirty reprinted editions during those years, while the theme produced 'a veritable flood of popular novels' during the twentieth century (Bekkaoui 2003, 30). That said, there is very little in *The Female Captive* that might not have been invented by a writer with the imaginative skills of a Daniel Defoe. Certainly, by the mid-eighteenth century, the Protestant captivity narrative had developed well-established features, and Marsh's book displays most of the key conventions developed since the late sixteenth century.[3] The narrator declares her belief in a providential deity who assists her eventual delivery from bondage. Fear of being converted to Islam, or of being thought to have converted, regularly animates the narrative. Lengthy and often detailed accounts of cruel and unusual sufferings at the hands of captors, with occasional testimonies to the kindness of exceptional foreign figures, are interspersed with ethnographic observations on the manners and customs of the alien culture, together with occasional descriptions of the landscape and architectural features of the places visited. Alongside these generic staples, *The Female Captive* includes historical and political asides that attest to its authenticity, as well as features of the sentimental novel, the picaresque and the romance. The immediate historical contexts of the plot involve the unsuccessful British embassy to Marrakesh of Vice-Admiral Sir Hyde Parker in 1756, and the invasion of British held Minorca by the French, followed by its eventual capture that same year, resulting from the perfidy of Admiral John Byng for which, amidst sensational reports, he was tried and shot.

---

[2]  Bekkaoui 2003; my thanks to Professor Bekkaoui for presenting me with a copy of his useful edition. Crisp 1769 can be found in the British Library at shelfmark 1417.a.5. See Nussbaum 2005, note 20 provides reference to the UCLA manuscript.

[3]  Snader 2000 provides a useful survey, but see also Matar 2001, 1–52.

Where *The Female Captive* may be said to add new, or at least unusual, elements to the genre is its use of the first-person female narrator who, throughout, shows herself preoccupied with domestic matters, such as her baggage and the furniture (or lack thereof) in the rooms to which she is confined; with clothing (her own and that of her captors); and with the quality of food she is offered but seldom able to eat. While material concerns weigh heavily upon our heroine's mind, body, and health, her inner life is raised to new and ever increasing heights of apprehension, anxiety, and fearful trepidations. *The Female Captive* inexorably 'moves' its readers, as Ros Ballaster would say,[4] fully into a world where female virtue is always in distress, and into a silent, inner world in which, like Samuel Richardson's Pamela, our heroine confronts the uncanny stillness and incomprehensible apparitions of gothic horror:

> My Room-door was thrown open with great Violence, as I pensively sat reflecting on the News I had heard; and a most forbidding Object presented itself to my View. He, for several minutes, fixed his Eyes upon me, without speaking a Word; and his Aspect was as furious as can possibly be imagined ... I was struck with Horror at his wild Appearance, and seemed rivetted to my Chair. (Crisp 1769, 2: 119)

We never again meet this muttering and 'forbidding Object' of 'furious aspect,' and his visit remains largely unexplained. But this, and other such passages, leaves readers with a startling image of the abjected narrator herself, and for that image of silent, terrified and immobile distress to move us to a compassionate condition of tremulous agitation and frustrated anticipation. In short, *The Female Captive* is as much a literary product of its age, aimed at a clearly established market of readers, as it is a documentary account of the events it purports to describe.

The chronotopes of *The Female Captive* are not the harems or the splendid and exotic palace courtyards familiar from oriental tales analysed by Ros Ballaster, though these do figure (Ballaster 2005, 112–16). Instead we are offered the dark, confined and closed rooms of captivity, or the equally appalling openness of the sun-scorched desert wastes across which she is taken. Sometimes there are spaces in between, moments of transition in which the captive's sense of self-importance might find temporary

---

[4]   See Ballaster 2005 for discussion of how 'oriental' tales 'move' their readers by means of a three-way relay between the actual reader, the teller of the tale, who is usually a subordinate female, and the listener, who is usually a dominant if not despotic male.

restoration, but even these prove to be sites of confinement and degradation in which she is paraded before the vulgar 'Multitude.' At the end
of volume one, after days and nights of unremitting torment being dragged
across three hundred miles of burning wasteland, our heroine finally arrives at the splendid city of Marrakesh – which she calls 'Morocco' – to
be given by her captors 'as a Present' to 'his Imperial Highness,' Sidi
Mohammed ben Abdallah, crown prince and effective ruler of Morocco
at that time (Crisp 1769, 1: 111). She then reports:

> I received a Message ... to change my Dress.
> The Meaning of this, according to the Interpreter's Explanation,
> was, that *I should make* fine Cloaths, which I did not readily under-
> stand; but my Friend, with concern, explained it thus: *that they would
> have me dressed*, in order to make some Figure at going into *Morocco*.
> I intreated to be excused from so disagreeable a Task, acquainting
> them, how very inconvenient it would be to unpack my Baggage, and
> dress in such a Place; but no Intreaties had any Effect, and I found it
> was their Ambition to carry in, adorned in this manner, Captives
> who, by Appearance, seemed above the Vulgar ...
> I was almost dead with Grief and Fatigue, and my Friend, every
> Moment, expected, that we should be thrown from the Mule; his Legs
> were scratched, in a terrible manner, with the Horsemen's Riding by
> us with great Fury; – but he did not seem to regard this, as his Atten-
> tion was intensely fixed on my Preservation from those Accidents
> that fell in my Way: – The Almighty, however, whose watchful Provi-
> dence had defended me from innumerable Dangers, continued his
> Goodness, and supported me through the Distresses of that dismal
> Day.
> About Noon, we arrived at Morocco, when my Friend and I were
> taken to an old Castle dropping to Pieces with Age, led up a Number
> of Stairs, and there left to our own Reflections: We were seated on the
> Floor, lamenting our miserable Fate, when a *French* Slave entered with
> some Water, a Loaf of Bread, and Melons; the latter was very agree-
> able, and all the Refreshment we had for many Hours. (Crisp 1769, 1:
> 116–29)

This passage illustrates several textual features I have already mentioned,
and introduces others; including the possibility that I am not alone in
finding Marsh's text regularly rather more funny than distressing. For
*The Female Captive* is a romance in a very specific sense. From start to
finish, our heroine is invariably at the centre of male attention and attentiveness. She is very seldom alone without some male figure appearing

to disturb or console her; everywhere she goes she instantly attracts threatening predators, or a bewildering variety of mariners, slaves and 'gentlemen' merchants who instantly go out of their way to serve her personal interests, frequently at their own inconvenience or expense and who, after parting from her company, tend to pine after and worry about her.

Indeed, marriage, class anxieties and potential husbands frame the narrative. Among the very first things we learn about her is that she is 'under an Engagement with a Gentleman, who was stationed' at Port Mahon in Minorca, where her father, also 'a Gentleman,' had through his 'Principles and Abilities procured ... a very respectable employment under the Government' (Crisp 1769, 1: 1–2). At the end of the narrative, however, she marries a different man, that 'Friend' whom we met on the entry into Marrakesh. Yet the final five pages of the book transcribe a letter from yet another suitor, one 'Mr. C— ,' a merchant living in Morocco, who regularly entertained her during her captivity and who cannot stop thinking about her. Throughout the entire account, our heroine's overarching preoccupation is little more than to find a suitable husband, one who will assure her a respectable position within polite society, gain the approval of her father and prove unrelenting in his attentiveness to the emotional needs of her refined and delicate sensibility. Hence, I tendentiously refer to Mrs Crisp rather than to Elizabeth Marsh, for the constant 'Friend' whom she marries can be named as the merchant James Crisp, a lineal descendant of Sir Nicholas Crisp, nominated Baronet in the time of King Charles I.[5] And it is the achievement and justification of that married name, for better or for worse, which serves as the guiding motive of the narrative. I say 'for better or for worse' because, while unmarried, Elizabeth finds her own sentimental attachments often directed elsewhere – to the powerful, exotic and fabulously wealthy prince, Sidi Mohammed, and to the letter-writing merchant, 'Mr. C—' who may be named as Mr Court. Moreover, the publication date of *The Female Captive* in 1769, thirteen years after the events it details, corresponds exactly with James Crisp's bankruptcy and public humiliation, resulting in his fleeing to India where Elizabeth would follow two years later. Let me back up.

In the Preface, Elizabeth notes how 'Reflections made in Suffering make always a deeper Impression on Minds endowed with Sensibility' and then continues, rather cryptically:

---

[5]   See 'Ancestors and Relatives of JJ Heath-Caldwell,' at http://www.jjhc.info/crispeliza17xx.htm accessed 5 December 2005.

The Misfortunes I met with in *Barbary* have been more than equalled
by those I have since experienced, in this Land of Civil and Religious
Liberty. (Crisp 1769, 1: sig A3v)

By her own account, our heroine is 'endued with a superior share of Sensibility' (Crisp 1769, 1: 55) and, at several points, declares that she is
driven to near despair of her life. But on each occasion marriage, rather
than captivity, is at issue. When the ship on which she is travelling under
the protection of James Crisp is taken captive, 'My Friend . . . had taken
on himself the Character of my Brother (in order to be some little Protection to me)' (Crisp 1769, 1: 43), but she soon discovers that this deception proves inadequate. Anticipating the arduous trek from Salé to
Marrakesh, she reflects once more on the benefits of sensibility:

> Such is the human Mind, that, where there is the least Glimmering of
> Hope, we love to cherish it; and it is happy we do so, for otherwise
> Souls, endued with a superior Share of Sensibility, instead of surmounting Difficulties with Fortitude, would plunge into Despair in the Hours
> of Affliction; – a Calamity, which those of less elevated Sentiments
> would be exempted from. (Crisp 1769, 1: 54–5)

Having thus reassured herself, Elizabeth introduces us to one Don Pedro,
'a *Minorquin* Slave, who was ... uncommonly affected at my unhappy
Situation, and was of infinite Service to us both as an Interpreter and a
Friend' (Crisp 1769, 1: 56). Nonetheless, it is Don Pedro who first declares a problem with the pretence that James and Elizabeth are siblings
and suggests instead that they should claim to be husband and wife. This
advice, she writes:

> Greatly alarmed me; and I earnestly wished to be removed from a
> World, wherein I had no Reason to expect any Felicity.
>     Tears gave me some Relief, but I remained in a very melancholy
> condition, until the Dawning of the Day, when a severe Shock of the
> Earth gave a Turn to my Thoughts, roused me from that State of Despondence I had indulged the preceding Night, and occasioned some
> religious Reflections, which, in a great Measure, resigned me to my
> Fate. (Crisp 1769, 1: 57–60)

Momentarily rescued by that providential earthquake, Elizabeth and the
other captives set out for Marrakesh accompanied by Don Pedro who
repeats his advice which this time is approved by her 'Friend':

This sudden Change shocked me beyond Expression, and I could only answer with my Tears; my heart was too deeply oppressed to give my Opinion for or against it, and, indeed, I was unable to determine. But, as the Arguments the Slave had used were very reasonable, I thought it most prudent to submit to their Judgment. (Crisp 1769, 1: 78)

Days of extremely uncomfortable travelling, however, cause her resolution to wear thin. After a fall from her mule, Elizabeth once more finds herself close to despair, a condition intensified by hindsight:

I earnestly invoked Heaven to put an End to my Days, which gave me a dismal Prospect of nothing but Misery; and, tho' I was preserved, yet it was for still greater Sorrows, and in *my own Country*, than any I ever experienced, even in *Barbary*. (Crisp 1769, 1: 85)

From this point on, no physical suffering causes Elizabeth as much agony as the strategic deceit that she is pretending to be married to a man to whom she is not.

On arrival in Marrakesh, Elizabeth's emotional condition vacillates as the number of amorous and attentive men increases. At her first meeting with 'his Imperial Highness' Sidi Mohammed, the female captive becomes preoccupied with her own appearance and how others regard her:

I had put on my Riding-Dress, and my Face had extremely suffered by the scorching Violence of the Morning Sun; which the Prince took notice of to the Slave who attended me, saying, that I had not been taken the Care of which he had commanded; and he seemed highly offended. (Crisp 1769, 1: 134–5)

Interrogated by Sidi Mohammed, her anxieties over her feigned marital status are instantly aroused and take on ontological proportions:

I was soon followed by the Prince, who, having seated himself on a Cushion, inquired concerning the *Reality* of my Marriage with my Friend. This Inquiry was intirely unexpected; but, though I positively affirmed, that I was really married, I could perceive he much doubted it, from his frequent Interrogations, as to the *Reality* thereof ...
    *Truth* was always my first Principle, but *Self-Preservation*, I hope, will plead my Excuse, *and*, especially, at such a Juncture. (Crisp 1769, 1: 138–41)

Her first reception by the Prince successfully over, volume one is about to draw to an end; but not quite. On returning to her 'dismal Habitation,' she reports that 'Amends, however, was speedily made for the Inconveniencies of the Place by the agreeable Company of two Gentlemen, Merchants, who resided in that Country ... they invited us to sup at their Lodgings' (Crisp 1769, 1: 142–3).

By now, few readers will be surprised to learn that the 'agreeable Company of two Gentlemen' affords her some 'amends.' But just in case any readers have been so careless as to miss the erotic frisson created by the arrival of these agreeable gentlemen, or have forgotten that, throughout, Elizabeth has represented herself as singularly suited to attracting the desiring gaze and attentions of any gentlemen seeking a desirable female body that has been inured to hardship – one which has, we might say, taken the rough without giving in, while remaining vulnerably compliant – volume two opens with the startling line: 'I instantly took off my Night dress,' and then proceeds to elaborate further on one of those 'two Gentlemen':

> I had the Pleasure of Mr. C[ourt]'s Company to Breakfast, who, perceiving me ill for want of Rest, went in quest of another Lodging, though he was not so fortunate as to succeed. (Crisp 1769, 2: 4)

Barely has Mr Court returned when '*John Arvona*, the Slave,' appeared bearing gifts from 'his Imperial Highness, who had ordered him to inquire particularly concerning my Health,' and with Arvona's assistance, Mr Crisp is able 'to procure me a more comfortable Apartment' in 'part of a new House, which belong to some *Jesuits*' (Crisp 1769, 2: 4–5).

At the centre of all this attention, from Princes, slaves and gentlemen-merchants, our female captive starts to feel rather better about the world and her place in it. Settling in to her new 'Apartment,' with no fewer than three chests of personal belongings, Elizabeth cannot disguise her growing pleasure at being right at the centre of so much gentlemanly concern, though of course it was all rather compromised by her pretence of being an already married woman:

> I therefore flatter myself that great Allowances will be made for my present Character, which, though *fictitious*, gave me the greatest Uneasiness, as it rendered me apprehensive, that the ill-disposed part of the World would unmercifully, though unjustly censure my Conduct; but I had no Reason to be under any Apprehensions from the man whom Providence had allotted to be my Protector. (Crisp 1769, 2: 10–11)

Elizabeth's concern for her reputation, and for that of the man she will eventually marry, does not prevent her from passing 'A very agreeable Day' with her new friend, Mr Court, who increasingly occupies her thoughts (Crisp 1769, 2: 13). Next morning, however, respectability is put on hold when she receives a request from 'his Imperial Highness':

> Accordingly I dressed myself in a Suit of Cloaths, and my Hair was done up in the *Spanish* Fashion':
> Just as I had made myself ready, Mr. C[ourt] visited me as usual; but he seemed to be surprised at my Appearance, and walked very pensively about the Room, without speaking a Word, which I could not then account for. (Crisp 1769, 2: 14–15).

Immediately putting aside, or perhaps even provoking, Mr Court's jealous distractions, Elizabeth is clearly impressed by the opulent surroundings and flattered by the prince's attentions during this visit. Left alone together, he makes tea with all the care and delicacy of a London hostess 'and he presented me a Cup of it, – *which*, as it came from his Hand, I ventured to drink, though I should have refused it from the Ladies, for very substantial Reasons' (Crisp 1769, 2: 20).

As Felicity Nussbaum points out, Elizabeth fears the women she meets in Morocco more than any of the men. And rightly so, since it is while in their company, and in the presence of a young French slave, that she inadvertently mimics some words that imply she has converted to Islam. Nussbaum also notes that Elizabeth 'is slyly explicit about the charms of the exotic Prince, of eligible age and demeanour, who courts her with "rarities" and "curiosities"' (Nussbaum 2005, 127). When, however, Sidi Mohammed suggests that, were she to accept his religion, she might stay on with him and enjoy unimaginable wealth and prestige, Elizabeth is again overwhelmed by feelings of suicidal despair at the prospect of an unsuitable marriage:

> This Shock was so severe, that it was with Difficulty I supported myself from falling; and I invoked Heaven for Assistance in my Distresses, they being excessively great, and nobody near me that I knew ...
> My Tears, which flowed incessantly, extremely affected him; and, raising me up, and putting his Hands before his Face, he ordered that I should be instantly taken away. (Crisp 1769, 2: 38–9, 41–2)

Once outside the gates, she is comforted by 'My worthy Friend ... his Hair all loose,' who 'took me in his Arms, and, with all possible Expedition' returns her to 'our Lodgings,' where 'I was kindly received by Mr. C[ourt], who discovered a silent Satisfaction at my Deliverance' (Crisp 1769, 2: 42–3, 45). Clearly sentimental lovers from her own nation appeal more than the charms of a suave Moroccan prince.

Elizabeth's romantic affections for Mr Court increase without entirely displacing James Crisp. It takes several days before the Prince allows the captives to leave Marrakesh, and several more before they are granted permission to leave Morocco. At issue are the diplomatic wranglings that brought them there in the first place and which are nothing to do with Elizabeth's refusal to stay on in the palace. Throughout, Mr Court emerges as being regularly in attendance and constantly in her thoughts. 'I was,' Elizabeth notes, 'much entertained with his agreeable Company, his Conversation being always new and improving; and Providence was particularly kind in indulging me, in that Country, with the Acquaintance of so amiable a Man' (Crisp 1769, 2: 52–3), and she is delighted that he accompanies them on the journey to Safee, 'which contributed to render short and pleasing an otherwise troublesome Journey' (Crisp 1769, 2: 69–70).

Divided loyalties and affections, however, have a price. Once arrived on the coast, Elizabeth finds herself increasingly depressed, despite being the centre of attention among the merchant community, and frequently being entertained at dinner parties where Mr Court 'sang in a most agreeable Manner' (Crisp 1769, 2: 81). 'Such Amusements,' she continues:

> Would have been delightful to me, had my Mind been at Ease; but alas! the Situation I was in abated its Charms, and Solitude being the principal Object I desired, made any Recreation irksome to me.
> Dress was a Pain to me, any farther than what Decency required … my Spirits were oppressed, and my Sorrows heightened by the Reflection that I had formerly enjoyed many happier Days … and I often wished to be taken from this World, as it afforded me no Consolation. (Crisp 1769, 2: 80–1, 83, 85)

While no specific reasons are ever offered for her depression at a time when she might be full of optimistic expectations, the narrative continually points to her acute anxieties over marriage and the problem of which candidate, and for what reasons. The thought of death has no sooner overcome her when, on cue, Mr Court appears with shocking news: he must leave her in Safee and return to Marrakesh. 'This unwelcome News so greatly afflicted me, that I bade Adieu to Chearfulness … and I was intirely miserable' (Crisp 1769, 2: 85, 87). Once again, right on cue, events take over as if to intensify and indicate the causes of her abject despondency:

> I was alone, the next Morning, and extremely Melancholy, when the Sound of *Moorish* Music drew me to the Window; I saw a great Croud, and, inquiring into the Meaning thereof, I was informed, that it was the Procession of a *Moorish* Wedding …
>
> These People having passed, Mr. C[ourt] came to take his Leave of us … he embraced my Friend and me, sending up to Heaven a pathetic Wish for our speedy Deliverance out of Captivity; and then he departed from us, with all Expedition: But, though I was extremely distressed by such a cruel Separation, I still relied on Divine Providence for support in all my Afflictions. (Crisp 1769, 2: 87–8, 90, 91)

Like all good captives who resign themselves to a benevolent providence, Elizabeth is swiftly rewarded: a letter, the first of three, soon arrives from the absent Mr Court, full of pathos and selfless affection. 'You engross much of my Thoughts,' he writes, 'and I can, with great Truth, affirm I shall not enjoy a Moment's Peace of Mind, until I hear you are gone from this Country, and happily restored to your Family and Friends' (Crisp 1769, 2: 103–4). Passing no comment on the letter or its contents, Elizabeth fails to find the first glimmerings of happiness until she is finally aboard a ship taking her to Gibraltar and her parents. The Captain, of course, gives her 'his State-room':

> I cannot express the comfort I felt in having an Apartment allotted to myself, after the cruel Restraint I had been under in Barbary, and the Uneasiness I had suffered on Account of passing for what I *really* was not … I had, besides, an additional Satisfaction, *viz.* that of having it in my Power to acquaint my Relations to whom they were indebted (next to Providence) for my Preservation, as my Friend had, in every Respect, fulfilled the Promise he had made to my Father (Crisp 1769, 2: 142–3)

On her arrival in Gibraltar, another letter arrives from Mr Court, full of restrained passion. Once more, Elizabeth leaves the letter to speak for itself, and then instantly reports how Mr Crisp finally declared to both her and her family his 'stronger Attachment than that of Friendship [and] of his Love for me' (Crisp 1769, 2: 153–4). With all the coolness imaginable, Elizabeth comments, 'I was not much surprised at this Declaration' and then, having explained that her father had already cancelled her former engagement, summarily notes how 'after adjusting some Family

Affairs, not necessary to this Narrative, we were married, and embarked for England' (Crisp 1769, 2: 154–5). But, as I have already pointed out, the final words are given to Mr Court whose third letter arrived before their departure. 'Madam,' he begins:

> It was with extreme Pleasure that I received your very obliging Favours of the 7th of December, and the 7th of January, the first signed with the name wherein I had been used to address you, and the last with that you has so long feigned in *Barbary*, and which is now become *real*. (Crisp 1769, 2: 156–7)

And so, on this plangent note of ontological reassurance, Elizabeth Marsh, the female captive, enters history as Mrs Crisp, a woman whose adventures led her to marry for all the right reasons but, perhaps, in despite of her own affections. 'Endued with a superior share of sensibility,' Mrs Crisp invites us to share in her self-displacement – the masquerade of marriage to her 'Friend' James Crisp that becomes all too real, the possibilities of further romance foreclosed.

For my part, the proleptic argument I am seeking to make is this: If Professor Colley's agent has not already started to inflame a Hollywood bidding-war over the film rights to 'The Ordeal of Elizabeth Marsh,' then Colley should sign on with Ed Victor immediately, for the tale told in *The Female Captive* offers all the anguished sufferings of the Christian captivity narrative combined with the languid erotic attenuations and innuendos of *Pamela*, and it does so within an exotic and orientalizing setting without ever losing sight of the heterosexual romance ending in marriage without which, it seems, no Hollywood film can be made. Times and tastes change but, as C. Bathurst of Fleet Street surely knew in 1769, such a combination of popular generic elements, when presented in the voice of a sensitive, genteel and proper young lady from an upwardly-mobile petit-bourgeois colonial background, could not help but find a wide and sympathetic audience among readers of equally proper inclinations and sensitive dispositions who were thrilled by tales of risks survived and dangers overcome in the cause of serving the Great British Empire. 'The Ordeal of Elizabeth Marsh' is bound to be a popular success. The possible risk is that its major achievement may be no more than to reassure those who need reassurance that, during the age of the trans-Atlantic slave trade, white Christian folk from Britain were also being taken into North African captivity by Muslims of a darker skin.

In fairness to Colley, her treatment of historical facts in *Captives* is pretty reliable, if sometimes partial and tendentiously selective. And

careful readers will agree that the stylistic exuberance of her book rightly
earned the large sales and laudatory reviews that it received in both the
trade and academic press. That she provides us, for instance, with the
view of what she calls 'the official mind' in describing life in the British
colony in Tangiers rather than the rather more sordid version of rampant
corruption and enforced promiscuity that appalled even Samuel Pepys –
hardly renowned for being narrow-minded in such matters – may seem
rather beside the point, since the aim of her book is, after all, to focus on
the hardships suffered by those unfortunate Britons who, seeking to further the cause of empire, found themselves captured and sold off in the
slave markets of Algiers, Tunis and Salé.[6] 'The Subject of these Volumes,'
Elizabeth Marsh writes in the prefatory epistle to *The Female Captive*, 'is a
Story of real Distress,' and indeed such stories – as Colley amply documents – really were many, real, distressing and make for compelling reading. The dilemma is that the very features that make these tales so compelling can encourage prejudicial attitudes among some readers.

*Robert Davis and Christian Slaves*

It seems unlikely that, in seeking to author a best-selling history book
aimed at attracting a broad cross-over market, Colley had any idea that
she would be playing into the hands of racist bigots in the US who have
championed her historical research in order to mitigate the transatlantic
trade in human lives. Such, however, cannot be said of Robert Davis
who, in his sensationally titled study *Christian Slaves, Muslim Masters:
White Slavery in the Mediterranean*, seeks to prove that, whatever crimes
that white, Christian Europeans inflicted on black Africans, similar crimes
were being committed by black and Muslim Africans against white Christians of European background. These, he thinks, have been unduly ignored.

Davis's conclusion, which has caused quite a stir, is that 'between 1530
and 1780 there were almost certainly a million and quite possibly as many
as a million and a quarter white, European Christians enslaved by the
Muslims of the Barbary Coast' (Davis 2004, 23). 'Almost certainly,' 'quite
possibly'; Davis is careful to hedge his bets.

---

[6]   Colley 2002, 28; but compare Pepys' version of life there in Chappell 1935,
discussed in MacLean 2007.

Davis cleverly makes his case by strictly observing scholarly protocols, providing statistical evidence and ingenious calculations, and even tactically acknowledging the complexities involved in evaluating and interpreting the very evidence he cites even when it undermines the very case he is striving to make. He also ignores significant contexts to suit his case, and indulges in selective quotation. The concluding chapter notes: 'The experience of so many tens of thousands of white slaves ... [what happened to the million or so?] made sure that slavery in early modern Europe was not conceived just in such color-conscious terms as many modern observers would have it.' Then, on the same page, it admits that for most Europeans taken into North African captivity 'the chances were that their master was a renegade, as white and European as themselves' (Davis 2004, 91): a crucial point he has managed to keep largely suppressed from earlier chapters. With this casual and final concession in mind, let us recall that Davis claims that he is attempting to put the North African slave trade into a global perspective, and then recall that, between 1500 and 1650, an annual average of 10,000 slaves – seized from Poland-Muscovy and Circassia – were traded via the Crimean port of Kaffa (Inalcık 1997, 284–5). That's a million and a half 'white European' slaves being traded in 150 years, not a million and a quarter in two and a half centuries. But until making a few final but all-too crucial concessions, Davis clearly wants to focus on a putative black-Muslim versus white-Christian trade, and would rather not have to consider complications such as those presented by a Black Sea market that was both vaster in extent and not conducted by North Africans, many of whom were Europeans in drag, but by Crimean Tatars who were descended from pre-Islamic Mongols, working with Jewish, Armenian, Venetian and Genoese merchants to serve the Ottoman Empire. In terms of a global perspective on the slave trade at the time Davis is examining, questions of religion and skin colour were relatively minor factors in a vast commerce directed by imperatives of profit and empire.

Throughout the book, Davis rhetorically finesses the complexities to which he finally admits by making sure that on nearly every page certain key words – 'white,' 'European,' 'Christian' – are placed in strategic opposition to 'black,' 'Muslim' and 'African,' thereby establishing and reinforcing throughout a Manichean dichotomy that has excited, encouraged, and emboldened not simply white racist hate groups throughout the US, but has also served the turn of even white liberals eager for relief from the tedious burden of feeling guilt for the crimes of their forebears. 'The more we study it,' concludes Piero Scaruffi, 'the less blame we have to put on the USA for the slave trade' (Scaruffi 2005). Scaruffi's comments on Davis's book offer the following arguments: what happened in the US was no worse than elsewhere; white US citizens inherited slavery from Europe; statistically, few whites actually practised slavery in the US; whites in the US were the first to condemn slavery and the slave trade; only colonization of Africa by white Europeans began to put an end to the slave trade within Africa.

Scaruffi's position really is, in contrast with some others, a liberal one. Within ten days of Davis's book being published in the US, comments sent to the white-supremacist website 'American Renaissance' might lead one to conclude that illiteracy and strong feeling are somehow inextricably linked with racist bigotry. 'The horrific stories recounted, include English and even Icelandic People being kidnapped and sold into slavery by these animals and requires a strong stomach,' observed 'Sissy White,' while someone signing as 'Aristotle' waxed lyrical:

> And the EU is considering letting Turkey join – amazing to anyone with the least bit of historical knowledge. The book will be unwelcome as it challanges the african american monopoly on slavery as an explanation of all there ills. If whites have a history of slavery, as they do at the hands of muslims, then whites too should be placed in the american pantheon of victims. One would think that this would fill it up to bursting – but I can already hear the complaints that somehow white slavery wasn't as bad as black slavery – I personally would much rather have been down home on the plantation then in some Turkish galley.[sic][7]

Other contributors declared intentions of buying the book, while many joined Davis in using statistics to score points about the past in order to shape the present. A correspondent called 'European' observed: 'We imported 6–700,000 slaves from Africa and end up with over 30 million "slave mentality" blacks, in little over 200 years no less. The rest of the world took the bulk of the 12 million slaves and none of the guilt. Only stupid White Americans. BTW, I ordered the book as well.' Meanwhile 'The Dalry Lama' took up the magical effect of numbers for similar ends:

[7]   These and subsequent passages are quoted from the Comments section following a reprint of Rory Carroll's review of Davis's book first printed in *The Guardian* (11 March 2004), and can be found in 'New Book Reopens Old Arguments about Slave Raids on Europe' at the 'American Renaissance' website: http://www.amren.com accessed 5 December 2005.

'The import of 1,000,000 Whites into the North African gene-pool also helped raise those countries up. It's a pity that the import of 700,000 Black slaves into the US had exactly the opposite effect.' I have no idea where these numbers or genetic observations come from; certainly not Scaruffi who gives the 'number of Africans deported to the Americas by the Europeans' as 'about 10–15 million' while 'about 30–40 million died before reaching the Americas' (Scaruffi 2005). In these Scaruffi follows the reliable estimates provided by Hugh Thomas's authoritative 1997 study, *The Slave Trade*, which Davis relegates to a single footnote reference while ignoring those probably uncountable millions who died on the middle-passage (Davis 2004, 195n).[8] For those who wrote in to the American Renaissance website, however, fantastic and ingenious factoids count for a great deal, while for others Davis's research offers an answer to that perennial question of 'what's in it for me?' Someone called 'Steve' simply declared: 'I'm putting in a request for reparations,' while 'W. O'Leary' was both more specific and more generous: 'White Christians throughout the world should demand through the U.N. oil reparations from Arab Islamic countries now! At least 40 barrels of oil and a Rolls Royce per white Christian.'

From the scholarly point of view, the problem I am trying to describe in anticipation of responses to Linda Colley's new book on Elizabeth Marsh, is that Davis's project is as entirely laudable as hers. Davis wants 'to rethink the story of European enslavement in the early modern Mediterranean world' and to place it 'in the larger context of slave studies world-wide' (Davis 2004, xxiv), so it really is a shame that by the end of the book, he has shown no knowledge of, interest in or consideration for slavery in a world wider than the North African littoral and some parts of North America. The eminent Ottoman historian Colin Heywood, in reviewing Davis's book, observed that 'it would be rewarding to perceive the Atlantic and African slave-based economies of the early modern period as only one part of a vast global economic phenomenon, stretching as far (at least) as Central Asia, where the slaving expeditions into Persia of the Turcoman khans of Khiva did not come to an end until the Russian conquest in the mid-nineteenth century,' and concludes with the optimistic hope that other scholars will take up the vast areas ignored by Davis (Heywood 2005, 490). Let us hope that someone is listening.

---

[8]   Hugh Thomas's figures are summarized in Thomas 1997, Appendix Three: Estimated Statistics, on 805–6, not 861–2 as given by Davis.

But Davis, having received research grants and fellowships from the Fulbright, Guggenheim, and numerous other foundations, was doubtless under considerable pressure to make the results of his findings appear to be as stunning and as original as possible, and he carefully sculpts his sentences to sound as sensational as studied scholarly qualifications will allow while, at the same time, contributing to knowledge, or, at least, changing the way some people think. 'One of the things,' he writes, 'that both the public and many scholars have tended to take as given, is that slavery was always racial in nature – that only blacks have been slaves. But that is not true. We cannot think of slavery as something that only white people did to black people' (Davis 2005). Evidently Davis is not the only one who believes that there really are other people somewhere, scholars among them, who think such things, and his aim is to enlighten them by returning to the Mediterranean world of the sixteenth and seventeenth centuries where such a view would have been impossible to believe. He informs us:

> In Barbary, those who hunted and traded slaves certainly hoped to make a profit, but in their traffic in Christians there was also always an element of revenge, almost of *jihad* – for the wrongs of 1492, for the centuries of crusading violence that had preceded them, and for the ongoing religious struggle between Christian and Muslim that has continued to roil the Mediterranean world well into modern times. (Davis 2004, xxv)

Davis is not alone in imagining that Muslims engaged in the North African slave trade were inspired by revenge. In 'The Holy War in the Mediterranean,' the tendentiously titled opening chapter of his much-cited study, *Corsairs of Malta and Barbary*, Peter Earle went even further and declared: 'Unlike normal wars the war of the corsairs had neither beginning nor end. It was an *eternal* war' (Earle 1970, 1). Such emphatic declarations of timelessness may look good on the page, but neither Earle nor Davis provides a single bit of evidence to support such a notion, most likely because neither of them have consulted any Arabic sources – Davis, by the way, casually remarks that there are none. On the other hand, scholars who have worked with Arabic sources, such as L. P. Harvey, insist that, while the Christian conquest of Granada in that signal year of 1492 'was of course of transcendental importance to the Muslims of Spain,' evidence of anything resembling systematic revenge simply cannot be found. 'The victory at Granada in 1492,' Harvey continues:

Might have been expected to evoke a military response, a counter
attack from somewhere in the Islamic world ... The Mediterranean
seacoast [of Spain] might be open and vulnerable to pirate raids from
the far Islamic shore, so that at times there was almost a Spanish psy-
chosis related to the cry 'Moros en la costa' (the Moors have landed),
but in fact there was no landing in strength on Spanish territory by
troops from any Muslim power, no attempt to regain what had been
lost. (Harvey 1990, 324, 325)

What we have in Davis's claim that 'there was also always an element of
revenge, almost of *jihad* – for the wrongs of 1492' is not simply ignorant
and uninformed history, but something rather more chilling: evidence of
paranoid Christian projection in the service of Islamophobia. Jihad has
nothing to do with revenge, whatever some hysterical self-appointed
imams have been saying of late, and it is not insignificant that while
questions of vengeance preoccupy both books of the Judeo-Christian Bible,
the Qur'an mentions it not at all. While anyone educated in the biblical
tradition cannot help but develop views early on in life about vengeance,
and to whom it might rightly belong, those brought up in the Qur'anic
tradition are not so educated. The fact that there was no retaliatory response to the expulsions does not mean that Muslims were not angry;
rather that revenge was not on their agenda. Muslim travellers to Spain,
as Nabil Matar has pointed out, 'repeatedly wished for the destruction of
the Christians,' but their 'repeated invocation for God to destroy or shame
them, *damarahum al-Lah* and *khadhallahum al-Lah*' make plain that retribution for the violence and the expulsions must come from elsewhere
(Matar 2003, xxviii). Crudely put, revenge was not a problem for Muslims until Christians tried to make it so. That said, I should, of course,
recall that in the contexts of the North African slave trade of the sixteenth and seventeenth centuries, many of the so-called Muslims engaged in this business were themselves not born into Islam but were renegades native to ostensibly Christian countries – Davis regularly calls
them 'apostates' which tells us something of his attitudes and purposes. It
may well be that, in the accounts by Christians taken into captivity, claims
that their captors taunted them with talk of revenge are to be found. But
to argue that revenge on the part of Muslims has led them to wage an
'ongoing religious struggle ... well into modern times' as Davis does, is to
show his complete failure to understand the history and beliefs of those
about whom he claims to be writing. History that makes the past speak to
the present is one thing, but projecting the beliefs of one group onto
another in order to justify a tendentious position is bad history. As for

'modern times,' Charles Glass has recently contrasted the revenge killings of as many as ten thousand French men and women suspected of
collaborating with the Nazis – killings tolerated by the American forces
of liberation – with the complete absence of reprisals by Hizbullah against
those who had collaborated with the Israeli occupation of Lebanon between 1978 and 2000.[9] Revenge belongs to those brought up on the
Bible, not the Qur'an.

One final point about Davis's use of sources and his critical vocabulary in doing so: he regularly selects and quotes lurid passages from a
number of Christian captivity narratives in order to emphasize – I could
say exaggerate – the horrifying torments endured by those who suffered
captivity at the hands of Muslim masters (who are termed 'patrons' in
most such writings) without showing any understanding of the circumstances that brought such works into being. And he seems oblivious to
the fact that these works were invariably written by captives who were
able to do so because they had been ransomed or escaped, and who consequently faced rigorous interrogation on return to their native countries
since the fact of their survival was regularly taken to be evidence that
they must have converted to Islam. In such cases, the burden of proof
rested entirely on the credible testimony of the former captive, so it is far
from surprising that strenuous declarations of piety and persistence in
the Christian faith mark all such narratives. The surest testimony that a
returned captive could offer to prove they had not abandoned their native faith was to recount at length, and in excruciating detail, all the
multiple forms of suffering they had been forced to endure at the hands of
their captors. This imitation of Christ was the best evidence of steadfast
faith and, while sufferings there no doubt were, imaginative elaborations
regularly played a part in these accounts too. By confusing these self-
serving reports of suffering with what really happened, Davis either proves
himself to be as gullible as the readers for whom these narratives were
originally written, or once again seeks to disguise some darker prejudices.
'Slaves,' he writes, 'had their place, albeit a humble one, in the Maghreb's
social hierarchy … Slaves, as individuals without rights or personhood in
law, made up the bottom rung' (Davis 2004, 103). The terminology is
revealingly anachronistic: 'rights'? 'personhood'? in the mid-seventeenth
century? Elsewhere Davis tendentiously adopts the inflammatory vocabulary of the era, regularly writing about 'Turks' when he means 'Ottomans,'
of 'apostates' when he means 'renegades,' and repeatedly referring to

[9]    Glass 2006: 8–9.

'Christian slaves' suffering at the hands of 'Muslim masters' without keeping it clear that the trade in European slaves was largely organised by
former 'Christians.'[10] Instead, in an obvious attempt to cash in on today's
fixations with a 'conflict of civilizations,' he writes of 'White Slavery,' a
commerce that was little more than multi-national business as usual at a
time when questions of 'individuals without rights or personhood in law'
had simply not been imagined.

I am not attempting to exonerate those involved in slaving, to dimin-
ish or sideline the sufferings of those from many nations and creeds who
were deprived of what we now call basic human rights; nor am I trying to
take sides and argue that one lot were worse than any other lot in this
grotesquely profitable business of trafficking in human lives, labour, and
liberties. My polemic is rather directed at historians of slavery such as
Davis – and there are others – who cannot not know what they are doing,
whose obvious though skilfully muted aims are to dig up the past in order
to excite present passions and who knowingly adopt language that serves
to arouse suspicion, fear and loathing.

So, what will readers make of Linda Colley's study of the first authenticated account by a woman of being held captive in North Africa? If
Colley's working title is anything to go by, the white supremacists at
American Renaissance will most likely pay it no attention, but one can
never tell. After all, in the century after the publication of *The Female
Captive*, US publishers found a ready market for spurious tales of European women taken captive by North Africans.

## Works Cited

*Electronic*

'American Renaissance.' At http://www.amren.com accessed 5 December 2005.
'Ancestors and Relatives of JJ Heath-Caldwell.' At http://www.jjhc.info/
    crispeliza17xx.htm accessed 5 May 2005.
Aslan, Reza, 2005. Review of Giles Milton, *White Gold* in *The Washington Post*
    (26 June 2005); at www.washingtonpost.com/wp-dyn/content/article/2005/
    06/23/AR2005062301612_pf.html accessed 5 August 2006.

---

[10]   The accusation of authors who use 'deliberately perverse terminology' is also
made by Reza Aslan reviewing a popular work in part inspired by Davis's study,
Milton 2004, in the *Washington Post* (26 June 2005); at www.washingtonpost.com/
wp-dyn/content/article/2005/06/23/AR2005062301612_pf.html accessed 5 August 2006.

Colley, Linda, profile. At http://his.princeton.edu/people/e102/colley/profile.html
accessed 5 August 2006.

Colley, Linda, interview. At http://his.princton.edu/people/354/
linda_colley_intervi.html accessed 5 August 2006.

Davis, Robert C., 2005. Press release at 'White Slavery Was Much More Common Than Believed,' at www.newswise.com/articles/view/503630, accessed 5 December 2005.

Scaruffi, Piero, 2005. 'The Origins of the African Slave Trade,' at www.scaruffi.com/politics/slavetra.html accessed 5 December 2005.


*Printed*

Ballaster, Ros, 2005. *Fabulous Orients: Fictions of the East in England, 1622–1785*. Oxford: Oxford University Press.

Bekkaoui, Khalid, ed., 2003. *Elizabeth Marsh, The Female Captive: A Narrative of Facts which Happened in Barbary*. Casablanca: Moroccan Cultural Studies Centre.

Chappell, Edwin, ed., 1935. *The Tangiers Papers of Samuel Pepys*. Greenwich: Navy Records Society.

Colley, Linda, 2002. *Captives*. New York: Pantheon.

Colley, Linda, 2003. 'The Narrative of Elizabeth Marsh: Barbary, Sex, and Power,' in Felicity A. Nussbaum, ed., *The Global Eighteenth Century*. Baltimore, MD: Johns Hopkins University Press. pp. 138–50.

[Mrs. Crisp], 1769. *The Female Captive: A Narrative of Facts Which happened in Barbary, in the Year 1756*. 2 vols in one. London: C. Bathurst.

Davis, Robert C., 2004. *Christian Slaves, Muslim Masters: White Slavery in the Mediterranean, The Barbary Coast, and Italy, 1500–1800*. 2003; rpt. Basingstoke: Palgrave, 2004.

Earle, Peter, 1970. *Corsairs of Malta and Barbary*. London: Sidgewick and Jackson.

Glass, Charles, 2006. 'Learning from its Mistakes,' *London Review of Books* 28: 16 (August 2006).

Harvey, Leonard Patrick, 1990. *Islamic Spain, 1250 to 1500*. Chicago: University of Chicago Press.

Heywood, Colin, 2005. Review of Robert Davis, *Christian Slaves, Muslim Masters*, in *Mariner's Mirror*, 91: 3 (August 2005): 489–90.

Inalcık, Halil, 1997. *An Economic and Social History of the Ottoman Empire, Volume One: 1300–1600*, eds. Halil Inalcýk and Donald Quataert. 1994; rpt. Cambridge: Cambridge University Press, 1997.

MacLean, Gerald, 2007. *Looking East: English Writing and the Ottoman Empire before 1800*. Basingstoke and New York: Palgrave, forthcoming 2007.

[Marsh, Elizabeth], 1934. 'Narrative by Miss Elizabeth Marsh of her Captivity in Barbary in the year 1756,' *Blackwood's Magazine*, 236 (November 1934): 573–96.

Matar, Nabil, 2001. 'Introduction' in Daniel J. Vitkus, ed., *Piracy, Slavery and Redemption: English Captivity Narratives in North Africa, 1577–1704*. New York: Routledge. pp. 1–52.

Matar, Nabil, ed. and trans., 2003. *In the Lands of the Christians: Arabic Travel Writing in the Seventeenth Century. First English Translations*. New York:

Routledge.

Milton, Giles, 2004. *White Gold: The Extraordinary Story of Thomas Pellow and Islam's One Million White Slaves*. New York: Farrar, Strauss & Giroux.

Nussbaum, Felicity A., 2005. 'British Women Write the East after 1750: Revisiting a "Feminine" Orient,' in Jennie Batchelor and Cora Kaplan, eds., *British Women's Writing in the Long Eighteenth Century: Authorship, Politics and History*. Basingstoke: Palgrave, pp. 121–39.

Okeley, William, 1675. *Eben-Ezer: or, A Small Monument of Great Mercy, Appearing in the Miraculous Deliverance of William Okeley, William Adams, John Anthony, John Jephs, John —— Carpenter, From the Miserable Slavery of Algiers, with the wonderful Means of their Escape in a Boat of Canvas; the great Distress, and utmost Extremities which they endured at Sea for Six Days and Nights; their safe Arrival at Mayork: With several Matters of Remarque during their long Captivity, and the following Providences of God which brought them safe to England*. London: Nat Ponder.

'S., Y.,' 1851. 'The Female Captive.' *Notes and Queries* 3: 83 (1851): 423.

Snader, Joe, 2000. *Caught Between Worlds: British Captivity Narratives in Fact and Fiction*. Lexington, KY: Kentucky University Press.

Thomas, Hugh, 1997. *The Slave Trade: The History of the Atlantic Slave Trade, 1440–1870*. London: Picador.

# 'Go West, Old Woman': the Radical Re-visioning of Slave History in Caryl Phillips's Crossing the River

## MAROULA JOANNOU

TWO CENTURIES after the British Abolition Act proclaimed the end to slavery in the British Empire the institution of slavery continues to haunt the American literary imagination and to throw its long shadow as a pre-history and pre-text to many works of fiction in the United States. While the significance of the 1807 legislation and its cultural legacy continues to exercise the historian and the literary scholar alike no British work of fiction has ever exerted a comparable hold on the popular imagination or penetrated as deeply into the national psyche and consciousness as *Uncle Tom's Cabin*, *Roots*, *Huckleberry Finn* or *Gone with the Wind*. Like the first generation of black British novelists who migrated to London after the Second World War (Sam Selvon, V. S. Naipaul, Edgar Mittelholzer, George Lamming and others), who mapped their concerns as immigrants over the white literary culture that they encountered in Britain, contemporary black British writers such as Salman Rushdie, Zadie Smith, Monika Ali and Hanif Kureishi, have been more interested in exploring the issues raised by hybridity, cultural diversity, urban thematics and the post-colonial legacy than the problematics of slavery. Moreover, living in times which have witnessed many instances of the attempted extermination of entire peoples, from the Holocaust to the victims of more recent wars in Africa and the Balkans, a second or third generation of black British intellectuals has sometimes questioned the continuing importance to them of a slave history that seems remote from the present and peripheral to contemporary concerns, raising the question; is discussion about slavery now exhausted? What if anything still remains to be said?

The contemporary black British novelist who has re-visioned the history of slavery the most extensively in his writing over a period of more than twenty years, as unfinished business in terms of its continuing impact on the sense of self and on relationships between black and white people in the modern world, is Caryl Phillips. Asked why any writer in the 1990s should still be writing about slavery, Phillips answered that slavery was 'the biggest of those shadows where the history of Europe meets the history of the Americas' (Phillips 1994, 26). Phillips has explored the history and cultural legacy of slavery in both his discursive writing and his fiction, including *Higher Ground* (1989), *Cambridge* (1991) and *Crossing the River* (1993), from a perspective that differs significantly from many black intellectuals in the United States where he currently spends much of his time. Born in the island of St Kitts in the Caribbean, to which he returned in a visit of self-definition at the age of twenty-two, he was taken to England by his parents when a few months old. Many of his ideas were shaped through his formative experience of growing up and being educated in the north of England:

> But what I find in America – like the rich, strange, fertile relationship between those of African origin and mainstream society – is interesting, but it's not me. My primary axis of frustration is what happens between the Caribbean and Britain – particularly Britain … [my ellipsis] If people say I'm British, I say fine; if they say I'm Caribbean, I say fine – because I'm both. (Phillips 1994, 29)

Like Thomas Hardy's *The Mayor of Casterbridge*, which opens with a man selling his wife and giving away his daughter, Phillips's fifth novel, *Crossing the River* (Phillips 1993) opens with a father selling his children and finishes with the man's anguished recognition of his own folly. While separation and loss are the hallmarks of slavery in Phillips's novel the 'signifying on' *The Mayor of Casterbridge*, as well as the inclusion in his text of the white working-class English GI bride whose poverty gives her no choice but to give away her son to the care of the local authority, makes the point that exchanges of this kind are not peculiar to those of African descent. *Crossing the River* is divided into four sections; 'The Pagan Coast', 'West', 'Crossing the River' and 'Somewhere in England'. Three of these refer to the subsequent fate of the children; two sons and one daughter. The first sentence of *Crossing the River* is voiced by an unnamed mythical ancestral African and reappears as a refrain on the last page but with the addition of one word: 'The crops failed. I sold my beloved children' (237). The adjectival insertion here signals a culturally specific form of inter-textuality, anchored to African-American literary traditions: Phillips 'signifies on' Toni Morrison's *Beloved* which is based on the story of the runaway slave, Margaret Garner, who put her baby to death in a profoundly protective act of maternal love rather than allow the child to be taken into slavery in 1856. In contrast, the initial narrator of *Crossing the River* is a grieving and absent father who has acquiesced in such a transaction in order to make possible his own economic survival.

The theme of much of Phillips's fiction is displacement as a defining experience of the African Diaspora and he is not only concerned with slavery as a historical phenomenon but also with how the experience of displacement makes possible a trans-national perspective in the reconfiguration of modern black identity and consciousness. *Crossing the River* is concerned with the narratives of slaves and their descendants who are represented as the subjects of history in a context that is both global and local, *actively* making history; as pioneers migrating to the west of America (rather than taking the better-known route of the wagon trains from the south to the north), as missionaries in Liberia, and as members of the allied forces of liberation during the Second World War.

Phillips attempts to reconstruct the underlying commonality of the people of the African Diaspora by instilling a totalizing order in the narrative: the separation of a father from his children is a *leitmotiv* throughout. *Crossing the River* proclaims its generic hybridity through the use of a variety of intertexts, ranging from the journal of an eighteenth-century slave trader to the mass-observation diaries kept by hundreds of volunteers from the 1930s onwards on which the final section of the novel, the only one to be set in England, is based. The use of an historical document as an intertext in a modern work of fiction ensures that the meanings of the original document are not restricted to the moment in which it was written, but that the historical material acquires modern connotations which resonate far more widely. Phillips's heavy reliance on *bricolage* and his penchant for 'rifling' or 'borrowing' the historical documents that find their way into his own work in altered but recognizable form has provoked comment and controversy. Evelyn O'Callaghan, for example, argues that his writing deliberately calls attention to its own intertextuality and that the particular historical documents that he favours, such as the slave narrative, the travel journal, and the diary, are often those with first-person narrators: conventions of rhetoric and structure that emphasise their fictionality and are 'shown to be rather insidiously fictional in their claim to "the truth"' (O'Callaghan 1993, 34).

Phillips writes in a tradition against slavery that takes in William Blake, Jonathan Swift, Daniel Defoe, William Wordsworth, Olaudah Equiano, Mary Prince, Grace Nichols, David Dabydeen, Edward Kamau Brathwaite and Derek Walcott. I wish to show how attention to its form and narrative structure provides us with an entry to *Crossing the River* which situ-

ates what it has to say to the reader about slavery between the relativism
of the tendency within postmodern theory (that refuses to take any position whatsoever) and the literalism that defends the historical sources
of knowledge as sacrosanct and regards any modern variant produced in
the context of fiction as an attempted erasure of the chronicler and an
assault upon the integrity of the original text. I have found the ideas of
Mikhail Bakhtin particularly helpful in my own reading of the literary
work.

Crossing the River is a polyphonic text that stipulates absolute equality
amongst its voices even as it requires the absence of a transcendental
authorial presence (Bakhtin 1984, 6). No two characters in the novel
use exactly the same linguistic register and each character's speech is
carefully nuanced in terms of their social class and education. The voices
of Edward and Nash ('The Pagan Coast'), Martha ('West'), Captain
Hamilton ('Crossing the River') and Joyce ('Somewhere in England')
represent individual, social, and thematic perspectives on the institution of slavery. The distinctive language given to each character ranges
from the formal to the vernacular and is refashioned, activated and
dialogised within the novel. In Crossing the River, the situation of the
individual voices in relation to the author's speech ensures that the characters have the capacity to compete with the author, to disagree with
him, and to hold values to which he does not subscribe. Moreover, the
authorial voice weaves in and out of the novel, disappearing and re-
emerging, so that the reader is given a plurality of narratives of equal
standing rather than a narrative illuminated by any single informing authorial consciousness. Heteroglossia enters the novel by means of the
speech of the author, narrator, and characters and the use of inserted
genres, each of which permits a 'multiplicity of social voices and a wide
variety of their links and interrelationships (always more or less
dialogised)' (Bakhtin 1981, 263). Through the use of such devices Crossing
the River radically re-visions the history of slavery by giving expression to
a plurality of independent and unmerged consciousnesses each with its
own particular authority.

The central issue that Crossing the River explores is the relationship
between the black person who is the real, material subject of his or her
individual and collective history and the cultural and ideological com-
posite 'other' of discourse, scientific, literary, historical or anthropological, as the case may be. Stuart Hall has suggested that black Caribbean
identities have always been 'framed' by two axes or vectors, simultaneously
operative: the vector of similarity and continuity, and the vector of

difference and rupture. What matters is the dialogic relationship between these two axes. The one 'gives us some grounding, some continuity with the past. The second reminds us that what we share is precisely the experience of a profound discontinuity' (Hall 2003, 226, 227). Phillips's fiction oscillates between an emphasis on continuity, signalled by his belief in the necessity of rootedness and an equally insistent emphasis on discontinuity. In *The European Tribe* he writes of the importance of rootedness, prefacing his concluding remarks with an epigraph from Simone Weil: '*to be rooted is perhaps the most important and least recognized need of the human soul*' (Phillips 1987, 119). Phillips recognizes the importance of historical knowledge to those who have been denied knowledge of their own past, as well as the potential dangers of history as a cul-de-sac in which the black person may be trapped with no means of escape. He writes of history as the 'prison from which Europeans often speak, and in which they would confine black people' (Phillips 1978, 121). Phillips has spoken of the crucial importance of history to his own writing: 'I and many other writers who are non-white, have the need to work against an undertow of historical ignorance. Our history is also our bank balance. And we have a responsibility to the people who produced us.' (Phillips 1994, 29). Moreover, 'in a situation in which history is distorted, he recognizes that the literature of a people often becomes its history, its writers the keepers of the past, present and future' (Davison 1994, 96).

Phillips is part of a group of university educated contemporary writers for whom a sophisticated understanding of the theory of the novel is axiomatic. *Crossing the River* is distinguished by its theoretical awareness of both history and fiction as human constructs and its rethinking and reworking of the literary forms and historical legacies of the past. The novel uses specific historical facts and consciously rearranges them in a new explanatory pattern. This re-ordering counteracts an accepted version of events and reflects a type of historical enquiry which, as Hayden White has put it, is determined less by 'the necessity to establish *that* certain events occurred than the desire to determine what certain events might *mean* for a given group, society, or culture's conception of its present tasks and future prospects' (White 1986, 487).

*Crossing the River* challenges the received views of the past in order to replace them with an interpretative rearrangement of processes and events. Historical detail is incorporated and assimilated into the novel in order to lend an aura of verisimilitude but at the same time the sense of a continuous, stable and homogeneous identity, whether of an individual, a group of people or a nation, is displaced and replaced with a history of fragmentation, discontinuities and exclusions. As Martha Rosler puts it, 'the elevation of an unknown or disused past emphasizes a rupture with the immediate past, a revolutionary break in the supposed stream of history, intended to destroy the credibility of the reigning historical accounts – in favor of the point of view of history's designated losers. The homage of quotation is capable of signalling not self-effacement but rather a strengthening of consolidating resolve.' (Rosler 1981, 81).

'The Pagan Coast' is an attempt to settle accounts with one of the founding texts of literary modernism, Joseph Conrad's *Heart of Darkness* (1899). This section begins in America in the 1830s, moving from there to the country of Liberia which was populated by released slaves under the auspices of the American Colonization Society. Phillips uses the literary devices of modernism; provisionality, intertextuality and fragmentation, to disrupt the totalizing order in the narrative thus reconfiguring the historical narratives contingent upon Africa's co-option into European modernism through the institution of slavery (Owusu 2000, 439). This section shows his fascination with the historical archive based on the author's communications with historians in Britain and the United States who specialized in the history of the nineteenth-century slave letters (Phillips 1994, 26).

Like Cambridge, in the eponymous novel, Nash Williams is subjected to a rigorous programme of Christian education by his liberal, white slave-owner, Edward Williams, and is made to adopt a white mask of culture which testifies to the success of cultural erasure. Taught to despise his African heritage and his pagan past he becomes deeply pious, a process which, as Fanon suggests, produces complete alienation from the self (Fanon 1967). There is a radical disjunction between the position of the black man as object (slave and 'other' to the white man) and as a subject (a free man and the author of highly literate missives to his former master). The assimilated Nash, one of several fatherless children in the novel, comes to revere Edward as a surrogate father while Edward finds himself sexually drawn to the racialised 'other', to the abjected black body synonymous in his culture with dirt, labour and degradation, so that the 'natural' basis of his own domination as a white man is no longer credible. The slave-owner's narrative is interspersed with letters from Nash, some with the salutation, 'Dear Father' which gloss over the violence of the severance from his cultural roots: 'You were kind enough to take me, a foolish child, from my parents and bring me up in your dwelling as something more akin to son than servant.' (Phillips 1993, 21).

Nash's is the only first-person voice in 'The Pagan Coast' and his letters, written as a pastiche of early nineteenth-century English to his master are interesting as examples of Bakhtinian varidirectional discourse, the perfectly calculated stylization of another's words in such a way that an element of ridicule is introduced and the effect produced is the opposite to the intention of the original. (Bakhtin 1984, 193). Nash may believe fervently in all that he professes but we are equally convinced of his alienness, his 'otherness', while he himself lacks any awareness that despite his impressive linguistic and cultural acquisitions others will find his claim to be a Christian gentleman suspect. However, the very brilliance of Nash's mimicry in the fictive correspondence between Nash and Edward, written in language designed to bring the exact vocabulary, cadences and phrasing of the genuine slave letter to mind, foregrounds the textuality of representation at the same time as it prompts the reader to ask whose history is known and by what means?

The representation of desire, difference and denial in 'The Pagan Coast' not only confounds the recognized parameters of slavery and the dominance of the white body over the black, but contest the very categories of ruler and ruled and the markers of racial difference and cultural distance which lay at the heart of the slave-owning societies. This is not just in respect of Nash whose very fluency invites suspicion about any first-hand experience of the humiliations of slavery, about which he remains silent, but also in respect of Edward whose homosexual orientation marks him as an outsider in his own society. Moreover, his sexually charged interest in Nash is a synecdoche of relationships between master and man, at once perpetuating the hierarchies of the slave-owner relationship while rendering problematic the assumptions on which such a relationship is premised. Slave-owners insisted on their own moral and cultural superiority while indulging their sexual desires and practices (both heterosexual and homosexual) in ways which did not involve the compromises and restraints inherent in sexual relationships with white women of their own class.

Like Marlow in *Heart of Darkness*, whose journey to Africa culminates in the discovery of the hollowness of Kurtz's *soi disant* civilizing mission, Edward makes the long voyage to Africa (but from America rather than Europe) in search of a missing envoy only to arrive too late to prevent Nash from 'going native' and abandoning the Christian precepts he has been taught. But Nash's fate is not represented as the familiar catastrophic reversal from the civilized to the barbaric of *Heart of Darkness*. On the contrary, we are presented with the reinscription of the cultural memory wiped out during the slave's acculturation in the New World. In Nash's acceptance of his African cultural heritage, in the act of remembrance, the reader is provided with an alternative narrative incompatible with the imperial mission of colonial literature and the lineaments of evangelizing Christianity.

As I have said, what makes Phillips's writing distinctive is his interest in the British historical context, in which slavery was officially brought to an end through parliamentary legislation in 1807 and 1833, rather than the very different context of American history in which slavery was finally declared unlawful much later, after the American Civil War (1861–1865) which ended in victory for the abolitionists. However, racial discrimination remained lawful until after the Civil Rights Movement of the 1950s and 1960s. Whereas American literature provides countless instances of novels dealing with slavery and its aftermath, literary references to slavery in the British colonies are much less common. Jean Rhys's *Wide Sargasso Sea* (1966), which begins with the suicide of a slave owner in the Caribbean after the emancipation of slaves in 1833, is perhaps the best-known. Phillips had already explored slave-experience in the Caribbean in his previous novel, *Cambridge*, which takes place on an early nineteenth-century slave plantation. As if to show how the histories of Europe and America converge, Travis, a black GI whose ancestors were slaves in the deep south of America, is sent to England, a country with which he has had no previous connection, at the historic moment when the United States entered the war to assist an endangered Europe.

Bénédicte Ledent cites the inability of Travis to recognize and put a name to a common English flower, the daffodil, as one example of how slavery had impacted differently on those of Caribbean origin who had had a British education in the colonies, and been taught the famous poem by Wordsworth (Ledent 2002, 133), and others of African-American descent who had not. The irony of which Phillips is acutely aware is that although they were treated as inferiors in their own army, black American servicemen were often more popular with the local people in wartime Britain (who were unlikely to have seen many black people) because they were perceived as less threatening, aggressive and arrogant than white American servicemen. As Peter Fryer puts it, their reception in Britain was often a 'strange mixture of genuine welcome and genuine discrimination – the latter often instigated (indeed, insisted on) by white American troops' (Fryer 1984, 359).

Phillips wrestles with the complications of love between black and white partners in the 'Crossing the River' section of his novel. Travis never appears except as a presence in the life of Joyce, the white, working-class, twice married, shop-keeper who loves him and keeps a diary between the years 1936 and 1963. Phillips had originally intended to give Travis a voice in the first-person but had difficulty in replicating a convincing southern accent and so his story is told exclusively from Joyce's point of view (Phillips 1994, 27).

'Somewhere in England' is predicated on the irony of a black American descended from a slave fighting to free the world from Fascism while being treated as a second-class citizen in the segregated Jim Crow military. This is carefully researched. Phillips drew upon documents about the segregated American forces in Britain in Washington, DC, and the archives in the Sheffield Public Libraries for information about Yorkshire village life during the Second World War (Phillips 1994, 26). The intertext for 'Somewhere in England' is the day-to-day record of life in Britain written by thousands of 'ordinary people' who volunteered to be part of the Mass Observation project in the 1930s and 1940s. The diarist, Joyce knows her own mind and refuses the communal pressure to conform. In Bakhtinian terms she can be considered one of 'life's maskers' – those fools who have the right to be other in the novelistic world and see the 'underside and falseness in every situation' (Bakhtin 1981, 59).

Joyce speaks in the Yorkshire dialect of Phillips's remembered childhood and writes colloquially and without formality or pretension, referring to the politician, Neville Chamberlain as a 'silly brummie bugger' (Phillips 1993, 176). The chaotic and elliptical diary entries that constitute the whole of this section are arranged in fragmented, non-sequential order reflecting the chaotic order of her life and requiring the reader to impose the narrative order that is lacking. The knowledge of the self that the diary reveals is at once social and individual, undermining the social pieties of the closed Northern community in which Joyce lives as an 'uninvited outsider' (129). At the same time the diary contests the patriarchal and patriotic discourse of wartime Britain and the racism that underlies this. Joyce too is a child who grew up in a brutal environment and without a father. Her diary records the back street abortions, petty crime, domestic violence and abusive aspects of subaltern white working-class life. The discontents and ambivalent feelings of the civilian population that the diary reveals are often sharply at variance with the official rhetoric of Churchill with its telling omissions. Joyce watches the cinema to find out what is going on in the war but 'they just showed the Tommies. Never the Yanks. And if they did, never the coloreds.' (223).

The other sense in which Joyce performs the functions of one of 'life's maskers' in the narrative is through her 'naivety expressed as the inability to understand stupid conventions' (Bakhtin 1981, 162). Joyce appears ignorant of racial prejudice and meets Travis, who is to die in the allied landings in Italy in 1945, at a dance in 1943 shortly after the first American troops arrived in Britain in the spring and summer of 1942. The crucial fact that Travis is black appears to be of little consequence to her and is withheld from the reader until a casual aside that his hair is 'well combed, with a sort of razor parting on the left. It's short like thin black wool, but he puts some oil or something on it because it shines in the light.' (Phillips 1993, 167). Travis obtains permission to marry as long as he doesn't try to take Joyce back to the United States where inter-racial marriages were illegal in many states. Their relationship in Britain although legal is dangerous and circumspect: 'Your father and I, Greer. We couldn't show off. We had to be careful and bold.' (223). The outcome of their union is the son, Greer, with whom his mother is eventually reunited but whom his father is destined never to see.

'West' is based on information about American slave trails derived from the catalogue of an exhibition in the Smithsonian Institute in Washington in the mid–1980s entitled 'Blacks in the West'. In an interview with Maya Jaggi, Phillips explains that he chose as his subject one of the black pioneers who joined the wagon trains and headed west because 'being a masochist, I chose to go with the aspect in which there was the least research because there was more latitude for the imagination' (Phillips 1994, 26). He also decided to write from the point of view of a woman because there was very little known about black women and their role in opening up the West.

Faced with the prospect of being sold back into slavery by her white masters, an ageing slave, Martha Randolph, runs away to find freedom and to be reunited with her lost daughter. This episode harks back to well-known nineteenth-century slave narratives. As Sarah Meer has pointed out, Harriet Beecher Stowe's Uncle Tom's Cabin (1852) uses the sanctity of motherhood as its most powerful argument against slavery: Eliza, the slave, who runs away to the North to avoid being separated from her child, is shown to possess the true humanity that the slave-owner, Marie St Clare lacks (Meer 1995, 90). Moreover, anti-slavery writers such as Frederick Douglass in his autobiography, My Bondage and My Freedom (1855) frequently indicted slavery because it separated the mother from her children, and argued that black people could feel familial love as passionately as did white (Meer 1995, 94).

Unable to give voice to her own desires in the custody of white people, it is through interior dialogization that Martha is able to resist the objectifying discourse about herself and to deny the right of others to discipline and control. Martha's 'westward soul' (Phillips 1993, 94) determines to find a place 'where your name wasn't "boy" or "aunty" and where you could be a part of this country without feeling like you wasn't really a part' (74). However, it is not white people but the predatory black traders patrolling the Missouri whom Martha knows that she must avoid because they would have no qualms about catching her and selling her back into slavery. Here, as in relation to the terrible act of human trafficking which the novel begins, Phillips touches upon a controversial aspect of slavery that many other black writers have been reluctant to tackle; the complicity of slaves in their own enslavement and the part played by some black people in selling others, including members of their own family, to slave traders, a practice that was cited to justify the treatment of Africans as less than human.

Although the black elites of West Africa were incriminated in the working of the Atlantic slave trade, and at moments when Africa was riven inter-ethnically the historical record shows that black people fought and enslaved each other (Blackburn 1997, 102), it is likely that stories of familial abuse were much exaggerated by Europeans and had become apocryphal in the eighteenth century. In his *The Journal of a Slave Trader* John Newton records having been told often that parents sold their children into slavery, and *vice versa*, although he 'never heard of one instance of either, while I used the Coast' (Newton 1962,109). Newton conjectures that the purpose of such anecdotes was to prove that the Africans, 'however hardly treated, deserve but little compassion' since 'they are a people so destitute of natural affection' (109).

What gives Martha the courage to run away at last are rumours she hears about the existence of communities of free slaves newly established in California and Colorado: 'Apparently, these days colored folk were not heading west prospecting for no gold, they were just prospecting for a new life without having to pay heed to the white man and his ways.' (Phillips 1993, 73–4). Here Phillips works into his narrative a sense of a wider black community with its own values and practices as a source of support for Martha and as an alternative to the family unit that the slave owners had destroyed. Through its use of a black woman character, whose maternal feelings have not been extinguished by a system of property ownership that perpetuates itself by separating children from their mothers and procreation from love, the novel is not only in dialogue with *Beloved* but with other modern narratives with black women protagonists.

One such example is Sherley Anne Williams' *Dessa Rose* (1986), a modern re-visioning of the nineteenth-century slave narrative which shows that slavery represented far more for women than abjection and defeat: 'I now know that slavery eliminated neither heroism nor love; it provided occasions for their expression' (Williams 1986, author's note).

The 'Crossing the River' section differs from the rest of the novel in that it is written from the point of view of a narrator whose professional business is the slave traffic. The fictional James Hamilton, the captain of a slave-ship, speaks with the diction and authority of a slave-trader who has acquired his position and his possessions through inheritance: he is also the son of a slave-trader whose unexplained death has left behind another of the bereft, and grieving, fatherless children with whom the novel abounds. His is the voice of dominance, the monologic voice of authority that the other voices of slaves in the novel contest. Hamilton's language is embedded in imbalances of power and saturated with traces of historical usage. Although essential to the novel it does not, however, dominate the text's overall polyphonic structure. Phillips borrows the title for his novel, which also serves as the title of the third section of the book, from the subtitle in Edward Kamau Brathwaite's epic poem about the slave trade, *The Arrivants: a New World Trilogy* (1973). The river to which the title refers is the river Missouri which ran along the border between the slave-owning and the free states of the United States. The title of the novel is also a reference to the notorious Middle Passage.

Like an earlier novel, *Cambridge*, which draws heavily on the diction of the eighteenth-century slave narrative *The Interesting Narrative of the Life of Olaudah Equiano* (1789), Hamilton's journal is a parodic version of the original on which it is based and is double coded in political terms in that it both legitimizes and subverts that which it parodies. The third section of the novel consists exclusively of extracts from a journal supposedly kept on ship by Hamilton and is closely modelled on that of John Newton, a friend of the poet William Cowper, and the author of the hymn, 'Amazing Grace', whom Wordsworth depicts as the castaway who teaches himself Euclid in Book VI of *The Prelude* by drawing diagrams in the sand. Newton began his professional career as a slave-trader but underwent a life-changing spiritual conversion and was ordained Rector of St Mary Woolnoth's in the City of London and made spiritual advisor to William Wilberforce, ending his life as a dedicated abolitionist. Although there was considerable awareness of the inhumanity of the slave trade by the 1750s, opposition grew rapidly between the time of Newton's first voyage and the time he was called to give evidence against the trade to a parliamentary committee in 1790, two years after the publication of his influential *Thoughts Upon the African Slave Trade* in 1788. The Abolition Society was formed in 1787. During his time at sea Newton wrote many affectionate letters to his devoted young wife, Mary, some of which were published in 1793 after her untimely death as *Letters to a Wife*. His journal covers three voyages in slave ships between 1750 and 1754. In his acknowledgements at the start of *Crossing the River* Phillips expresses his 'particular obligation' to Newton who 'furnished me with invaluable research material for Part iii.'

The language attributed to the fictional Hamilton, particularly in those sections of the diary which depart the furthest from Newton, exposes the contradictory impulses of a man who aspires to be virtuous but whose idea of virtue appears to be overly dependent on sexual continence: Hamilton will not condone the debauchery of his sailors on or off ship and will have nothing to do with prostitutes: ('they say I am slave to a single woman; I claim that they are a slave to hundreds, of all qualities') (Phillips 1993, 109). In contrast, it is likely that Newton did avail himself of prostitutes in the course of his voyages (Hindmarsh 1996, 57–8). As Hamilton uses the word here, slavery denotes a pleasurable addiction rather than the enforced labor and exploitation inherent in an economic system of exchange. The question which the diary raises for the modern reader, and of which Hamilton is unaware, is that pinpointed by an anonymous reviewer of the novel in the *Times Literary Supplement*: 'How was it possible for *anyone* to be virtuous in a world in which it was acceptable for children to be bought and sold?' (Anon. 1996, 22).

Many of the textual changes to Newton's journal that Phillips makes appear purely arbitrary although a few tie the modern, fictional version more closely into the thematics of the rest of the novel. On 19 May, Hamilton is 'approached by a quiet fellow' from whom he 'bought 2 strong man-boys, and a proud girl' (Phillips 1993, 124), a reference to the purchase of Martha, Travis and Nash. Newton's sea voyage took place from 30 June 1752 to 29 August 1753 on board a ship called *The African* whereas Hamilton's expedition in *Crossing the River* takes place from 24 August 1752 to 21 May 1753 and the vessel is *The Duke of York*. The year in which Hamilton sets sail is the same as another slave ship, *The Liverpool Merchant*, sets sail in Barry Unsworth's Booker prize-winning novel, *Sacred Hunger* (1992), which indicates the importance of the only extant complete record of an eighteenth-century slave voyage to writers of historical fiction other than Phillips. While the entries in Hamilton's diaries and Newton's are of a similar style and length, the factual contents bear no exact correspondence. In the month of December 1752, for example, Newton provides eight diary entries and Hamilton five. The only date of the month common to both journals is 23 December and the entries for this date bear no resemblance. The authorial interest in the 'real' here is beset by a knowledge of the fictionality of all textual representation. In refusing to camouflage the oscillation between mimesis and artifice, which a more exact correspondence between the two diaries would have disguised, the author reminds the reader of the inauthenticity of Hamilton's diary and of the textuality of both Newton and Hamilton's. There is an ironic renegotiation of the relationship between style and substance and style becomes a means of negotiating with history.

In *Slavery, Empathy, and Pornography* Marcus Wood has provided a sustained and incisive critique of the problems inherent in appropriation of the eighteenth-century slave-trader's diaries entitled 'Telling Tales: Fact as Fiction in Caryl Phillips's Abuse of Newton'. In a meticulous, sophisticated discussion of the purpose and significance of what Wood shows to be slight, but nevertheless telling, differences between the diary entries that Phillips produces for his fictional Hamilton and those made by the real Newton, Wood registers his unease at the effect of these changes. In this he is clearly impelled by his desire as a custodian of the historical archive to protect the 'ghastly authenticity' and integrity of Newton's original words: 'Maybe those words cannot be changed, except in their smallest details, because they have an authority which a late twentieth-century consciousness desperate to reclaim the past cannot mimic.' (Wood 2002, 54).

One reason why the historical John Newton is effaced and reinvented in the fictional guise of Captain Hamilton is that the historical Newton and the fictive Hamilton are substantively different in that nothing is known about Hamilton beyond that intimated by the words attributed to him on the page. Hamilton exists for the reader without the accompanying paraphernalia of Newton's conversion to Christianity, as a participant in the slave trade and not as the concerned opponent of the trade that he subsequently became. Unlike Newton he cannot be conscripted into the orthodox histories of the abolition of slavery as the achievement of enlightened Englishmen like Wilberforce which some scholars argue have minimized the role of black activists like Olaudah Equiano and Robert Wedderburn in securing their own freedom. As Julia Swindells points out, 'the movement's achievements cannot be usefully summarized in terms of the commitment of one, or even two or three prominent men, but people of every class of society and from most regions of Britain rallied to the anti-slavery cause, to the extent that the character of petitioning and mass mobilization changed for ever' (Swindells 2001, 45).

David Dabydeen contends that there is a difference between black writers of the eighteenth century like Equiano, who trudged all over England organizing anti-slavery rallies, and British poets such as Wordsworth and Coleridge who nominally opposed the trade, arguing that 'there is little evidence though to suggest that any of these poets devoted any personal time or effort, or dug deep into their pockets, to support the abolition cause.' (Dabydeen 1985, 44) Moreover, Dabydeen suggests that the revolts in the slave factories on the West African coast and on board the ships taking them to the colonies, and on the plantations and 'the bloodletting and barbarities they unleashed, made more impact on the dismantling of slavery than the poems issued by English writers' (46). As if in support of a version of the history of abolition in which the role of the white mediator is minimized, Hamilton's diary tells of an abortive slave insurrection on ship which serves as a marker to the courage of those African captives who refused to submit in silence: 'Nearly 30 of them had broken their irons ... Should they have made their attempts upon the coast, when we had a half-dozen out of the ship, I cannot imagine the consequences.' (Phillips 1993, 124).

Stuart Hall has questioned whether it is 'only a matter of unearthing that which the colonial experience buried and overlaid, bringing to light the hidden continuities it suppressed? Or is a quite different practice entailed – not the rediscovery but the *production* of identity. Not an identity grounded in the archaeology, but in the *re-telling* of the past' (Hall 2003, 224). In an interview conducted by Carol Margaret Davison, Phillips expressed his longstanding desire to 'make an affirmative connection, not a connection based upon exploitation or suffering or misery, but a connection based upon a kind of survival' (Davison 1994, 93). 'Signifying on' Alice Walker's *The Color Purple* (1981), perhaps the best-known and the most redemptive of modern-day African-American slave narratives, *Crossing the River* ends with the fabular reunion of long-lost family members across space and time and the symbolic reparation of the family unit broken by tragedy, bereavement and loss but extended, strengthened and augmented by a significant symbolic co-option: 'My Nash. My Martha. My Travis. My daughter, Joyce' (Phillips 1993, 237).

The potential of the former slave for collective strength, solidarity and survival depends on learning the lessons of history in order that the past and the present become mutually informing and the old patterns of disempowerment identified, avoided and destroyed. The disembodied voice of the ancestral African father which guides his children to safety intimates that there can be no return 'to a land trampled by the muddy boots of others. To a people encouraged to war among themselves. To a father consumed with guilt'; it is no longer simply a question of 'being'. For those whose personal and collective history has been intimately tied up with the history of slavery (including those like Joyce for whom the ties have been sealed by love and marriage rather than birth) it is also a question of 'becoming'. There is guarded optimism in the unnamed father's vision of the future and in his confidence that his children have the inner resources to survive whatever trials may befall them: 'Only if they panic will they break their wrists and ankles against Captain Hamilton's instruments.' (Phillips 1993, 237). There is also, as Phillips puts it, an 'underlying passion which informs the ability to survive' (Phillips 1994, 28).

In *Crossing the River*, then, the experience of people of African descent is represented in all its contradictory complexity: global, political, cultural, and historical – a history of mixed failures and achievement, that avoids romanticizing and takes account of violence on the part of black as well as white, and of black dictators as well as black revolutionaries; from Toussaint L'Ouverture's inspiring slave rebellion of the 1790s to the hated regime of Papa Doc Duvalier in modern Haiti, from the freedom fighters in the Vietnam war to the vision of universal 'brotherhood' in Martin Luther King's 'I have a Dream' speech that summed up the hopes of the American Civil Rights movement that have yet to be fulfilled, and the anguished *Notes of a Native Son* by James Baldwin, the first writer whom Phillips had ever met and whose influence was greater than any other black writer during the 1950s and 1960s. The musical legacy that the children of the Diaspora have bequeathed to humanity includes inner city blues; Marvin Gaye's anthem of sorrow at the world plummeted into environmental crisis; jazz; the sophisticated improvisation on Iberian classical music by 'king of the trumpet', Miles Davis and Motown; the charttopping syncopated rhythms of Diana Ross and the Supremes.

> For two hundred and fifty years I have listened. To the haunting voices. Singing: Mercy, Mercy Me. (The Ecology) Insisting: Man, I ain't got no quarrel with them. Vietcong. Declaring: Brothers and Friends. I am Toussaint L'Ouverture, my name is perhaps known to you. Listened to: Papa Doc. Baby Doc. Listened to voices hoping for: Freedom. Democracy. Singing: Baby, baby. Where did our love go? Samba. Calypso. Jazz. Jazz. Sketches of Spain in Harlem. In a Parisian bookstore

a voice murmurs the words Nobody Knows My Name. I have listened
to the voice that cried: I have a dream that one day on the red hills of
Georgia, the sons of former slaves and the sons of former slave-owners
will be able to sit down together at the table of brotherhood. (Phillips
1993, 236–7)

In this passage Phillips is at pains to resist all totalizing imperatives. What
is at play is a multiplicity and mêlée of voices linked and interrelated
dialogically which enter the novel through the interplay between authorial speech, narrator speech, inserted genres and character speech (Bakhtin
1981, 263). What I have argued has been common to all the voices in
the novel, with the exception of Captain Hamilton, is purposeful dissi-
dence: each expresses its own resistance counterposed to the discourses
of dominance. The play of voices in the text reveals both the configurations of power and the potential resistance to those configurations.
Phillips's is essentially an anti-authoritarian project which plays with language to parody the language of the missionaries and the slave-masters.
What is deployed in *Crossing the River* is a type of literary discourse in
which the individual character, Nash, Martha, Joyce, James Hamilton,
has free play *against* the author. The emphasis is on rebellion, on a return
to lost origins and on different kinds of freedom, including the freedom
of the individual voice to be raised against constituted authority.

Like Toni Morrison's *Jazz*, *Crossing the River* is contrapuntal and syncopated. As Pilar Cuder-Dominguez points out, the structure of the novel
with the father calling to the fatherless children who each respond in
turn resembles the call-and-response patterns of traditional African music and song. Cuder-Dominguez also suggests that antiphony is perhaps a
more appropriate term for the structure of the novel than polyphony 'in
so far as each voice utters his or her song alternately, and not simultaneously' (Cuder-Dominguez 2005, 371). Phillips himself commented that
he didn't want to leave the novel 'as an analysis of fracture' because he
'felt such an overwhelming, passionate attachment to all the voices, and
I kept thinking it seemed almost choral. These people were talking in
harmonies I could hear.' (Phillips 1994, 28).

As a character in Salman Rushdie's *The Moor's Last Sigh* points out,
'Children make fictions of their fathers, re-inventing them according to
their childish needs. The reality of a father is a weight few sons can bear.'
(Rushdie 1995, 331). *Crossing the River* is allegorical: the voice of the
250-year-old father selling his children at the start of the novel may be
read as the voice of Africa. However, a political reading of fatherhood as
a metaphor by no means exhausts the meanings of the father and child

relationship in a novel which resonates with the author's personal interest in exploring the theme of parental separation and loss. Phillips himself was brought up by his mother after his parents divorced when he was about eight and he never properly knew his father. The longing for reunification with the father to whom the child has hitherto been little more than a stranger is fulfilled in the redemptive ending of *Crossing the River*. Questioned about his most recent novel, *A Distant Shore* (2003), in which a survivor of African tribal conflict finds refuge in modern Britain, Phillips admits to having become more interested in 'identity' than in 'race': 'The latter is just one component in the former, along with religion, gender, nationality, class, etc.' (Phillips n.d.). In the experience of the diasporan subject the effects of displacement on the human psyche are revealed at their most intense. As Stuart Hall puts it, 'the loss of identity which has been integral to the Caribbean experience only begins to be healed when these forgotten connections are once more set in place'. Moreover, narratives of cultural displacement and dispossession 'restore an imaginary fullness or plenitude, to set against the broken rubric of our past'. As a radical and optimistic revisioning of the experience of slaves and their descendants, which offers hope but no easy solutions, *Crossing the River* offers us 'resources of resistance and identity, with which to confront the fragmented and pathological ways in which that experience has been reconstructed' (Hall 2003, 224).

## Works Cited

Anon., 1996. '*Crossing the River*', *The Times Literary Supplement*, 22 May.

Bakhtin, Mikhail, 1981. *The Dialogic Imagination: Four Essays*, ed. Caryl Emerson and Michael Holquist. Austin, TX: University of Texas Press.

Bakhtin, Mikhail, 1984. *Problems of Dostoevsky's Poetics*, ed. and trans. Acryl Emerson. Minneapolis: University of Minnesota Press.

Bakhtin, Mikhail, 1986. *Speech Genres and Other Late Essays*, ed. Caryl Emerson and Michael Holquist. Austin, TX: University of Texas Press.

Blackburn, Robin, 1997. *The Making of New World Slavery: From the Baroque to the Modern 1492–1800*. London: Verso.

Brathwaite, E. K, 1988. *The Arrivants. A New World Trilogy: Rites of Passage, Islands, Masks, 1967–1969*. Oxford: Oxford University Press.

Cuder-Dominguez, Pilar, 2005. 'Roots versus Routes in Caryl Phillips's *Crossing the River* and Dionne Brand's *At the Full and Change of the Moon*', in *Revisiting Slave Narratives/Les avatars contemporains des récits d'esclaves*, texts collected by/textes réunis par Judith Misrahi-Barak. Montpellier: Les Carnets du Cerpac 2, Université Paul Valéry, Montpellier: 365–378.

Dabydeen, David, 1985. 'Eighteenth-Century English Literature on Commerce', in *The Black Presence in English Literature*, ed. David Dabydeen. Manchester: Manchester University Press. 26–49.

Davison, Carol Margaret, 1994. 'Crisscrossing the River: An Interview with Caryl Phillips', *Ariel: A Review of International English Literature* 25.iv (October): 91–9.

Fanon, Frantz, 1967. *Black Skin, White Masks.* New York: Grove Press.

Fryer, Peter, 1984. *Staying Power: The History of Black People in Britain.* London: Pluto Press.

Hall, Stuart, 2003. 'Cultural Identity and Diaspora', in *Identity: Community, Culture and Difference*, ed. Jonathan Rutherford. London: Lawrence and Wishart. 222–38.

Hindmarsh, Bruce D., 1996. *John Newton and the English Evangelical Tradition between the Conversion of Wesley and Wilberforce.* Oxford: Clarendon Press.

Ledent, Bénédicte, 2002. *Caryl Phillips.* Manchester: Manchester University Press.

Meer, Sarah,1995. 'Sentimentality and the Slave Narrative: Frederick Douglass' *My Bondage* and *My Freedom*', in *The Uses of Autobiography*, ed. Julia Swindells. London: Taylor and Francis. 89–97.

Newton, John, 1962. *The Journal of a Slave Trader*, ed. Bernard Martin and Mark Spurrell. London: The Epworth Press.

Newton, John, 1962a. *Thoughts Upon the African Slave Trade* [1788], reprinted as an appendix in Newton 1962. 97–120

O'Callaghan, Evelyn, 1993. 'Historical Fiction and Fictional History: Caryl Phillips's *Cambridge*', *The Journal of Commonwealth Literature* 29.ii, xxix. 34–47.

Owusu, Kwesi, ed., 2000. *Black British Culture and Society*, London: Routledge.

Phillips, Caryl, 1987. *The European Tribe.* London: Faber and Faber.

Phillips, Caryl, 1989. *Higher Ground.* London: Viking.

Phillips, Caryl, 1991. *Cambridge.* London: Bloomsbury.

Phillips, Caryl, 1993. *Crossing the River.* London: Picador.

Phillips, Caryl, 1994. Interview: '*Crossing the River*, Caryl Phillips talks to Maya Jaggi', *Wasafiri* 20: 25–30.

Phillips, Caryl, 2003. *A Distant Shore.* London: Secker and Warburg.

Phillips, Caryl, n.d. 'A Conversation with Caryl Phillips', http:www.nathanielturner.com/distantshore2.htm

Rosler, Martha, 1981. *3 Works.* Halifax, Nova Scotia: Nova Scotia College of Art and Design.

Rushdie, Salman, 1995. *The Moor's Last Sigh.* London: Jonathan Cape.

Swindells, Julia, 2001. *Glorious Causes: The Grand Theatre of Political Change, 1789–1833.* Oxford: Oxford University Press.

White, Hayden, 1986. 'Critical Pluralism'. *Critical Inquiry* 12: 480–93.

Williams, Sherley Anne, 1986. *Dessa Rose.* London: Macmillan.

Wood, Marcus, 2002. *Slavery, Empathy, and Pornography.* Oxford: Oxford University Press.

# Index